Deterrence in the Twenty-first Century

Proceedings

London, UK
18–19 May 2009

September 2010

First published the Air University Press, Maxwell, AL, USA
This edition published by Books Express Publishing, 2011
ISBN 978-1780390-50-5
To purchase copies please contact info@books-express.com

Contents

Preface

Deterrence has long been a cornerstone of interaction among states. This was especially true when state interests clashed and when political leaders sought to avoid direct military conflict. In traditional deterrence relationships, calculations of military, economic, and diplomatic power determined the degrees of deterrence effectiveness. This seemed to change with the advent of the Cold War. The potential destructiveness of nuclear weapons combined with the relatively small numbers of states that possessed them suggested a need for new concepts of deterrence tailored to govern the nuclear competition among the Soviet Union, the United States, and their allies. Deterrence thinking came to mean nuclear deterrence—and as the Cold War wound down, there was a general perception that the absence of nuclear confrontation among the great powers required less emphasis on deterrence as a key feature of national strategy and a corresponding decrease in the instruments of deterrence that had prevailed during the Cold War.

As the collapse of the superpower confrontation became more distant, however, states began to confront threats that were present during the Cold War but were perceived to be less important—what some have termed *lesser included* threats. These threats involved state failure, mass migration of populations, and drug, small arms, and human trafficking. Also included were environmental and humanitarian disasters, traditional state competition, proliferation of weapons of mass destruction and their components, and the emergence of nonstate actors empowered by new communication and information technologies that give them global reach. Taken individually, few of these threats have the potential to overthrow established and functioning states—especially in the developed world. However, these threats present challenges that policy makers struggle to meet using traditional diplomacy. Economic sanctions and incentives have exerted little apparent effect toward solving some of these post–Cold War challenges. In the end, states—and particularly the United States and its partners and allies—relied on military intervention to cope with an increasingly complex set of challenges and crises.

To help understand and begin to develop alternative policy frameworks that fit the current and emerging security context, the US Air Force's Air Force Research Institute (AFRI), the Royal United Services Institute (RUSI), and King's College, London, hosted a two-day conference at the RUSI offices in London on 18 and 19 May 2009. We sought to bring together some of the best thinkers on deterrence to examine how to reinvigorate this essential tool for today's policy community.

The conference exceeded our expectations, as readers will observe from the excellent products in these proceedings. From the pre-conference "thought pieces" by RUSI's Michael Codner and AFRI's Adam Lowther—the presentations by the keynote speakers and case study developers—to the post-conference "Quick Looks" by AFRI personnel, the outcome reflects the creativity and the seriousness with which the attendees and the planning staffs approached the topic.

We see this conference as a beginning conversation that has the potential to inform policy makers on how to develop richer options for coping with the increasingly complex and lethal security challenges of the world in which we live. We are grateful to the participants and to those who contributed to the success of the endeavor.

Chapter 1

Framing Deterrence in the Twenty-first Century
Conference Summary

Adam Lowther

The evolving challenges of an unstable international security environment—aggravated by the global financial crisis—set the context for renewed interest in strategic deterrence. After nearly a generation of near-constant operations, pitting the world's most powerful military against rogue regimes and nonstate actors, scholars and strategists are struggling to adapt the theories and vocabulary of deterrence to a post–Cold War context that is very different from the context in which deterrence theory and policy was developed.

The structure of the bipolar international system in which the United States and Soviet Union maintained an uneasy peace during the Cold War focused deterrence theory and policy on its nuclear aspects. Such theorists as Hermann Kahn, Bernard Brodie, and Thomas Schelling clearly emphasized that conventional conflict could escalate into nuclear war, thus requiring careful attention on the part of statesmen. The special circumstances of the Cold War kept attention focused on *preventing* nuclear war rather than analyzing the continuities between nuclear and "lesser included" conflicts.

The watershed events represented by the end of the Cold War and the terrorist attacks of 11 September 2001 called into question the relevance of deterrence as a strategic approach. With their falling out of favor immediately after the Soviet Union's collapse, democratization, globalization, and a focus on second and third world economic development displaced the focus on hard power. Nuclear operations seemed less relevant in a world characterized by diverse challenges such as failed states, humanitarian disaster, genocidal conflict, counter/nonproliferation, terrorism, and asymmetric conflict. Thus, if deterrence is to be relevant, current questions should center on linking deterrence to desired effects. In other words, states that adopt deterrence as part of a comprehensive strategy should be able to determine, with a fair degree of certainty, that the policies and initiatives intended to deter some behavior

1

actually achieve their objective. This is where the notion of deterrence in the twenty-first century begins to break down.

Theorists and practitioners agree that at its core, deterrence is about convincing an adversary, or ally, that the costs of an undesirable action are greater than the rewards, thus preventing a challenge to the status quo. This requires an understanding of the adversary's motives, decision-making processes, and objectives. While the Cold War structure may have evolved to give strategists some degree of confidence that the principal adversary was deterred by American capability, force structure, and alliances, today's diversity of challenges increases the complexity of formulating deterrence strategies. In fact, not all adversaries may be deterrable. This may be particularly true of nonstate actors.

Some analysts postulate that globalization has fundamentally transformed the security environment, making unilateral state action impractical and ineffective. Those who adopt this perspective argue that the threat-based nature of deterrence creates a diplomatic and military environment that precludes constructive conflict resolution. Others claim that the fiscal costs of developing and maintaining the military platforms necessary to sustain a credible deterrent are prohibitively expensive and ineffectively consume limited resources that could be more efficiently used to better humanity. Others see the primary utility of deterrence as remaining focused on nuclear weapons and their potential to prevent or cause major conflicts.

The lack of focus and clarity that prevails among theorists and practitioners combined with the nuclear focus of the Cold War has produced a situation in which there is no common foundation for understanding what deterrence means and how it applies to national security. The result is a lack of clarity and rigor in policy making that could result in ineffective and inefficient investments. Ultimately, this could lead to failed policies. Force structures that rely on the Cold War legacy without the existential threat posed by the Soviet Union have the potential to be too expensive to maintain in the long term while also removing capabilities that would be better employed against other near-term threats. Attempting to apply deterrence as a template without understanding the specific social, cultural, military, and political characteristics of the adversary could be futile at best and disastrous at worst. In other words, deterrence must be specific to the context and characteristic of the threat.

Purpose of the Conference

To shed new light on this important subject, the Royal United Services Institute (RUSI), the Centre for Defence Studies at Kings College—London, and the US Air Force Research Institute co-sponsored a two-day conference in which military leaders, policy makers, and senior academics were brought to RUSI's head-quarters in Whitehall for two days of discussion. *Framing Deter-rence in the 21st Century* took place on 18–19 May 2009 with the intent of answering four fundamental questions:

- What is deterrence?
- What are the instruments of deterrence?
- Why does deterrence fail?
- What are the consequences of deterrence policies?

In the process of examining these and related questions, the British and American participants explored the challenges fac-ing the United States and Europe and the ends, ways, and means at their disposal.

Over the two-day conference, participants were briefed on five sub-topics: (1) conceptions of deterrence, (2) deterrence and counter/nonproliferation, (3) nonstate actor attempts to deter states, (4) state attempts to deter nonstate actors, and (5) state versus state deterrence, with a keynote address and a case study preceding participants breaking into discussion groups. There they were asked to examine one of the four ques-tions as it related to the points raised in the keynote address and case study. Data was captured from these discussions and presented to the entire group, by each of the small group fa-cilitators, before the conference's closing.

In designing the conference in this manner, the sponsors sought to answer key questions, develop policy recommenda-tions, and discover those areas requiring further research. Each of these objectives was completed—to some degree—and served as the basis for the remainder of the proceedings.

3

What Is Deterrence in the Twenty-first Century?

There are possibly more questions than answers in the field of deterrence studies. Those who expect quick, concise, and immediate practical answers are destined to be frustrated by the highly theoretical nature of deterrence conversations. Others may experience similar frustration as the conversation quickly becomes constrained to notions of nuclear deterrence, arms control, and counter/nonproliferation. There are, however, several insights that can inform policy discussions.

First, deterrence may not apply to all situations. Some adversaries are not likely to be deterred by any practical means at the disposal of states. These challenges must be either contained or eradicated. However, understanding the culture, interests, and objectives of an adversary has the potential to decrease the number of adversaries who cannot be deterred. Possessing a value system that differs from Western norms does not make an adversary irrational. It requires greater knowledge and understanding on the part of the United States and its allies, if deterrence is to be successful.

For those situations in which statecraft does apply, situations can and should be shaped without resorting to the threats inherent in deterrence interactions. This implies that states adopt coherent and comprehensive approaches that are relevant to the global security environment and that they purposely employ all instruments of power to achieve desired objectives. In such a context, states would focus and tailor their strategies according to the demands of the threat.

In those situations where deterrence may apply, policy makers must determine the appropriate instruments, ensuring that the desired state of affairs is effectively communicated and accepted by the target audience. Additionally, the success of deterrence depends on the ability to accurately assess an adversary's behavior and likely counter moves. Without such assessment, deterrence will remain a theoretical construct with little relation to actual conditions as they exist in the adversary's camp.

There may be ways to deter nonstate actors. This is an area requiring further research aimed at developing an understanding of their objectives and values. Only by understanding a nonstate actor can the United States and its allies target what it values most. While it is often said that Islamic fundamentalists are undeterrable, they do seek to achieve tangible worldly objectives. This presents an opportunity to develop an effective set of deterrence policies that may include all aspects of diplomacy, information, military, and economics. To the extent that criminals, insurgents, terrorists, and other groups represent challenges to state and international security, they operate outside the accepted laws of conflict out of weakness, not an inherent preference for the "tactics of the weak." To suggest that nonstate actors are—by nature—irrational would be a grave mistake.

Finally, as long as states possess nuclear weapons and as long as there are those willing to share weapons of mass destruction (WMD) information and technology, deterrence remains a valid strategic approach. Where states have acquired such capabilities, deterrence is the primary approach that provides a foundation for governing interaction with adversaries. For those states that seek to acquire WMD, deterrence provides a robust set of theories and approaches for states to use counter/nonproliferation.

What Are the Instruments of Deterrence?

A generation ago, the instruments of deterrence would not have generated significant interest. They were well understood. However, the collapse of the Soviet Union on Christmas Day 1991, followed a decade later by the 11 September 2001 terrorist attacks on the United States, caused a shift in US foreign and military policies. Most importantly, these events undermined the foundation upon which Cold War deterrence was built. Before 25 December 1991, it was widely understood that deterrence and nuclear weapons went hand in hand; the end of the Cold War decoupled the two.

Into the space created by the Cold War's end rushed globalization and democratization, which quickly moved to the forefront of foreign policy as deterrence waned in strategic significance. Although the United States experienced terrorist attacks on more than a few occasions before 9/11, it was not until the attacks on New York City and Washington, DC, that national security policy focused on the defeat of Islamic fundamentalism. Nonstate actors became the primary threat to security and the

5

elimination of al-Qaeda and other terrorist networks became the objective of US foreign and military policy. As this shift occurred, deterrence was given little attention because nonstate actors were seen as irrational and undeterrable. Kinetic force became the primary instrument of power.

With the election of a new administration (November 2008) and a prolonged recession, there is a new opportunity to examine the usefulness of deterrence in an international system where the primary threats to security and stability are, and will remain, rogue regimes and nonstate actors.[1] For deterrence to play a prominent role once again, the instruments of deterrence must be applicable to current threats.

Unlike the Cold War, Islamic fundamentalism does not pose an existential threat to the United States. However, this does not mean that the United States should not maintain its capabilities (instruments) at all levels of conflict (fig. 1).

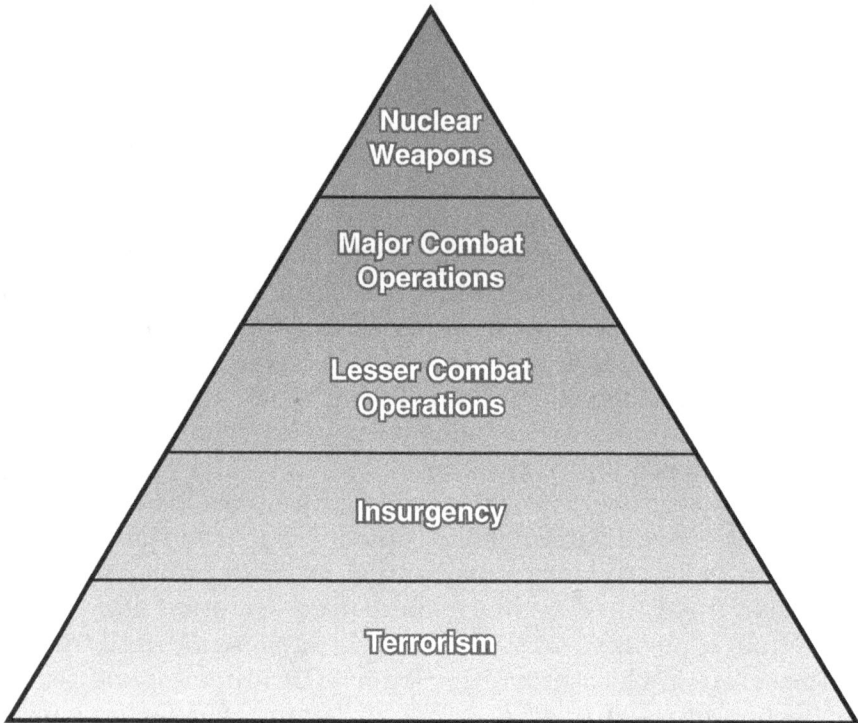

Figure 1. Conflict Pyramid

Maintaining a credible nuclear deterrent is recommended to deter current and future peer and near-peer nuclear powers. While the threat of nuclear conflict is greatly diminished from its Cold War height, disarmament would allow and encourage adversaries operating at the lower end of the conflict spectrum to seek equality with the United States. Thus, it may be possible to deter nuclear proliferation by maintaining a credible nuclear deterrent.

The variety of threats to security and stability existent in the international system requires the creation of a new set of "red lines" that effectively communicate boundaries to potential adversaries. Not only do rogue regimes and nonstate actors pose significant threats, but they also threaten to use terrorism, WMD, and cyber attacks as their primary tactics. These adversaries also operate with an alternative rationale from the one the United States and its allies grew accustomed to during the Cold War.

It may be more useful to think in terms of weapons of "mass effect" than to think in terms of weapons of mass destruction. In an era when cyber warfare is becoming an increasingly important capability of state and nonstate actors and terrorism remains a tactic that aims at altering an adversary's public policy, the role of kinetic force is diminishing. This stems in large part from the military dominance of the United States. Deterring current and future adversaries will require an expanded set of tools that will rely more on the diplomatic, informational, and economic elements of national power.

Intelligence will play an increasingly important role in supporting policies of dissuasion, denial, and deterrence. American Cold War strategists operated under the assumption that Soviet leaders were rational actors. The same cannot be said of modern adversaries who do not operate within the same rational framework as their Western adversaries. Intelligence plays a vital role in providing the knowledge and understanding required to develop credible deterrence policies.

Effective communication shapes the battle space undermining an adversary's attempts to establish the narrative and capture the moral high ground. As recent experience demonstrates, nonstate actors are experienced at manipulating media coverage and the sympathy that often accompanies coverage of the "underdog." They are also adept at maximizing the public relations benefits of mistakes made by adversaries. Successful nonstate actors are masterful in articulating a set of grievances that draw support from target audiences. Countering the communications and public relations efforts of nonstate actors has the potential to undermine their success and deter future efforts.

Rather than allowing nonstate actors to deter states through superiority in information/communication operations, states must develop the capability to deter nonstate actors. This may prove particularly difficult for democracies that are often unwilling to develop effective propaganda capabilities.

Efforts to modernize the instruments of deterrence for an international security environment different from its Cold War predecessor are long overdue and may yield unanticipated benefits. Doing so does not, however, guarantee the success of deterrence. Like all strategies, deterrence is prone to shortcomings that require alternative courses of action. As the following section illustrates, deterrence is not a magic bullet.

Why Does Deterrence Fail?

Actors operate within a strategic environment where, even if rational, variables limit a decision maker's ability to make optimal choices. Some scholars suggest that decision makers operate within a framework of bounded rationality where variables such as stress, fear, exhaustion, and imperfect information abound. This says nothing about cultural, historical, linguistic, political, or religious differences that may lead decision makers to see their adversary very differently than they actually are. These limits in rationality and understanding can lead to a lack of situational awareness, poor signaling, misinformation, confusion, and the misreading of signals.

The United States often does not understand its adversary. As mentioned earlier, American decision makers often operate without understanding the culture, history, language, politics, and religion of an adversary. Mirror imaging frequently occurs, leading decision makers to develop deterrence policies that are less effective than potentially possible. The war in Iraq is one example where a more complete understanding of these variables may have led to the development of policies that could have deterred a domestic- and/or foreign-led insurgency.

A "credibility gap" can develop between capability and will.
Although the United States possesses unrivaled economic and
military might, decision makers often do not respond to deterrence failures with sufficient punitive action to restore the status quo and American credibility. This opens a gap between
economic and military capability and will. Thus, future adversaries are not deterred because of previous American responses
to challenges. For example, Osama bin Laden stated in a post–
9/11 interview that weak American responses to previous
al-Qaeda attacks created an expectation that President Bush
would respond in a limited fashion to the 9/11 attacks as had
previous administrations.

*Too great a degree of ambiguity in policy can send the wrong
signal.* While ambiguity is a necessary element of a deterrence
strategy, communicating too ambiguous a policy can mislead
an adversary and, as history demonstrates, incorrectly suggest
that the United States will accept a change in the status quo
when it will not. Ambiguity has worked best when uncertainty
surrounds the severity of a response, not the possibility of a
response. The most widely used example of too great a degree
of ambiguity are the 25 July 1990 comments of US ambassador to Iraq April Glaspie, who stated to Saddam Hussein that
the United States had "no opinion" on the conflict between Iraq
and Kuwait. This opened the door for the Iraqi dictator's invasion of his neighbor.

The strong often fail to deter the weak. One scholarly study
suggests that approximately 30 percent of conflicts are initiated by the weak with an attack on the strong. Despite the
probability of defeat or annihilation, strong states frequently
fail to deter weaker adversaries because weaker states are
highly motivated (asymmetry of interests), misperceive the
probable response, and seek to take advantage of an acute military vulnerability. Although risks often outweigh rewards,
weaker states frequently feel risks more acutely. The Japanese
attack on Pearl Harbor is the most familiar example of a weaker
state attacking a much stronger adversary despite an admit-
tedly low probability of winning a prolonged conflict. For the
Japanese, the risks of not attacking far outweighed the risks of
an American response. This was the result of clear misperception of American will by the Japanese High Command.

9

More often than not, deterrence fails because of a combination of the points listed above. Rarely is there one variable that causes an adversary to seek a change in the status quo, despite the potential ramifications for doing so. It is, however, clear that the United States and its allies can reduce deterrence failures by more effectively communicating with an adversary that is understood by American decision makers and believes the United States to be credible. Successfully deterring current and future adversaries will depend on these variables.

What Are the Consequences of Deterrence Policies?

Undoubtedly, this final question is the most difficult of the four. Among conference participants, few sought to address a question that requires significant speculation. In examining the consequences of deterrence policies, however, three points were raised.

Decision makers (political and military) in democratic systems are most often focused on immediate threats to security. Deterrence, on the other hand, is not successful when decision makers are reactive rather than proactive. Its success depends on developing effective policies well in advance of an adversary's attempt to alter the status quo. Decision makers are required to think, devise a tailored strategy and policy, effectively communicate objectives, and respond to potential threats well in advance of a deterrence failure.

Extended deterrence remains a primary concern for American allies protected by the nuclear umbrella. As the United Kingdom contemplates the reduction or elimination of its nuclear arsenal and Japan remains committed to a nonnuclear defense posture—despite growing threats—the credibility of US extended deterrence weighs heavily in the strategic calculation of America's allies. Further reduction in the operationally deployed strategic nuclear force is, for example, of great concern to the Japanese and a potential cause for proliferation should the nuclear umbrella lose its credibility.

There can be little doubt that a loss of credibility with respect to extended deterrence is the potential policy consequence of greatest concern for the United States. With the Nuclear Posture Review under way and a renegotiation of the Strategic

Arms Reduction Treaty planned to take place before its December expiration, the nation's allies are closely observing the direction that the United States takes. It will be incumbent on Pres. Barack Obama to reassure America's allies that the guarantees of the Cold War remain and that the United States is not abandoning its security obligations. If this does not occur, Japan and other allies have the potential and necessary security concerns to quickly join the nuclear club.

It is difficult to have a public discussion and debate about deterrence. During the Cold War, Herman Kahn, the respected nuclear strategist, advocated a policy that would have enabled the United States to survive and win a nuclear conflict with the Soviet Union. His frank and calculating approach led policy makers, journalists, and scholars to dismiss his ideas. Today, it is equally difficult to discuss deterrence in public venues. The often-unpleasant policy choices that are required lead policy makers, journalists, academics, and the American public to reject the entire discussion. As one British participant noted, this is even more accurate a description of the mood in Europe, where such debate is quashed.

Although Herman Kahn found it difficult to foster the public debate on nuclear strategy he desired, it is only marginally easier now to discuss the requirements for a credible deterrence policy targeting rogue regimes and nonstate actors. As in the past, today's threats require that decision makers contemplate unseemly and undemocratic options, which the public finds at odds with our values.

Recommendations and Questions for Future Research

The difficulty deterrence presents to experienced strategists and policy makers was evidenced during the two days of intense discussion. Neither was unanimous agreement reached, nor was a "magic bullet" discovered that would penetrate to the heart of the issue. Deterrence, like all human endeavors, is imperfect in its creation and execution. The goal, however, was to improve on the knowledge and understanding currently available. To that end, the conference was a success. It also led to five broad recommendations, each of which will require further research if it is to be executed efficiently and effectively.

If deterrence is to play an important role in national security policy in the future, policy and theory must develop beyond their Cold War origins. Strategic deterrence policies must focus on deterring adversaries across the spectrum of threats generated by peer competitors, rogue regimes, *and* nonstate actors. It is the latter two that are currently the greatest threat to the United States and its allies, but this may not be so in the future. To develop effective policies that will deter the most likely threats, deterrence must be tailored to the specific actors that threaten American interests. This requires an improved understanding of these actors and their objectives. Again, a focus on the current fight should not lead to shortsightedness. By design, deterrence requires a long-term approach and a focus on preventing undesirable action before it occurs.

Extended deterrence will continue to play an important role in American foreign policy, as allies remain dependent on US security guarantees, particularly as the number of nuclear powers increases. America's allies are deeply concerned about continued reductions in the US nuclear arsenal, which threatens the credibility of the nuclear umbrella. Although it is often underappreciated in the United States, ensuring the continued credibility of extended deterrence is at the forefront of security concerns in European capitals, Tokyo, Seoul, and across the Middle East.

Additionally, in the wake of the present economic crisis, the United Kingdom is reviewing its options in relation to nuclear deterrence. A credible US nuclear umbrella allows options that might not otherwise be available to the present or future governments.

Nonstate actors pose the greatest **immediate** *threat to the security of the United States and its allies. In addition, like peer competitors and rogue regimes, nonstate actors are potentially deterrable.* However, if the United States and its allies are to deter nonstate actors, they must expand deterrence as a concept and set of policies. Nonstate actors operate under a fundamentally different rule-set than that governing interstate relations. This requires a detailed knowledge and understanding of each group's objectives, leadership, culture, and other characteristics. Since nonstate actors often operate within a framework that is unlike Western rationalism, it is increasingly important that the United States follow Sun Tzu's dictum "know thy enemy." The same is true of the leader-centric rogue regimes that also pose a threat to US national interests.

Cyber attacks are growing in their frequency and sophistication. Deterring these attacks will become increasingly important in the decades ahead. As the most technologically advanced nation in the world, the United States faces a serious threat in cyberspace, as do its technologically advanced allies. In addition, while the United States may not face weapons of mass destruction in cyberspace, "weapons of mass effect" are a real threat. With advanced technology playing a major role in propelling the US economy and in supporting the nation's defense, cyber attacks are attractive options for current and future adversaries. As new phenomena, cyber attacks provide no "red lines" that communicate to a potential adversary the value of America's information infrastructure and the repercussions for attacks against it. Thus, credible cyber deterrents will require coordinated interagency collaboration to design effective policies. They will also necessitate a better understanding of the dangers posed to critical infrastructure in the cyber domain.

Deterring the acquisition and use of weapons of mass destruction will grow in importance and difficulty as additional states acquire these weapons. There was near-unanimous agreement that the proliferation of WMD knowledge and technology cannot be completely staunched. It is, however, possible to raise the costs of acquisition by improving export controls, strengthening punitive measures for treaty violations, and creating a viable multilateral strategy for counter/nonproliferation.

Currently, the United States frequently describes actions that threaten nonproliferation objectives as "unacceptable" or "grave" while taking no action when adversaries violate American declarations. This undermines the credibility of deterrence and of established counter/nonproliferation regimes. A more effective mix of dissuasion, denial, and deterrence is required to slow the proliferation of WMD knowledge and technologies. Moreover, such efforts must be led by the United States and other technologically advanced nations.

In addition, as one arms control specialist suggested during the plenary session, the arms control and deterrence communities

13

would be wise to work together in developing a comprehensive strategy rather than viewing one another as competitors.

Conclusion

Perhaps the most striking result of *Deterrence in the Twenty-first Century* was the need for additional research in the areas described above. Even with more than three dozen of the most knowledgeable and experienced practitioners and scholars from the United States and Great Britain, many questions were left unanswered. In fact, the conference may have generated more questions than solutions. As one of the principals pointed out in his discussion of the conference's findings, "Nuclear deterrent behavior seems significantly different from other types of deterrent behavior." He then asked, "How should we refine the system to represent what we want?" In asking this question, the speaker struck at the heart of the matter. In addition, perhaps inadvertently, he illustrated the work yet to be done. Nevertheless, the success of future efforts may hinge on the ability of the United States and its allies to develop clear national strategies that offer an enduring course of action. When it was suggested that neither the United States nor the United Kingdom "does strategy anymore," many participants agreed. Such a state of affairs does not bode well for the future of deterrence.

Conference sponsors and attendees alike left with a clear understanding that nonstate actors, extended deterrence, and cyberspace offer untilled soil for further research. There is little doubt, however, that this will not be the last conference of its kind, as the United States and its allies continue to seek solutions for the most pressing problems of national security.

Note

1. Peer competitors are, however, the only adversary who poses an existential threat to the United States and will again pose the greatest threat to the United States in the future.

Chapter 2

DEFINING 'DETERRENCE'

Framing Deterrence in the 21st Century
18–19 May 2009, RUSI, London

Michael Codner

RUSI
www.rusi.org

Introduction

This note addresses military deterrence in the broadest sense. During the Cold War the word was generally associated with nuclear weapons. After the collapse of the Soviet Union, there was more interest in conventional deterrence. However, in the United Kingdom Ministry of Defence (MoD), there was a high-level view that any study of conventional deterrence would imply dependence on conventional capability at the expense of the nuclear deterrent and that nuclear deterrent policy would be weakened by the process.[1]

North Atlantic Treaty Organisation (NATO) military operations in the Kosovo War focused the spotlight on military coercion, in particular the ineffectiveness of air power to force the Bosnian Serb leader, Slobodan Milosevic, to withdraw Serbian forces from Kosovo within the timelines envisaged by NATO at the start of the campaign. This failure was the genesis of a discussion on both sides of the Atlantic into "Effects Based Operations (EBO)" and "the Effects Based Approach Operations (EBAO)". While there was nothing new in the notion that military action should be planned and executed to deliver the required military and political effect, this focus emphasised the importance of the cognitive domain in delivering military effect. There has been something of a presumption in the Western military community that a full understanding of the cognitive domain in any particular operation will be the philosophers' stone for success. Typically, in doctrinal work and other military analyses, *deterrence* and *coercion* are presented as two aspects of military activity in the cognitive domain.

The Physical and Cognitive Domains

At this stage it is useful to draw the distinctions between the physical and cognitive domains in the application of the military instrument. The defining purpose of the military is the state-owned, organised use of violence for combat. *Combat* means the use of violence to effect a decision—that is, to overwhelm an opponent. The military uses violence in two broad ways. First, it can deny the opponent his military capability by destroying it or removing access to it physically. Second, it can coerce the opponent into conceding by influencing his decisions in the cognitive domain. Denial and coercion are closely related. Most wars and conflict situations are ultimately terminated in the cognitive domain by a decision to accede by such authority as may remain. However, destructive action at the tactical level may persuade leadership at the operational level to retreat—in turn allowing physical advantage at the strategic level. Conversely, a tactical force may disperse or withdraw through fear allowing physical advantage at the operational level, which in turn may persuade strategic leadership that the case is hopeless.

The manoeuvrist approach, which has dominated Western military doctrine since the 1980s, emphasises domination of wills—that is, winning in the cognitive domain through coercive effect. However the effect in the cognitive domain is less predictable than physical destruction. Effective coercion in combat typically requires evidence of dominant capability as well as evidence of intent and reputation.

The focus of this discussion of deterrence is of course on posture and actions short of full-scale combat. However, it is important to bear in mind that coercive effect in the cognitive domain is every bit as relevant in combat as in the context of deterrence. Indeed deterrence itself continues into combat with regard to the choice of weapons (deterrence of the use of nuclear capability and other weapons of mass destruction), to the geographical scale of conflict (deterrence of escalation outside a particular theatre) and deterrence against other forms of escalation such as the targeting of civilians or decapitation of political leadership.

The focus of the remainder of this note is on the cognitive domain, but this relationship should be borne in mind.

Typologies

Also during the Cold War there was a parallel area of study into naval suasion. The classic work on this subject is James Cable's *Gunboat Diplomacy*.[2] Cable's presentation of the types of 'gunboat diplomacy' as the 'definitive', 'purposeful', 'catalytic' and 'expressive' uses of force is vivid. However it is somewhat literary. It does not stand up to the test of strategic analysis and is not particularly useful for military practitioners. A lesser known monograph, Edward Luttwak's *The Political Uses of Sea Power*, contains a more systematic typology of naval suasion.[3] It is comprehensive enough to be extended to suasion generally, and this is the launch point of this note.

In Luttwak's typology (fig. 1), active deterrence against a particular target entity is the negative subset of coercion—preventing a specific opponent from doing something the opponent may wish to do. The positive subset is compellence—forcing an opponent to do something that the opponent would not wish to do.

Importantly, there is also a latent deterrent mode. Here, a target entity is not specifically identified. Military capabilities are generated and deployed. A potential opponent is not specifically targeted by this behaviour or any accompanying rhetoric, whether diplomatic or informal. However, potential opponents would be expected to draw conclusions about capacity and will which would inform their own posture and actions.

This latent deterrent mode has been variously described as inherent, undirected, or existential deterrence. One might

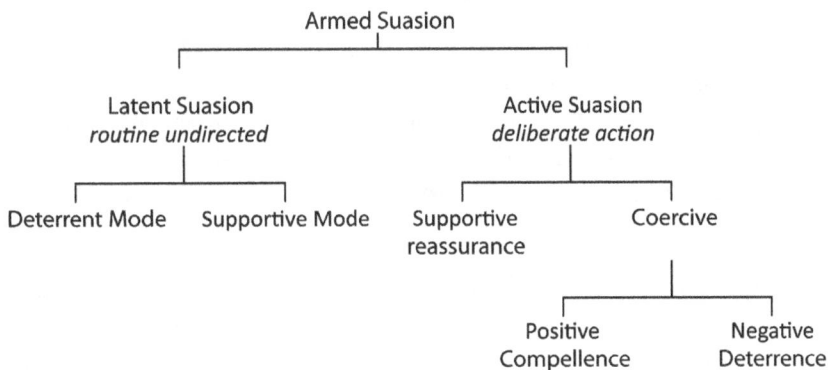

Figure 1: Typology of Armed Suasion (Luttwak)

associate shades of meaning with these three words, but the concept is clear.

When applied to Cable's terminology, the purposeful use of force–the application of force to change the policy or character of the target government or group–constitutes robust active suasion, whether compellent or deterrent. Expressive use of force–the use of forces to send a political message–would be symbolic, active suasion. Definitive use of force to create or remove a *fait accompli* is arguably not an act of suasion at all.[4]

The interesting category is the catalytic use of force, which Cable treats as a phenomenon where the purpose is not defined but forces are deployed to buy time. There is a touch of cynicism in his language here. In Luttwak's typology, this is latent use of suasion, which could embrace a spectrum from robust to symbolic.

When the authors of the first edition of the United Kingdom's strategic maritime doctrine, *The Fundamentals of British Maritime Doctrine: BR1806*, were faced with the challenge of addressing suasion in a practical way, they simplified this fusion of Cable's and Luttwak's analyses into three broad categories:[5]

- **Coercion**, which embraces both compellence and active deterrence, as Luttwak argued, but which implies robust posture and deployment including the limited use of violence.

- **Symbolic** uses, which could be directed or undirected, and supportive or deterrent, but would constitute posture and deployment without the use of violence–naval presence is in this category of undirected symbolic use.

- **Preventive, Precautionary, and Pre-emptive** uses where there is not a specifically defined mission or purpose except in the widest sense of avoiding maldeployment, expressing interest, and being prepared to address a range of possible objectives. This expression attempted to capture Cable's meaning of catalytic without the irony.

A version of Luttwak's analysis (fig. 2), which addresses the current environment in a practical way, uses the word inducement rather than suasion, a word not widely used except amongst scholars.[6]

Military Inducement

Latent Inducement — Active Inducement

Inherent Deterrence — Precautionary Posture

Supportive Action — Military Coercion

Compellence — Active Deterrence

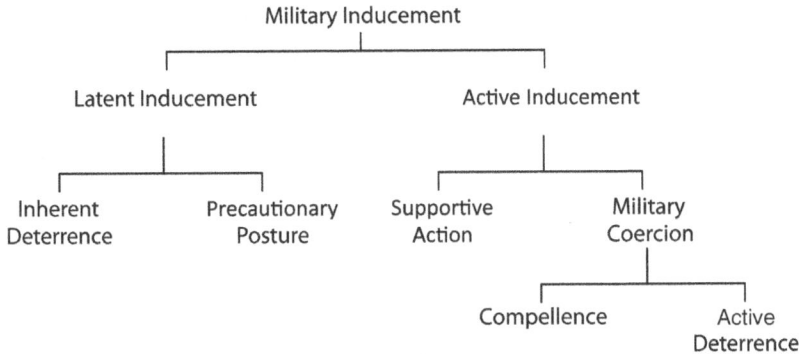

Figure 2: Typology of Military Inducement

Superimposed on this typology is the degree of inducement expressed by capability and rhetoric. Figure 3 displays a spectrum of armed inducement.

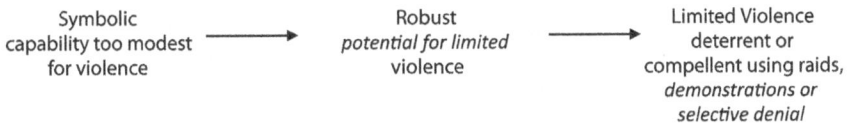

Symbolic capability too modest for violence ⟶ *Robust potential for limited violence* ⟶ Limited Violence deterrent or compellent using raids, *demonstrations or selective denial*

Figure 3: Spectrum of Military Inducement

Note also that inducement can shift from latent to active very rapidly and that this is the essence both of a precautionary posture and of an inherent deterrence. For instance, a Continuous at Sea Deterrent (CASD) based around a submarine-borne nuclear missile may be providing inherent deterrence, but CASD specifically permits a rapid transition to active deterrence and indeed use of the weapon if deterrence fails. In conventional cases the maritime environment typically permits nuanced shifts from latency to active inducement. This feature explains the emphasis on naval inducement in doctrine and the provenance of some of this analysis. The typology is, however, equally appropriate to the land and air environments and, indeed, to cyberspace.

Elements of Deterrence

The factors essential to understanding inducement are generally that effect is achieved through influencing the **perceptions** of actors–whether these are actual or potential opponents, actual or potential friends, or the wide number of different stakeholders for whom the consequences may be a spectrum of engagement from consent through to assent to mere acquiescence. Three elements to all forms of inducement apply to deterrence: these are **perception of capability to deliver violence, perception of will,** and **reputation** of the ability to implement intentions effectively.

Directed deterrence will usually be aimed ultimately at elements of the leadership of a potential or actual opponent entity with whom the decisions will rest. This entity may be a state government or a nonstate actor of some description. However, deterrence may be effective against some elements of a multiple leadership or at some levels of leadership with the result that the leadership as a whole may be effectively deterred. Furthermore, deterrent action may affect support for leadership. The effect on, say, a population could be to undermine the leadership's decision to continue with a course of action. Equally, a population could become more united against a common opponent as a result of coercive action, and this support would strengthen the hand of a leadership.

It bears mention that it is a feature more of compellence than deterrence that populations may habituate to coercive action, particularly if the effect is incremental. It is, however, relevant to deterrence in that this may be reinforced by limited denial or punishment. However, the use of limited violence in this way could harden the resolve of a population against the deterring power.

One final factor is the perceived **legality and morality** of deterrent action. This could influence the support to a leadership that is the target of deterrent action amongst the population or by other groups for whom support could be valuable (for instance, potential friends and allies). It is also relevant to the support given to the leadership of the deterrent power by friends and allies and its own population.

It has been suggested that there is a useful **distinction** between **dissuasion** on the one hand and deterrence on the other. Dissuasion could be used to mean purely diplomatic action to prevent actors from taking particular courses of action, while deterrence would imply that military capability and intentions would be a contributing factor. The problem with this distinction is that *'dissuasion'* was used by France in the Cold War as the

French translation of deterrence. France pursued an independent nuclear strategy from NATO, and *dissuasion* using French pronunciation has legacy meanings embracing the *préstrategique* concept and *tous azimuths* targeting. In any event, if the distinction is not apparent in translation into the language of a nuclear power, it is probably not a useful one to pursue, except in that in English 'dissuasion' might have a gentler nuance.

Understanding the Cognitive Domain

The point has been made earlier that the cognitive domain is less predictable than the physical domain. In the debate over the effects-based approach, it is frequently overlooked that positive effects are only a subset of consequences of military action and that many other effects could be negative. The cognitive domain is complex because of the vast number of variables. Furthermore, students of complexity in its technical sense would argue that unpredictability is a defining factor of complexity. Another feature of the cognitive domain is that the academic disciplines that explore it (sociology, social psychology, anthropology, etc.) are immature in comparison with the exact sciences. An important conclusion is that any strategic or operational plan that is heavily dependent on an understanding of the cognitive domain in a particular theatre is extremely high risk. Solutions cannot be engineered. The de-risking of such plans requires branches and sequels that are not so dependent on managing the cognitive domain.

Once again, compellent strategies and operations are most at risk in this respect. Intuitively, a nation, alliance, or coalition cannot be totally dependent on conventional deterrence, whether inherent or directed, and there will usually be plans to address its failure. Nevertheless, nations will typically see strategic choices that emphasise deterrence as more economical financially, particularly in the context of alliances and economies which might be made in plans to address the failure of deterrence.

One method of de-risking deterrent strategies is to have a commonly accepted international framework of understanding (which may be expressed in law and agreed practices) in which deterrence operates. There were presumptions of such a framework during the Cold War which fortunately were never tested. In the present environment there is no truly comprehensive conceptual framework. In any event, such a framework would most probably exist among and between nation actors, and the most difficult security challenges are posed by nonstate actors operating within unshared conceptual frameworks and, perhaps, with transcendental aims.

Nuclear Deterrence

While nuclear deterrence fits into this general analysis, some important features need to be highlighted:

Inherent Deterrence

The issue of inherent deterrence is particularly salient in the present security environment. It is patently not helpful for existing nuclear powers to identify targets for deterrence in their declaratory policies, and, since the Cold War, most have avoided declaring direct deterrence. However, nuclear powers need benchmarks for their capabilities, which will probably be the existing levels available to the other nuclear powers, among other measures of requirement.

Deterrence of Other WMD

The issue of nuclear deterrence of nonnuclear weapons and of war is particularly testing. Declaratory policies typically do not imply that nuclear weapons have this role. Equally, uncertainty as to the occasions for use is a feature of inherent nuclear deterrent strategies. There is also a presumption that major nuclear powers are unlikely to confront each other in conventional war because of the risk of escalation, which raises the question of deliberate first use.

Probability of Response

There has been a shift from the Cold War nuclear deterrent message of a high level of probability that nuclear weapons would be used in certain defined situations (flexible response and the ladder of escalation) to messages of deliberate uncer-

22

tainty as to the circumstances of use. Intuitively, the world is hardly a safer place as a result.

Communications

A related issue is that of communication of nuclear policy and of intentions. During the Cold War clearly defined protocols involving formal signal traffic would have served to minimise misunderstanding amongst a relatively small number of actors. There is now a larger number of state and potentially nonstate actors with very different characteristics, operating in a more globalised environment with a host of informal means of communication involving the media and internet. In addition to the complexity problems mentioned earlier is one of reinforced misunderstanding through informal communications and ill-considered rhetoric.

Perception of Legality, Morality, and Entitlement

The framework of international treaties and agreements governing ownership of nuclear weapons and restraining proliferation may have international legal standing, but perceptions as to the morality of entitlement within strategic cultures will affect nations' decisions to pursue nuclear weapon capability. Existing nuclear powers should reinforce the moral standing of their ownership through their declaratory purposes if they are to justify nonproliferation measures and limit nuclear arms races. Declaratory devices such as **no first use** policies and **negative security assurances** are examples.[7] A crucial moral justification for major nuclear powers' ownership is extended deterrence: that is, the treaty obligation to provide nuclear deterrence to nonnuclear powers.

Conclusions

This analysis generates several broad conclusions, each of which merits further discussion:

- It is helpful to understand deterrence within the broad concept of inducement. Directed deterrence is a subset of military coercion. Its partner is compellence.

- Inherent, undirected, or existential deterrence is an important concept in the present security environment, allowing nations on the one hand to build relationships across difficult boundaries in a globalised world, while on the other hand preserving deterrent capacity to deny options for the use of the military instrument for bullying and blackmail without provoking arms races.

- While there is a distinction to be made between latent and directed inducement, and inherent and directed deterrence in particular, the posture and behaviour of forces can communicate a rapid shift from one side of the divide to the other.

- There is a spectrum of direct inducement, from symbolic actions to the limited use of violence. Deterrence may be reinforced by limited violence, but this runs the risk of unintended consequences.

- Inherent deterrence has particular relevance in the nuclear context, but there is the associated problem of deliberate uncertainty and the risks that this could spawn–particularly in an environment in which communication means are multiple, diverse, and open to misunderstanding.

Strategic culture is an intrinsically important variable in multipolar deterrence. If states or other actors do not share a common strategic culture when they communicate and respond to the intention to deter, there is a high risk that the deterrent message will not be delivered effectively and with predictable consequences. Strategic culture is fundamental to effective communication. Understanding the differences and shaping perceptions in an alien culture are key challenges.

Michael Codner
Director, Military Sciences
RUSI

Notes

1. See Michael Codner, "Coercion from the Sea," in Eric Grove and Peter Hore (ed.), *Dimensions of Sea Power: Strategic Choice in the Modern World* (Hull: The University of Hull Press, 2001). The author prepared a paper on conventional deterrence for the Naval Staff in 1993 at the request of the outgoing assistant chief of the Naval Staff, RADM Peter Abbott. The response of

the central Policy Department is not in the public domain, but was critical for these reasons. The paper was not taken forward, but its analysis was published in this chapter.

2. James Cable, *Gunboat Diplomacy 1919–1979: Political Applications of Limited Naval Force* (London: Palgrave Macmillan, 1986). There is a 1996 revision.

3. Edward N. Luttwak, *The Political Uses of Sea Power* (Baltimore, MD: The Johns Hopkins University Press, 1974).

4. In his classic analysis, Thomas Schelling contrasts brute force with coercion. Cable's "definitive use" is in Schelling's class of brute force. See Thomas C. Schelling, *Arms and Influence* (New Haven, CT: Yale University Press, 1966).

5. *BR 1806: The Fundamentals of British Maritime Doctrine* (London: HMSO, 1995). New editions have since been produced.

6. It is not, however, an academic neologism. 'The suasioun of swetenesse' features in Geoffrey Chaucer's *Troilus and Criseyde* (c. 1385).

7. The conditional undertaking is not to use nuclear weapons against a state which does not possess them.

Military Sciences Department, RUSI

The Military Sciences Department tackles the question 'What is Military?' in the complicated security environment of today and the future. It studies the purpose and roles of military forces and the many ways in which they affect security for good and bad throughout the world. Its mission is 'to contribute substantially to the wise use of the military instrument'.

There are four programmes which conduct research and arrange conferences, seminars, workshops, and other meetings:

- The Maritime Studies Programme
- The Technology and Acquisition Programme
- The Land Operations and Capabilities Programme, and
- The Armed Forces and Society Programme.

In addition, the programme heads and director form The Aerospace Group, which integrates research on the air and space operational environments.

For further details of conference and research work undertaken by this department, please visit http://www.rusi.org/research/militarysciences/.

Alternatively, please contact the Director of Military Sciences, Michael Codner, at codner@rusi.org.

Chapter 3

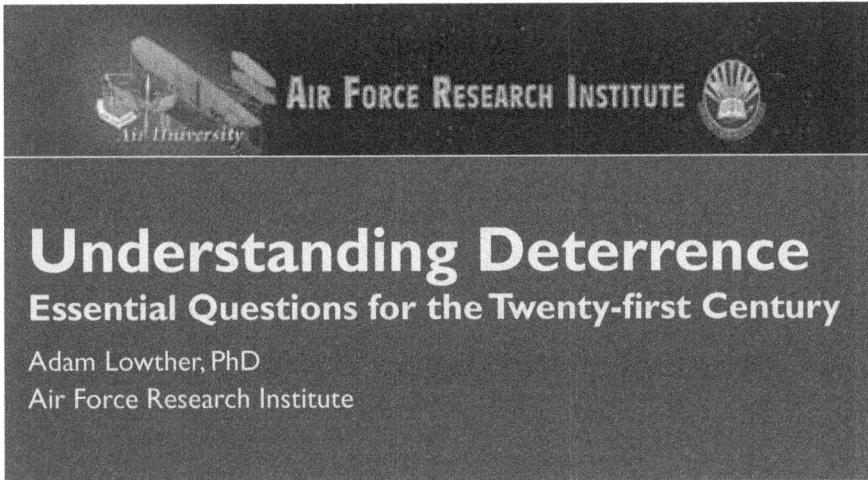

AIR FORCE RESEARCH INSTITUTE
Air University

Understanding Deterrence
Essential Questions for the Twenty-first Century

Adam Lowther, PhD
Air Force Research Institute

1. Is deterrence more than nuclear?

Joint Publication 1-02, *Department of Defense Dictionary of Military and Associated Terms*, defines *deterrence* as *"the prevention from action by fear of the consequences. Deterrence is a state of mind brought about by the existence of a credible threat of unacceptable counteraction."* Thus, deterrence is fundamentally about achieving a psychological effect. Since deterrence comprises capability and credibility, the success or failure of deterrence is premised on the deterrer's ability to convince the deteree that changing the status quo is not worth the potential costs. Prior to the advent of nuclear weapons, states clearly used deterrence concepts in their strategies for dealing with adversaries. However, during the Cold War, the nuclear capabilities possessed by the United States and the Soviet Union and the overarching structure of the bipolar conflict gradually constrained deterrence concepts in the nuclear arena. Following the end of the Cold War and, more recently, the terrorist attacks on 9/11, the United States has begun to take a larger view of deterrence theory. By definition, there is no reason deterrence must be nuclear.

US Strategic Command's Deterrence Operations—Joint Operating Concept (DO-JOC) clearly illustrates a wider view of deterrence beyond nuclear issues. In the case of the Air Force, deterrence can work across the spectrum of capabilities.

Although some treat dissuasion, denial, and deterrence as separate concepts, it is possible to think of deterrence as operating across the spectrum of conflict with the use of compellence intervening when deterrence fails.

If deterrence is understood as described, it is possible to develop deterrence strategies that apply to actors ranging from nonstate actors to peer competitors.

2. Is unilateral or bilateral nuclear disarmament a wise policy?

The most recent literature offered by advocates of disarmament clearly shows that there is only limited rationale for unilateral disarmament. The argument of "going to zero" relies largely on moral objections to the existence of nuclear weapons, rather than on identified national security issues. That is to say, there is no compelling evidence to suggest that nuclear disarmament will reduce threats in the international system, lead to greater international peace, or reduce potential threats to the homeland. To the contrary, historical evidence suggests that deterrence works best when deterrence threats are more severe.

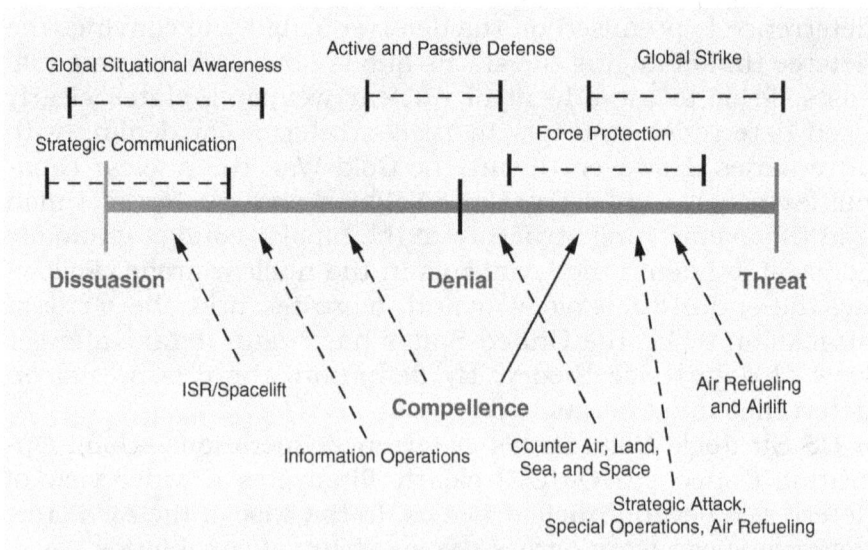

Russia

Bilateral reductions in operationally deployed strategic nuclear weapons are possible between the United States and Russia, but largely because Russian security concerns do not focus on the United States. Increasingly, Russia is focusing on Europe and China. While the United States remains the single greatest concern for Russia, the level of concern is at an all-time low.

Russia believes its nuclear arsenal is vital to national security for three reasons. First, nuclear weapons are a prestige weapon and the last symbol of Soviet empire. It should not be forgotten that the Soviet Union was once the largest land empire on earth. Russians have not forgotten their heritage. Second, the Russians believe nuclear weapons deter the United States from interfering in Russian affairs in the near-abroad, such as in the recent conflict with Georgia. Third, nuclear weapons deter a feared Chinese expansion into eastern Siberia, which the Russian army cannot deter with conventional forces.

With Russian security focusing closer to home, tactical nuclear weapons are increasingly important to Russia. Thus, President Medvedev is willing to support a new round of Strategic Arms Reducation Talks negotiations, but only if they do not include reduction in the Russian tactical nuclear arsenal. Fewer American operationally deployed strategic nuclear weapons means

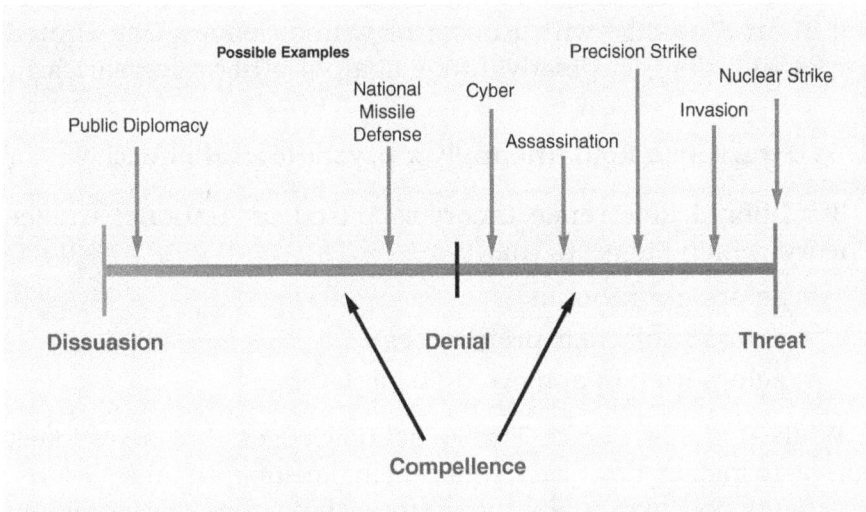

the United States can hold less Russian infrastructure at risk, which the Russians desire. Since they have no plans to wage war against the United States, fewer long-range strike weapons presents an opportunity for cost savings. It is the medium- and short-range weapons the Russians highly value.

To suggest that Russia will stop current modernization efforts because of US overtures is a mistake. President Medvedev and Prime Minister Putin are pursuing a clear strategy that preserves the maximum freedom of action—both nuclear and conventional—for Russia. The United States must come to grips with the fact that it is no longer the center of Russian security concerns.

China

The Chinese are currently increasing their nuclear arsenal by 12–16 weapons per year and will soon field 1,000 ICBMs/SLBMs. While the Chinese have a stated no-first-strike nuclear policy (minimum deterrence), there is no reason to believe that they would be willing to stop expanding and modernizing their forces to join the United States in arms reductions. China clearly sees itself as a rising state and the United States as a nation in decline.

Bilateral or unilateral arms reductions below current numbers threaten to place the United States in a position in which it would expend approximately 70 percent of its nuclear arsenal in an exchange with Russia or China, leaving the United States at a distinct disadvantage against other adversaries.

3. Is deterrence fundamentally a psychological effect?

Traditional deterrence theory is based on Rational Choice Theory, which suggests that:

- actors are rational
- actors rank their preferences
- actors seek to achieve their preferences

While Rational Choice Theory acknowledges that actors lack complete information and frequently make suboptimal decisions, the theory does not accept the premise that actors are irrational.

Much of the writing of early deterrence theorists such as Bernard Brodie, Thomas Schelling, Glenn Snyder, and others accepted the tenets of Rational Choice Theory and applied it to Soviet/American interaction during the Cold War. Assured destruction was an approach that applied perfect rationality to both the United States and the Soviet Union with the expectation that each state was a unified actor making rational decisions.

In *Arms and Influence*, Thomas Schelling explains the psychological nature of deterrence:

> It is a tradition in military planning to attend to an enemy's capabilities, not his intentions. But deterrence is about intentions—not just *estimating* enemy intentions but *influencing* them. The hardest part is communicating our own intentions. War at best is ugly, costly, and dangerous, and at worst disastrous. Nations have been known to bluff; they have also been known to make threats sincerely and change their minds when the chips were down. Many territories are just not worth a war, especially a war that can get out of hand. A persuasive threat of war may deter an aggressor; the problem is to make it persuasive, to keep it from sounding like a bluff (p. 35).

With the inherent uncertainty of international politics, states are always liable to make suboptimal decisions. Thus, later rational-choice thinkers developed the concept of bounded rationality, which accounts for incomplete information, stress, and other variables that can lead actors to take actions that do not result in desired outcomes.

The crux of successful deterrence lies in understanding what each actor values, what each is willing to risk, and in effectively communicating one's position. Not only is deterrence about psychology, it is about altering an adversary's psychology.

4. Extended deterrence—where does the size of the force produce a tipping point that leads to nuclear proliferation, especially as the United States reduces the size of the nuclear arsenal?

The two variables that matter in deterrence are capability and credibility, with credibility mattering more. This is perhaps even more accurate when considering US extended deterrence. The difficulty in attempting to determine the numbers of weapons at which extended deterrence fails is the logical paradox that deterrence can create.

For example, it is possible to be capable but not credible, and it is possible to be credible but not capable. Given recent statements suggesting that the United States will de-emphasize nuclear weapons in national security policy, aggressively move to zero, and forgo any modernization of the arsenal, the United States could appear less credible to allies and adversaries alike while remaining just as capable—at least until the policies begin to take effect.

Israel, on the other hand, is far less capable but has clearly demonstrated through the use of conventional forces that any threats it issues are credible. While Israel may lose a large-scale conflict with its principal adversaries, there is little doubt that the Israelis will inflict maximum damage. Thus, credibility potentially enhances the Israeli deterrent strategy more than its capability.

This combination of factors makes it difficult to determine a specific number at which extended deterrence becomes untenable. Japanese officials have responded recently to statements

32

concerning reductions in the US nuclear arsenal by expressing their desire to maintain current numbers. The Japanese view continued reductions as both undermining capability and credibility. German leaders are playing a different game. In public, for example, the German foreign minister recently called for the removal of remaining American tactical nuclear weapons. In private, Germany maintains that the small number of tactical nuclear weapons remaining in Germany is vital to its national security.

With the United States having already reduced its nuclear arsenal by 80 percent since the end of the Cold War, further reductions threaten to undermine extended deterrence credibility and may lead to proliferation. The primary factor that may prevent proliferation among states covered by American extended deterrence is the expense, which is particularly high for advanced nations with stagnant economies.

5. What is the relationship between capability and credibility?

A state's past behavior is perhaps the best indicator of the relationship between capability and credibility. If, for example, a state has a long history of bluffing, the relationship between capability and credibility may be low. If, however, a state has a history of carrying out threats, capability and credibility may be strongly correlated.

The cases of North Korea and Iran present two examples of a strong correlation between capability and credibility—leading to action. According to statements by North Korean and Iranian officials, the nuclear programs of both states are (to a large degree) predicated on the idea that a nuclear-armed North Korea/Iran can deter the United States from attempting a future invasion. In this case, US conventional capabilities are highly capable and, because of American post–Cold War foreign policy, highly credible. Thus, the North Koreans are willing to face international sanctions to deter a US invasion through nuclear-weapons acquisition.

World War II provides an excellent example of capability and credibility failing to correlate. After Neville Chamberlain and Édouard Daladier signed the Munich Agreement (1938) granting the Sudetenland to Germany, British and French threats to declare war on Germany should Hitler invade Poland lacked credibility when made in the months that followed Munich.

Thus, the answer to the question of whether capability or credibility is more important is, it depends. Adversaries look to a nation's past and its current interests when attempting to determine the credibility of deterrence and any threat that may accompany it.

6. What are conditions under which actors would use nuclear weapons?

The United States

The United States currently has no stated nuclear-use policy. During the Cold War, US national policy disavowed first-strike use of nuclear weapons. However, NATO policy differed. In the *National Strategy to Combat Weapons of Mass Destruction* (2002), President Bush suggested that the United States may respond with nuclear weapons to a WMD attack on the homeland, but as with all previous administrations, strategic ambiguity—the creation of purposeful grey areas—remains a core aspect of American nuclear policy.

During the Cold War, it was widely understood that "Mutually Assured Destruction" created a strategic balance in which there was no rationale for either side to launch a first strike

since both sides (US or USSR) would retain a sufficient second-strike capability to negate any potential benefits from a first strike. Thus, custom has created an approach to nuclear weapons in the United States where it is widely believed that the role of nuclear weapons is to prevent the use of nuclear weapons. This relegates them to a position in which there is only one viable option for their use—retaliation.

Russia

Throughout the Cold War, Russian policy was very much like that of the United States. And, much like the United States today, Russia has shifted its strategic nuclear weapons policy to reflect the post–Cold War strategic environment. Where the United States and Russia differ is in the apparent willingness of Russia to use its tactical nuclear weapons for political purposes (prestige and European blackmail) and to protect its large and porous border with China. Since Russian conventional forces are incapable of defeating the People's Liberation Army in a conventional conflict in the Russian Far East, President Medvedev must rely on nuclear weapons that target China to prevent any aggression against Russia.

China

China has a clearly articulated policy of no first use, which is part its minimum deterrence strategy. It is reasonable to sug-

gest that China would resort to nuclear weapons only in a retaliatory response.

India and Pakistan

The nuclear arsenals of India and Pakistan are specifically
intended to deter aggression from the other. The existence of
nuclear weapons has been successful in de-escalating a bitter
rivalry over the past decade. There is, however, some uncertainty as to where the line in the sand is drawn for nuclear use.
Pakistan lacks the conventional capability to defeat India in a
major war, making it more likely that Pakistan will resort to
nuclear weapons should India launch an invasion of Pakistan.
India would likely respond in kind if Pakistan were to use nuclear weapons.

France

With approximately 500 nuclear warheads, which are currently
being converted from land-based ballistic missile to sea-launched
ballistic missile roles, France's nuclear weapons policy can be
understood as political in nature. Unlike the United States, France
has not developed a counterforce nuclear strategy but would use
nuclear weapons to destroy an adversary's economic capacity to
wage war. This strategy is premised on the idea that France is a
small country that lacks the capacity to survive a full-scale
exchange. This approach would apparently favor using nuclear

weapons in an escalatory fashion, beginning with a limited strike to promote the de-escalation of a conflict.

Note also that France struggles to cover the cost of its nuclear program, which is leading to significant aging in warheads and delivery platforms with no clear signs of a desire to modernize the fleet.

Britain

Much like France, Britain does not believe it can win a nuclear war. Thus, it shares a similar strategy which already relies on a monad of four ballistic missile submarines. The flagging British economy and the end of the Cold War have seen pressure mount to reduce the program further with an eventual goal of eliminating it. Many in British government see the extended deterrence the United States provides as sufficient protection against potential Russian aggression in Europe.

NATO

There is some debate within NATO as to whether US tactical nuclear weapons should remain on European soil. Some suggest it makes NATO member states a target for Russia. Others suggest they prevent Russian aggression. As mentioned earlier, European publics are largely opposed to the presence of nuclear

weapons, but host governments are reluctant to support their removal. It is difficult to say if European NATO members would support using nuclear weapons under any conditions except in response to a first strike.

7. What alternative views inform our understanding of deterrence in the twenty-first century?

Some European states, such as the Nordic states, often view deterrence as a police action rather than as a military action. They deter within their own borders, not seeing an external threat. The most significant concern of most European Union (EU) nations is cross-border migration. Once migrants gain entry into the EU, they have free access across the entire union. Nations such as France and Germany are struggling with the concept of assimilation into their society. Currently enclaves exist within each nation where underprivileged minorities reside in congested proximity. The Islamic enclave in Paris erupted in 2005, rioting for weeks before police were able to restore order. The close proximity to the Middle East creates a different dynamic for all EU nations. France and Britain are not exceptions, but with nuclear weapons, they also see a rationale to deter externally (principally state on state).

The 2008 Sarkozy administration's white paper defined deterrence for French policy as nuclear only. It went on to discuss terrorism in a dissuasion context. The latest definition of deterrence was designed principally for an internal and EU audience. Historically, France has viewed deterrence in a larger context. For example, the Maginot Line was specifically designed to deter German aggression.

8. Can nonstate actors be deterred by nuclear or conventional means?

Nonstate actors, such as al-Qaeda, do not typically begin their efforts to change the status quo by resorting to terrorism. Deterring nonstate actors may be best understood within the context of the Kinetic Effects Pyramid. Nonstate actors prefer operating at the highest possible level, but because they are

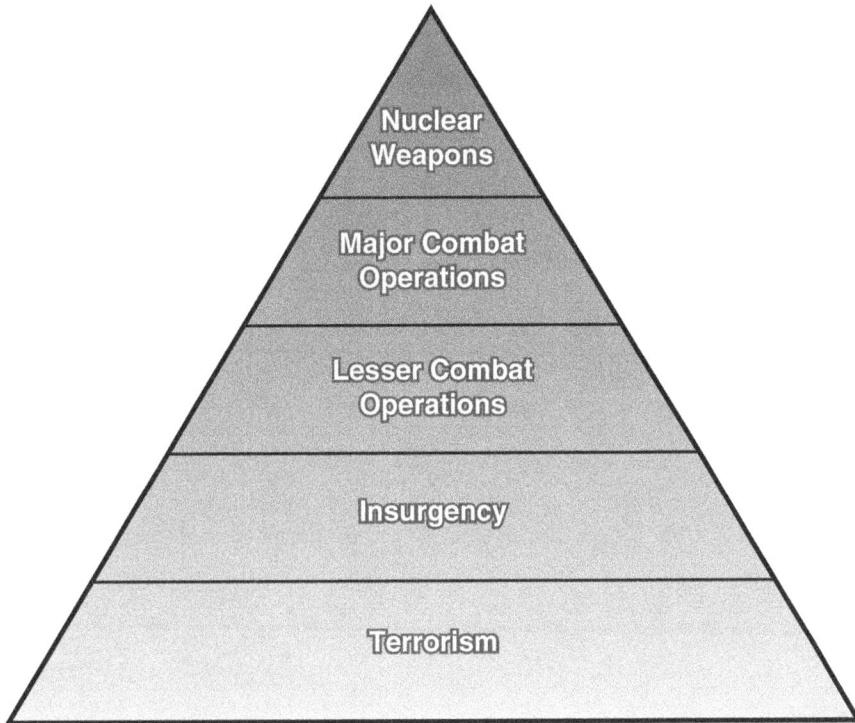

weak, are pushed to the bottom of the pyramid where they must resort to kinetic effects that present the least probability of altering the status quo. As Mao Zedong wrote, every terrorist/insurgent seeks to move through the stages of conflict until he can defeat his adversary in large-scale conflict.

According to the above logic, it is possible to develop an understanding of nonstate actors that attaches rationality to their behavior. If an adversary is rational, he can be deterred. And, just as with states, the success of deterrence depends on determining what a nonstate actor values, holding it at risk (capability), and effectively communicating a threat to the nonstate actor (credibility).

If terrorists were to acquire nuclear weapons, they would be more useful as a tool for blackmail or propaganda than as a weapon of mass destruction. Terrorists seek to change the status quo by targeting noncombatants who can then shift the policies of the target government.

Al-Qaeda's threatening to use a nuclear weapon against the United States is far more powerful than actually using it. In one instance, Americans may pressure their government to change a policy. But once nuclear weapons are used on American soil, Americans will demand vengeance and unleash the hounds of hell to reach those responsible. Osama bin Laden is well aware of the repercussions that will follow any WMD attack on the United States.

Chapter 4

Policy and Purpose
The Economy of Deterrence*

Norton A. Schwartz, General, USAF
Timothy R. Kirk, Lieutenant Colonel, USAF

The 2008 Air Force Association convention chief of staff keynote addressed the subject of deterrence, asserting that it is not a fading construct in national security. On the contrary, deterrence is reemerging and growing in importance as an aspect of US defense policy. The keynote speech invited the audience to think about deterrence in a broader sense and how the US Air Force can contribute in a fashion relevant to twenty-first-century national defense. The purpose of this article is to add to the growing body of literature that seeks a broader understanding of deterrence and how it fits with other forms of policy such as dissuasion, assurance, and insurance.[1]

Identifying and understanding the distinctions among these concepts and how they relate to US policy are fundamental to explaining the relevance of deterrence to our collective security. This task is certainly ambitious, but the need demands consideration. Deterrence policy has shown itself an exquisitely beneficial tool in obtaining national security objectives. On the other hand, deterrence—either misunderstood or misapplied—can form the basis for incomplete or ill-advised US policy, especially in terms of how and when to use military power to achieve high-stakes national security objectives. A variety of recent and historical examples attests to a vital requirement for understanding how disconnects among military capabilities, national policy, and the value of national purpose can cause unfavorable if not disastrous consequences.[2]

Such disconnects have often occurred because the policy paradigms or the associated strategies employed were frequently designed for a bygone or mismatched context. This situation has become more apparent as the rate of change in the global security environment exceeds that of policy design, making the

---

*Originally published in *Strategic Studies Quarterly* 3, no. 1 (Spring 2009): 11–30.

disconnects even more pronounced. In recent years, defense strategists persuasively postulated that "the United States needs to develop a more comprehensive approach to deterrence that looks beyond nuclear weapons . . . [and] tailor deterrence strategies and postures to each potential adversary." Initially, the primary reason for this new requirement was the emergence of a new strategic environment as "the Cold War is now over; the Soviet Union is gone. Advanced weapons capabilities have spread and will continue to spread to other parties . . . the behavior of numerous other parties must be watched and preferably controlled."[3] In addition to this contextual shift, Russia has succeeded the Soviet remnant, subnational extremist groups disrupt the international system, and ascending regional powers contest for resources in an increasingly competitive world. With these and other trends in mind, the implications suggest a need for innovative policy and supporting defense capabilities. It seems clear that Dr. Schlesinger's following observation applies to arms control in specific terms and more broadly, by implication, to defense policy in general, where "the future of arms control will depend on the willingness of our negotiators to shed obsolescent ideas."[4] We suggest the same is true for the future of deterrence policy and the form the military instrument takes to support its purpose.

Our intent is to promote expanded thinking about future deterrence policy's role and to provide perspective on how US Air Force capabilities can support policy's purpose. That being said, it is important to have a clear understanding of what deterrence is—and is not. To those ends, we will first identify some limitations of this theory and then address a fundamental question on the nature of national power, followed by a theoretical framework for policy. We will also examine some characteristics of different regions of the framework and the challenges they present to modern strategists. We examine the specific aspects of policy as they relate to both national and subnational actors in deterrence. The article concludes with an assessment of the economy of deterrence policy within the theory framework as we examine the implications for US Air Force strategists, leaders, and Airmen at large.

Theoretical Limitations

Our exercise here is academic, but our purpose is much more meaningful. The consequences of our failure to understand how military capabilities relate to applicable policy are unacceptably severe. When called upon, we must be able to help our civilian leaders design deterrence policies that are credible, supportable, and logical. We must know when and under what conditions deterrence is a likely policy candidate, the requisite supporting capabilities, and how our craft might achieve the desired purpose. The subsequent theory serves as the foundation for understanding policy, purpose, and the economy of deterrence. This construct is not meant to serve as doctrine, dogma, or a deterrence strategy, nor is it meant to be exhaustive; it presents no proven predictive ability with any degree of certainty. For the purposes of this article, it is limited to the military instrument, with an eye toward an expanded understanding of deterrence's interplay with the other instruments. Our examination will initially limit discussion to nation-state interplay and later will examine the interrelationships between national and subnational forces.

We acknowledge the scholarly wisdom that likely applies here. A great strategist once observed,

> I am painfully aware that scholars and officials, civilian and military, are apt to be mesmerized by their own conceptual genius. . . . We love our categories and our subcategories. Their invention gives us an illusion of intellectual control. . . . The results all too often are official definitions that tend to the encyclopaedic [sic] and are utterly indigestible.[5]

Our sincere hope is to avoid this trap and rather provide some compelling points to ponder for strategists and tacticians alike. If these issues do appear to emerge, please excuse them as unintended by-products of genuine efforts to encourage dialogue on, and consideration of, current and future challenges for military thinkers.

National Power, Legitimacy, and Control

The ideas here consider deterrence in proportion to other policy; however, policy and purpose must always have primacy in these discussions. As Patrick M. Morgan observed, "Understanding [deterrence] means facing up to the fact that it is inherently imperfect. It does not consistently work and we cannot manipulate it sufficiently to fix that . . . it must be approached with care and used as part of a larger tool kit."[6] Accordingly, this article attempts to treat deterrence with appropriate care by examining its use with respect to military means and the other metaphorical tools in the policy kit. We should recognize that each policy has some purpose or intent in mind and that the military instrument supports the policy in achieving that objective. The military instrument works in concert with the diplomatic, economic, and information instruments of national power to support policies aimed at achieving specific purposes (fig. 1).

A fundamental question to initiate our discussion is this: What is national power? The question is important because the answer presumably dictates precisely what the instruments of national power should seek to attain. National power takes on a variety of practical forms depending on geopolitical conditions. However, we can identify certain essential characteristics of national power. History is full of examples of nations mistaking the ability

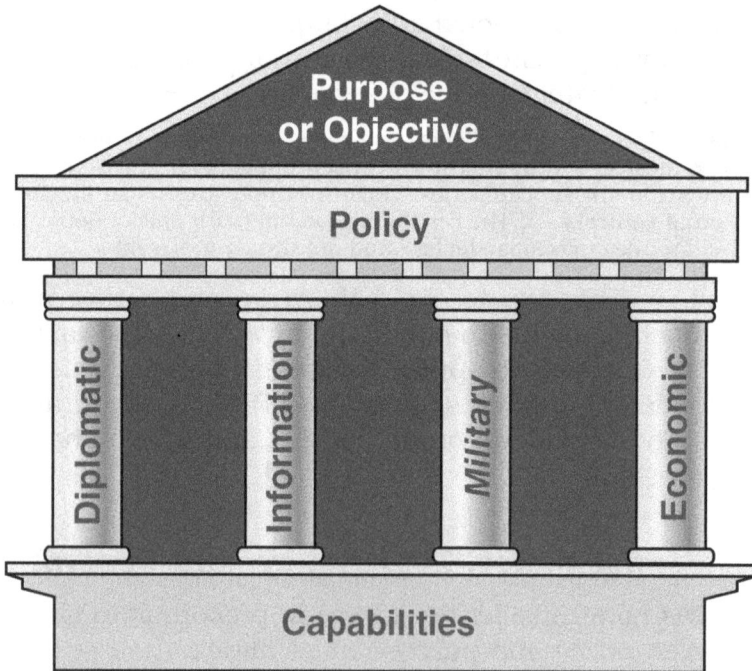

Figure 1. Policy and purpose relationship

to exert control as a dominant and durable form of national power. Likewise, we see historical examples of weak actors with superior legitimacy and political will defeating materially stronger foes. Perhaps we can estimate what is necessary for national power but not that which is both necessary and sufficient. We offer the assumption that nations seek some purpose or object of value to them, and they leverage their instruments of national power to achieve those ends.[7] We therefore express national power in terms of the total number of choices available to a nation and the maximum national value those choices are capable of achieving.[8]

Legitimacy and control are contributing components of national power. Nation-states derive legitimacy from their moral, resource, and humanitarian obligations to their citizens and to neighboring nations. Meeting these obligations establishes some level of legitimacy, and international norms and regimes form the basis of international relationships that allow nations to maximize their ability to meet these obligations. Norms and regimes form the basis of international law, economics, diplomacy, and warfare where the expectation of justice between states is founded upon nations meeting their obligations without infringing on other nations' ability to meet their own obligations.[9]

Control, on the other hand, is one nation's ability to affect the cost-and-benefit equation for other nations over time. Nations can reward each other by offering mutual benefits or can exact costs by depriving each other of something of value. The payoff or reward is the ultimate consideration in the exercise. Control leverages some set of ways and means to alter the cost-benefit-reward proposition in some way as to compel an actor to do something the actor is not naturally motivated or inclined to do.

We assume these two components share an economic relationship. Legitimacy and control coincide to determine the number of national choices available to a nation and the maximum national value those choices can achieve. They work together much like supply and demand. Economics explains how supply and demand determine the market price of a product and the total quantity of products that will be sold. In the exercise of national power, legitimacy and control determine how many choices are available and the value of those choices' outcomes. We will limit our discussion of this point to the relevant portion of our theoretical construct, for much more could be written about the economic dynamics of national power. For our purposes here, it is necessary to recognize that the instruments of national power work together to achieve something of value; they achieve that value by building legitimacy and exercising control with national resources. This forms an economy of policy; investment of national resources in the instruments of power enables collective action. These actions are choices taken to leverage legitimacy and control to attain value. This suggests that the best policy is one that maximizes value for a minimum investment; poor policy invests more than the value of return. The theoretical framework that follows utilizes the concept of national value in deriving specific aspects of policy and purpose.

At the most elementary level, policy and purpose form proximate considerations, and policy is subordinate to the object it seeks. This purpose provides the value and meaning to any policy associated with it, and all policy should link to some demonstrable purpose or object. This is certainly the ideal rather than consistent reality, and it is important to note that policy forms at the highest levels of national decision making where complexities abound; the practitioners of the instruments of national power are, at most, advisors to the makers of policy on the realm of the possible. The instruments of national power must support designated policy to a prescribed degree to achieve the desired object.

If we allow the assumption that this principle applies to both the conduct of war and the military instrument as constituted by all its ways and means, then we find a prescription for proper conceptualization of defense issues and strategy. We accept the conclusion that "the first, the supreme, the most far-reaching act of judgment that the statesman and commander have to make is to establish the kind of war [application of the military instrument] on which they are embarking; neither mistaking it for, nor trying to turn it into, something that is alien to its nature." This logic serves as a prescription suggesting our examination of deterrence, or any other policy application of the military instrument, should begin not with ways and means in mind, but rather ends—policy's object—followed by the requisite blend of the instruments of national power. We must also think of the interplay, both by design and coincidence, of inter-related policies and their objects in context.[10]

Theoretical Framework for Policy

Our examination deals squarely in theory, and we acknowl-edge that the question of policy and purpose in the realm of deterrence requires a stipulation that "in discussing the *theory* it is important to distinguish it from deterrence *strategy* . . . the theory concerns the underlying principles on which any strat-egy is to rest."[11] This article proposes no strategy but seeks to expand the understanding of strategic potential by illuminat-ing related policy as a whole. Both etymology and political par-lance offer the notional purpose of deterrence "to frighten away" an aggressor. Clearly there is much more to deterrence policy's purpose, but we can understand from this simple consider-ation that deterrence has a *negative* purpose; deterrent intent is to prevent an adversary's action. The concept offered here assumes this is the case and posits that each policy is ulti-mately governed by that primary nature and that any negative policy purpose can share a corresponding positive policy pur-pose—each aspect offering different features, yet inextricably affecting the other to some degree. In the case of deterrence's negative purpose in statecraft and strategy, we see an opposing positive purpose of attracting and assuring allies against the ranks of the potential aggressor. These two objectives of policy work together toward our national security, the value of which is enumerated by the rigor of our policy in preserving coopera-tive friends and preventing adversaries from hostile acts of vio-lence. In a similar fashion, we must consider policy implica-tions on both the nation-state and subnational actor levels while carefully confirming our assumptions regarding the ra-tionality of all the actors involved.

The ways and means available within the instruments of power are sets of capabilities designed to create effects that support the attainment of policy. This point cannot be over-emphasized, as capabilities should not substitute for the purpose in policy making; rather, they are subordinated to policy's work in obtaining its purpose.

Failure in recognizing this relationship leads to all sorts of problems as technologically sophisticated capabilities begin to drive policy independent of the purpose or value. To paraphrase Abraham Kaplan's Law of the Instrument, if all you have is a hammer then every problem looks like a nail.[12] This is not to say that policy is insulated from capability considerations, for no policy can hope to achieve its purpose without requisite capabilities. Military capabilities aid policy makers in deciding which objects can be achieved with acceptable means at a reasonable cost; capabilities must remain adjunct to policy and purpose in appropriate fashion.

The theory we offer here is designed to explain the interaction of positive and negative objects relating to deterrence and to help explain the challenges of moving from Cold War deterrence policy (as it was) to future deterrence policy. The framework is built upon a foundation of the gradient of allies and adversaries along with another of Clausewitz's notions. We will begin with the former and posit that our relationship with other nation-states can be expressed as a continuum of coexistence and cooperative potential. One end of the continuum represents our very best friend—a wholly vested partner committed to peaceful coexistence. The other represents a bitter adversary—one who is devoted to depriving us of our sovereignty and to ensuring our ultimate destruction. The latter notion is considered here as a treatment of Clausewitz's assertion that "the more powerful and inspiring the motives for war, the more they affect the belligerent nations and the fiercer the tensions."[13] The level of *power* behind the motives toward a policy's purpose will theoretically drive the level of *force* behind the policy. There are exceptions to this principle in bluff and blunder, but for the purposes of this examination, we will consider that in general the more powerful the motive for the purpose, the more forceful the policy. Furthermore, any policy's force can be generally characterized as fixed or flexible.

Two Types of Policy

Fixed policy is deterministic in nature and is characterized by a declared statement of intent and action, which can take on a variety of forms. We are interested here with the "if . . . then" nature of a fixed policy. Thomas Schelling describes this aspect of deterrence policy distinctly as "setting the stage—by announcement, by rigging the trip-wire, by incurring the obligation—and waiting."[14] In this type of policy, the threat or outcome is clearly and overtly communicated with a rational and perceived credibility in two forms. The first is to say to an adversary: if your nation does something specified that our nation finds unfavorable, then we will take this specified action against you. The second is to the friend: if another actor does something specified that both our nations find unfavorable, then we will take this specified action on your behalf. Our policy is fixed; we wait, and our response is *determined* by the choices of the other party.

Likewise, we can characterize the flexible form of policy as an associative one that suggests a response may follow to a varying degree. Our focus here includes the "if . . . maybe" form of flexible policy. In this type of policy, we associate by movement, posture, procurement, or inference that if another nation takes any unfavorable action, then we might take some unspecified action in response. The outcome may be *associated* with the choices of the other party but not necessarily so. We set our policy, go about our business, and retain the flexibility to act in response to the choices of the other party. The two policy types are distinct, serve different functions in achieving different types of objects, and derive their places based on the perceived value of policy's purpose.

Once we have defined these regions of the framework by their distinct characteristics, we can see a series of policy relationships form based upon their functions (fig. 2). The region we are perhaps most familiar with in dealing with a negative purpose toward our adversary is the upper-left quadrant. This region is the classic notion of immediate "deterrence." The far-upper-left portion of the quadrant is the extreme portion of deterrence when "mutually assured destruction" notions exist, and we will look at that portion in greater detail later. For now, we will refer to the deterrence region as Colin Gray describes it: "In its immediate form, deterrence is always specific. It is about persuading a particular leader or leaders, at a particular time, not to take particular actions. The details will be all important, not be marginal."[15] This describes the two factors in play in the policy toward a negative purpose, namely the fixed "if . . . then" policy dealing with

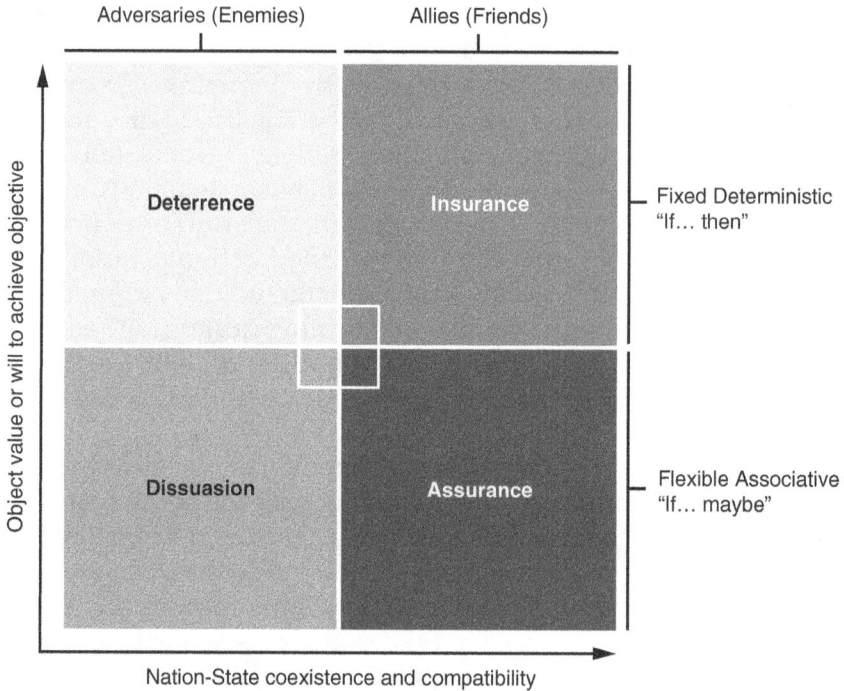

Figure 2. Policy types and relationship

an adversary nation-state. It features the element of predictable automaticity. The adversary can reliably expect if it performs the act, then it "would be assumed to have [its] address on it. The United States would then return postage. Automaticity of this kind concentrates the mind."[16]

The next region is the upper-right quadrant, where fixed policy is applied to allied or friendly nation-states. This region characterizes formal treaty agreements and mutual security arrangements of a specific nature, much like the North Atlantic Treaty Organization (NATO) treaty features a signatory agreement to go to war on another nation's behalf. We can refer to this region of the framework as policy of "insurance," as it is a stronger form of policy that insures some action on some occasion in the form of "if . . . then." These arrangements are formed explicitly on the basis of the perceived value of policy's purpose on our side primarily and potentially on a multilateral basis if other nation-states share a mutual valuation of the purpose.

The lower-right region of the framework is the flexible policy treatment of allied or friendly nation-states. This type of policy is commonly referred to as "assurance," where the United States presents some nonspecific form of support by agreement or expediency. As an example, consider times when the United States stations military forces in a foreign country at the invitation of the host without an explicit security agreement.[17] The United States is not bound by treaty to act in an "if . . . then" fashion but assures the ally and/or friends in the region with the presence. Obviously, assurance policy can exist without the physical presence of forces and even includes weapons research and development of small forms of shared economic investment at the lower extremes of the region. The flexible property of the policy suggests some value to the purpose worthy only of an "if . . . maybe" association with our willingness to act on another's behalf.

The final region is the lower-left portion of the framework that characterizes flexible policy toward adversaries or enemy nation-states. We will call this area "dissuasion" policy, denoting the original meaning coined for use in international influence theory minus the certainty of any overt threat communicated in policy statements.[18] Note here the distinction between *deterrence* as a policy and the "deterrent effect" in which a variety of actions result. For our purposes, *deterrence* refers to Schelling's policy concept of an overt communicated threat with requisite credibility, capability, and rationality. The *dissuasion* term refers to the notion of preventing unfavorable adversary actions (the deterrent effect) through a variety of methods unguided by an overt deterrence policy. This allows for a distinction in the level of certainty between the fixed and flexible properties of policy. Dissuasion in this sense includes both the classical notions of "general deterrence" as well as dissuasive moves as described in US defense strategies such as arms development and capability deployment. As a whole, it constitutes the associative effect of any potentially threatening gesture that suggests an "if . . . maybe" potential counter to an adversary nation. As Colin Gray describes dissuasion,

> Don't discount general deterrence, or dissuasion . . . the effect upon behavior, and upon the norms that help shape behavior, of perceptions of US military power and of the likelihood that it would be employed.

Possession of a very powerful military machine, and a solid reputation for being willing to use it, casts a shadow or shines a light—pick your preferred metaphor—in many corners of the world. That shadow, or light, may have a distinct deterrent effect, even in the absence of explicit American efforts to deter.[19]

The distinction should be noted here between the fixed and flexible qualities of policy. Since policy derives its force by the value placed on the purpose, the form policy takes should reflect the relative value of the purpose. The difference is reflected in the certainty of action against the negative ends. In the case of dissuasion, the value of the purpose does not warrant the explicit efforts to deter in a binding deterministic policy. The policy therefore presents the possibility of US action, however slight, with the ways and means supporting it. However, the contrast between these two forms with respect to commitment also tends to affect the policy options for branches and sequels. Fixed policy choices are commitments to action, are subject to tests of will and bluffing, and clearly reduce a policy maker's flexibility for future action. Likewise, associative policy choices keep more options available for follow-on action. Note this relationship, especially when the military instrument is committed to policy's objective. Without careful consideration of the properties prior to enacting policy, events can easily result in misapplication of the military instrument or artificial limits on military capabilities. The strategic context will determine which form is better suited to attain policy's purpose. Perhaps the most sophisticated example of these elements working successfully in concert is the Berlin airlift, where these policy types simultaneously dissuaded, deterred, assured, and insured the relevant actors in the theater and around the world. The relationship between the elements plays an important policy role discussed later in this article, but at this point it is vital to simply recognize that a distinction exists between the "if . . . then" effects of deterrence policy and the "if . . . maybe" effects of dissuasion policy.

The Intersection

We have defined the regions of the policy quadrant framework and now turn our attention to certain relationships between the regions and the effects of policy in one region upon another. As previously mentioned, there exists an interplay of action between these quadrants, either intentionally or coincidentally. A fundamental example of this is the Cold War relationship between the mutually assured destruction–flavored nuclear deterrence and the insurance-oriented NATO treaty. This protected central Europe with a design offering insurance to allied European nations through an agreement interpreting an attack on any member as an attack on all members. The deterrence counterbalance to this NATO insurance was the unambiguous threat of massive retaliation with nuclear weapons against the Soviet Union in the case of a first strike. The "if . . . then" nature of these two policies coincided with the desired positive and negative objects. The United States held the positive purpose of maintaining a free Europe alongside the negative purpose of preventing Soviet nuclear attack. The question of if these policies had corresponding assurance and dissuasion effects is difficult to prove or disprove.

As Colin Gray asserts, "Dissuasion is at work when a political leader rules out an exciting course of action from serious policy consideration because of the fear that it would trigger an American response. . . . Although common sense, logic, and historical experience all point to the significance of this deterrent phenomenon, it is utterly beyond research."[20] The same can be said of the assurance question when a political leader ruled "in" options of cooperation and mutual interest with the United States. But it seems safe to assume that the insurance and dissuasion policies of the Cold War did not serve in a policy vacuum; other nations had to take heed of how their policy choices would impact the order of the bipolar world, to their benefit or detriment. These effects of second-order nature are open to debate, but the clear relationship is the necessary balance between adversaries and allies in the deterrence and insurance policies. The nature of that balance becomes more complex and challenging as the area in question is closer to the intersection of the lines inside the quadrant. This is the region most likely to challenge policy makers in the future.

The challenges of policy and purpose are simpler at the extreme corners of the diagram. Questions of existential threat from a mortal enemy, a mortal enemy that poses no threat to anything of value, a friend who is completely vested in mutual interests, or an actor who is a friend though no common interests exist—these are cases that represent the least sophisticated of all policy conditions. On the other hand, the intersection of the elements offers the most challenging policy conditions. Enemies and friends are lukewarm, and loyalties shift easily; threats are moderate or only punctuated by existential-level threats; and allies share a modicum of interests and cooperative motivation. Current and potential policy conditions are closer to the intersection than the bipolar world of Cold War conditions. This is the area in which we must become comfortable and where the Air Force's inherently flexible nature is vital. It is the realm where challenges thrive as the value to our national interests rises to a degree that motivates our involvement, but the value is insufficient to warrant our exercise of all the ways and means available to us. The conditions also feature strained alliances, weakened friendships, and inconclusive diplomacy. Within this context, the military instrument must leverage limited ways and means in close concert with the other instruments of power without forsaking maintenance of a backdrop of capabilities with overwhelming potential. Successful policy and purpose achievements in this realm are the fruit of sophisticated strategists, diplomats, economists, and statesmen.

The implications for our military leaders are significant. The intellectual demands in technological advancement, interagency coordination, multinational cooperation, and nuanced public media relations will grow by orders of magnitude as conditions approach the intersection. Each theater of operations will present specific aspects of several points on this notional diagram; each policy point will have some degree of interplay on the other. Policy and purpose achievement at the extreme corners of the diagram are the work of brilliance; achievements at the intersection are the work of collaborative genius. This is relevance's price of admission in the foreseeable future of our nation's military instrument. The ultimate goal is to leverage military capabilities in cooperative fashion to maximize legitimacy and control to the degree necessary for achieving the purpose of national policy.

Policy and Purpose in the International System

If the conditions were not complicated enough at the intersection of our diagram, then the interplay of subnational actors within the nation-state order serves to further complicate. For the purposes of this examination, we will limit this term to a subset of the subnational agency. We do not refer to nongovernmental organizations or transnational bodies of diplomacy and economics. We will consider almost exclusively the groups that present proximate challenges to the military instrument in policy as purveyors of destruction and national anxiety. These are the subnational actors we commonly refer to as terrorist or extremist groups.

The question of how to deter extremist subnational actors has been addressed in recent works that present well-reasoned and elegant strategic thinking in fashion that ranks with Galula.[21] Other works focus on the form of warfare termed *irregular* in contemporary dialogue and illuminate the subject of strong states contending against weaker adversaries, including subnational actors.[22] It seems clear that no consideration of policy and purpose can be relevant without accounting for the interplay of subnational actors within the international system. However, the framework we have considered to this point deals only with how policy relates to nation-states. We must consider how effectively policy can achieve objects associated with subnational actors.

Deterrence and the Subnational Actor

The classic notions of policy deal primarily with nation-state rational actors. Contemporary issues demand a method of addressing subnational actors in the exercise of policy—no small feat in statecraft. Subnational actors now threaten the relevance of our contemporary nation-state system. It may turn out that the nation-state system is destined to go the same way as the medieval city-state system did long ago, but until such a time arrives we must assume the purpose of future policy will be to secure the requisite objects for preservation of a stable international system. Deterrence policy of the Cold War served the same purpose seeking to secure the negative purpose of preventing mutually assured destruction of nation-states within a bipolar context.

Deterrence policy in the future must continue to achieve that negative purpose, though apparently on a smaller scale in this modern, multipolar context. However, it must also achieve the requisite objects for preventing mutually assured chaos where subnational actors significantly damage or displace the international order with weapons of mass destruction (WMD). We choose the "mutually" moniker, recognizing that some nation-states (a milieu of rogue, failed, or phantom states) cooperate with subnational actors for some duration in pursuit of perceived common interests. Taking a longer-run view, however, opens the mind to the temporary nature of these shared interests, and the fact emerges that the ideologies that compel many subnational actors with a willingness to use WMD can conceivably lead those same actors to turn on their national sponsors at some point in the future. It is impossible to know with any certainty if this is the case or not, but the implication for future policy seems clear. In attracting nation-states to cooperate and coexist with us, we must present the possibilities of a better state of peace than the alternatives. For those nations that do not accept, we must carefully craft policies to deter and dissuade their collaborative efforts with subnational actors that threaten a stable international system. In sum, our policy remains unchanged, the objects are suitably similar though different in number and degree, and the number of relevant actors in the game is increasing.

These elements combine in various contexts to dictate their own form of policy requirement, and each friend or adversary demands its own carefully crafted policy of a type designed for the particular context of national fear, honor, and interests. The positive and negative objects create a dynamic environment in which each act supporting policy design in one aspect may also create a concurrent effect in the other. Astute theorists have previously observed that "coercing powers must also recognize when it is appropriate not to use an instrument . . . an instrument can fail, and it can also backfire . . . the failure of an instrument in one instance can undermine the credibility [in another]."[23] This dynamic interplay suggests that no act of policy to achieve the negative purpose fails to affect the positive purpose, and vice versa, in varying degrees. This interplay is part of what makes coercion so complex; every act taken to enhance our own security paradoxically decreases an adversary nation's security, and every act bears a potential for catastrophic outcomes. This in turn impacts the relevant threat potential of subnational actors. While it may seem unlikely that a policy our nation considers rational could succeed against an actor we deem as irrational, the complex nature of these actors does offer some promising potential for success.

Subnational actors can best be deterred in one sense but not in another. They can be deterred from acting outside the economy of policy with a fixed policy resembling "if you leave this system and act outside of it, then we will seek to deny you the means to do so and to constrict your influence." This type of policy is often tangentially referenced with a metaphor of draining the swamp. The ability to do so depends upon manipulating legitimacy and control in all four regions of the policy quadrant for insurance and assurance of cooperative nation-states to join the effort as well as dissuasion and deterrence of uncooperative nations from supporting subnational actors. This also suggests a need to offer legitimate courses of redress for subnational interests within the nation-state system in addition to building partner capacity to deal with subnational actors who resist. A successful deterrence strategy should address each of these elements in a carefully orchestrated effort to deter subnational actors from willfully acting outside of the international system.

Subnational actors cannot be deterred as though they were national actors playing inside the international system. These groups act subnationally to divest themselves of the obligations that come with legitimacy and sometimes seek to exact control based on a reward system that includes the afterlife. This is what we mean when we refer to these groups as extremist or irrational. Rationality in the international system is based on a this-life reward system. For example, when Hamas acted subnationally against Israel, it did so without the moral, legal, or humanitarian obligations of a nation-state and used tactics like suicide bombing that leveraged rewards in the afterlife for destructive control effects in the present. Death and destruction are viewed as rewards in and of themselves; destroying such actors rewards and legitimizes them (in their own system). However, once Hamas leaders were elected to national office, they crossed a line; they incurred the obligations that come with nation-state status. Ultimately, these obligations erode legitimacy quickly when afterlife rewards are included in national policy. The Revolutionary Armed Forces of Colombia–People's Army (FARC) is another example of this principle without the afterlife reward system. The FARC struggled with the obligations of legitimacy as the organization achieved territorial gains and had to meet the peoples' needs in addition to their criminal pursuits. This phenomenon should be viewed as a positive motive for bringing subnational elements back into the economy of policy but is also evidence that extremist subnational actors cannot be deterred as though they were a nation-state.

So What?

What has changed about the security environment, and how does the environment change our policy paradigm? How should we design deterrence strategies for the twenty-first century? How should we think about military capabilities to support national policy purposes in general? We offer that the regions of the policy quadrant in which the Cold War challenged us are represented by the extreme corners of the diagram, and the post–Cold War environment tends to offer challenges at the intersection of the quadrants—a much more complex policy proposition. We must approach deterrence not as an entity by itself, but rather as a policy component from a larger palette; assurance, dissuasion, insurance, and deterrence blend together to achieve policy's purpose. Ways and means are still important, but the proportional mix will shift based upon policy's purpose. For example, nuclear weapons remain a vital capability, but some contexts will undoubtedly require conventional means where nuclear means were once sufficient. Likewise, new contexts may emerge where nuclear capability is vital to the policy, but the policy is dissuasive rather than deterrent. Our challenge is to recommend to policy makers the proper identification and application of capabilities to support new strategies, which are relevant to the context, policy, and purpose.

The strategic environment will likely dictate policy portfolio engineering in place of traditional deterrence policy.[24] If the environment continues to emerge consistently with recent trends, we can expect a requirement to engineer policy that includes a mix of deterrence, dissuasion, assurance, and insurance with respect to three contexts. Major global powers, regional powers, and failing states will each demand a specific blend of these policy types to achieve US policy purposes. In addition, we must engineer global and regional policy portfolios designed to motivate subnational actors to work within the international system while denying them the means to act outside the system. Each of these contexts will present challenges in all four quadrants, and any successful strategy must address each quadrant's contribution to achieving the purpose.

This is where the economy of policy informs our recommendation. We must recognize the relationship between legitimacy and control, the impact they have on the number of choices available to policy makers, and the value prospect they generate. Additionally, each quadrant of this theoretical diagram presents different aspects, sources, and demands on legitimacy and control. Detailed economic analysis of these relationships is not within the scope of this article except to note: the higher the value for policies like deterrence, the higher the required value point generated by legitimacy and control. This illustrates an important point in expressing that it is not enough for us to simply add ways and means to the mix without building legitimacy in the context. This helps explain the need for recent initiatives designed for building partner capacity and irregular warfare as well as interagency and multinational cooperation. But there is so much more to this principle; each context will present lines with differing slopes and elasticity, depending on whether the context is conventional or irregular. The important lesson across the board is the special relationship between legitimacy and control. We can build all the capabilities known to man, but their contribution to national defense diminishes rapidly if we fail to build legitimacy in a corresponding fashion. Likewise, capabilities designed to exert control will be more effective if we design, produce, and employ them with greater legitimacy.

The US Air Force is working diligently to develop game-changing war-fighting capabilities for combatant commanders in today's fight and for future challenges. Likewise, we are developing new concepts, programs, and methods for building national legitimacy in the interest of preventing wars and promoting our ability should war become unavoidable. The global vigilance, reach, and power we provide the nation will continue to be a vital contributor to national defense. Our challenge is to think about deterrence in a broader sense than the limited Cold War application, including the related policies that support deterrence. Also, we simply must expand our thinking from a purely control-oriented focus to include both legitimacy and control in every case. Think about precision weaponry, the global positioning system that guides that weaponry, the humanitarian assistance we provide, the global mobility system that delivers that assistance, and the provincial reconstruction teams we serve—these are all cases where Air Force capabilities build legitimacy through precision and reliability. The same is true of our nuclear capabilities; weapons of this kind require precision and reliability with no margin for error, and our adherence to the highest nuclear mission standards builds legitimacy. That legitimacy is fragile; we can easily lose it should we fail to perform to those exacting standards.

This is the fundamental risk and reward of deterrence in the economy of policy; conventional and nuclear capabilities that support deterrence form a double-edged sword requiring constant vigilance. These capabilities contribute to purposes of the highest national value, yet negligence in safeguarding their constituent elements represents one of the most costly of national security errors because it so easily diminishes both legitimacy and control. When used appropriately, deterrence policy offers a maximum value for given investment; yet, deterrence incurs the highest obligations for the service that provides the necessary capabilities. We Airmen must think of our contributions to all forms of national security policy whether in dissuasion, deterrence, assurance, or insurance; and, we must likewise consider how our performance directly impacts national legitimacy and control as part of the military instrument.

The ideas presented here offer a way of thinking about policy, purpose, and the economy of deterrence. These ideas invite further study on many aspects of the elements, their inter-action, and the economic relationship between them. This serves as a challenging area of research for our Air Force strat-egists and defense academia. We need a more comprehensive view of how deterrence works with other policy to achieve its purpose, and that view must accommodate the ever-increasing complexity of the security environment. If we do so, we will succeed in improving the rigor and relevance of our thinking and the delivery of effective national security strategies now and in the future.

Notes

1. The latter two terms are used in a novel sense here with respect to policy, and we will expound on this later in the article, but consider these the soft-power attractions that go with coercion ideas of compellence and deterrence.

2. Examples of this are numerous, and we avoid acute contemporary ex-amples as a matter of discretion, but view the Korean War (1950–53), wars in Indochina (1947–79), the Bay of Pigs invasion (April 1961), the Yom Kippur War (October 1973), and US legitimacy crises in Lebanon (October 1983), Somalia (October 1993), and those ongoing since the Iraq Survey Group In-terim Report (October 2003) as candidates for consideration.

3. Leon Sloss, "The New Arms Race," in *Contemporary Nuclear Debates: Missile Defenses, Arms Control, and Arms Races in the Twenty-First Century (Washington Quarterly Readers)*, ed. Alexander Lennon (Cambridge, MA: MIT Press, 2002), 240.

4. James R. Schlesinger, "The Demise of Arms Control," in *Contemporary Nuclear Debates: Missile Defenses, Arms Control, and Arms Races in the Twenty-First Century*, ed. Alexander T. J. Lennon (Cambridge, MA: MIT Press, 2002), 252–55.

5. Colin S. Gray, "Irregular Warfare: One Nature, Many Characters," *Strategic Studies Quarterly* 1, no. 2 (Winter 2007): 37.

6. Patrick M. Morgan, *Deterrence Now* (Cambridge: Cambridge University Press, 2003), 285.

7. In the case of national power, we use the term *value* not in a mathemati-cal sense but rather as an expression of significance, utility, or importance.

8. Credit for the idea of power from the number of choices available is due to Everett C. Dolman for a compelling discussion of power in strategy in *Pure Strategy: Power and Principle in the Space and Information Age* (London: Tay-lor & Francis, 2007). We expand the case to include some relative value to a choice's outcome.

9. For more on sources and forms of legitimacy, see Max Weber, *The Theory of Social and Economic Organization*, trans. A. M. Henderson and Talcott Par-sons (Glencoe, IL: Free Press, 1947).

10. Carl von Clausewitz, *On War*, ed. and trans. Michael Howard and Peter Paret (Princeton, NJ: Princeton University Press, 1976), 88.

11. Morgan, *Deterrence Now*, 8.

12. Abraham Kaplan, *The Conduct of Inquiry: Methodology for Behavioral Science* (San Francisco: Chandler, 1964), 28.

13. Clausewitz, *On War*, 87.

14. Thomas C. Schelling, *Arms and Influence* (New Haven, CT: Yale University Press, 1966), 70–71.

15. Colin S. Gray, *Maintaining Effective Deterrence* (Carlisle, PA: US Army War College, Strategic Studies Institute, 2003), 30.

16. Charles Krauthammer, "What Will Stop North Korea," *Washington Post*, 13 October 2006, A-14.

17. Any number of examples serves where US forces are permanently stationed overseas where no formal incurrence treaty exists nor is there a commitment to fight on a nearby nation's behalf.

18. J. David Singer, "Inter-Nation Influence: A Formal Model," *American Political Science Review* 57, no. 2 (June 1963): 424.

19. Gray, *Maintaining Effective Deterrence*, 29.

20. Ibid.

21. Dan Green, "Winning the War against Religious Extremism," *Strategic Studies Quarterly* 2, no. 3 (Fall 2008): 120.

22. Gray, "Irregular Warfare"; and Jeffrey Record, *Beating Goliath: Why Insurgencies Win* (Dulles, VA: Potomac Books, 2007).

23. Daniel Byman and Matthew C. Waxman, *The Dynamics of Coercion: American Foreign Policy and the Limits of Military Might*, RAND Studies in Policy Analysis (Cambridge: Cambridge University Press, 2002), 124.

24. This policy portfolio engineering concept naturally occurs at the most senior levels in government, but the process will demand especially cogent military advice.

Chapter 5

Waging Deterrence in the Twenty-first Century*

Kevin Chilton, General, USAF
Greg Weaver

In recent years many national security policy scholars and practitioners have questioned whether deterrence remains a relevant, reliable, and realistic national security concept in the twenty-first century. That is a fair question. New threats to American security posed by transnational terrorists, asymmetric military strategies and capabilities, and the proliferation of weapons of mass destruction (WMD) by adversaries who see the world in profoundly different ways than do we have called into question America's reliance on deterrence as a central tenet of our national security strategy. Some experts advocate a move away from deterrence—and particularly the nuclear element of our deterrent force—toward greater reliance on other approaches to provide for our security in a complex and dangerous environment.

In our judgment, deterrence should and will remain a core concept in our twenty-first-century national security policy, because the prevention of war is preferable to the waging of it and because the concept itself is just as relevant today as it was during the Cold War. But its continued relevance does not mean that we should continue to "wage deterrence" in the future in the same manner, and with the same means, as we did in the past. As a starting point, it is useful to reexamine the fundamentals of deterrence theory and how it can be applied successfully in the twenty-first century. Next, we should consider how deterrence does—or does not—apply to emerging twenty-first-century forms of warfare. Finally, we should carefully consider the role that US nuclear forces should—or should not—play in twenty-first-century US deterrence strategy.

---

*Originally published in *Strategic Studies Quarterly* 3, no. 1 (Spring 2009): 31–42.

Reexamining Deterrence
Theory and Practice

In 2004, Strategic Command was directed by the secretary of defense to develop a deterrence operations joint operating concept (DO JOC).[1] In response the command reexamined both the academic literature on deterrence theory and the history of deterrence strategy and practice. We concluded that deterrence theory is applicable to many of the twenty-first-century threats the United States will face, but the way we put the theory into practice, or "operationalize" it, needs to be advanced.

One insight gained from our research and analysis is that a number of the "general" deterrence lessons we thought we learned in the Cold War may, in retrospect, have been specific to the kind of deterrence relationship we had with the Soviet Union. For example, many argue that deliberate ambiguity about the nature and scope of our response to an adversary's attack enhances deterrence by complicating the adversary's calculations and planning. Arguably, this was the case vis-à-vis the Soviet leadership after the Cuban missile crisis. However, the impact of ambiguity on deterrence success is likely to be a function of the target decision makers' propensity to take risks in pursuit of gains or to avoid an expected loss. Risk-averse decision makers tend to see ambiguity about an enemy's response as increasing the risk associated with the action they are contemplating; thus, such ambiguity tends to enhance deterrence. The deterrence impact of US ambiguity about our response to an attack by a *risk-acceptant* opponent, however, might be quite different. Risk-acceptant decision makers might well interpret such ambiguity as a sign of weakness and as an opportunity to exploit rather than as a risk to be avoided. Our deterrence strategies and operations need to take our potential opponent's risk-taking propensity into account.

A second difference from the Cold War experience is the potential for a lack of unity of command in certain twenty-first-century opponents (e.g., regimes with competing centers of power or transnational terrorist organizations). If there are multiple individuals in the political system capable of making and executing the decisions we seek to influence, our deterrence strategy will need to have multiple focal points and employ multiple means of communicating a complex set of deterrence messages that in turn take into account the multiplicity of decision makers.

Throughout our Cold War deterrence relationship with the Soviet Union, the focus of US grand strategy was to contain Soviet expansionism, in part by frustrating Soviet efforts to overturn the international status quo by military or political means. However, in the twenty-first-century security environment, the United States may at times find it necessary to take the initiative to alter the international status quo to protect our vital interests. Deterring escalation while proactively pursuing objectives that may harm an opponent's perceived vital interests poses a different, more difficult kind of deterrence challenge. As Thomas Schelling noted, such circumstances may require a deterrence strategy that pairs promises of restraint with threats of severe cost-imposition.[2] For example, to deter Saddam Hussein from ordering the use of WMD during Operation Desert Storm in the first Gulf War, the United States issued a threat of devastating retaliation but also made clear that the coalition's war aim was limited to the liberation of Kuwait.

Finally, the United States and the Soviet Union each recognized that in an armed conflict between them, the impact on each side's vital interests would be high and symmetrical (i.e., the survival of both nations and their respective political systems and ideologies would be at stake). In the twenty-first century, the United States could face a crisis or conflict in which our opponents perceive they have a greater national interest in the outcome than does the United States. This circumstance has the potential to undermine the credibility of US deterrent threats, especially if opponents have the capability to inflict harm on US allies and/or interests that they believe exceeds our stake in the conflict. Thus, we must devise deterrence strategies and activities that effectively address such situations.

How Deterrence Works—Achieving Decisive Influence over Competitor Decision Making

Deterrence is ultimately about decisively influencing decision making. Achieving such decisive influence requires altering or reinforcing decision makers' perceptions of key factors they must weigh in deciding whether to act counter to US vital interests or to exercise restraint. This "decision calculus" consists of four primary variables: the perceived benefits and costs of taking the action we seek to deter and the perceived benefits and costs of continued restraint.

Understanding how these factors interact is essential to determining how best to influence the decision making of our competitors. Successful deterrence is not solely a function of ensuring that foreign decision makers believe the costs of a given course of action will outweigh the benefits, as it is often described. Rather, such decision makers weigh the perceived benefits and costs of a given course of action *in the context of* their perception of how they will fare if they *do not* act. Thus, deterrence can fail even when competitors believe the costs of acting will outweigh the benefits of acting—if they *also* believe that the costs of continued restraint would be higher still.

Our deterrence activities must focus on convincing competitors that if they attack our vital interests, they will be denied the benefits they seek and will incur costs they find intolerable. It also emphasizes encouraging continued restraint by convincing them that such restraint will result in a more acceptable— though not necessarily favorable—outcome. The concept itself is fairly simple, but its implementation in a complex, uncertain, and continuously changing security environment is not. What, then, is required to implement this concept in the twenty-first century?

The Need for "Tailored Deterrence" Campaigns

Effectively influencing a competitor's decision calculus requires continuous, proactive activities conducted in the form of deterrence campaigns tailored to specific competitors. Competitors have different identities, interests, perceptions, and decision-making processes, and we may seek to deter each competitor from taking specific actions under varied circumstances.

One of the most important aspects of tailored deterrence campaigns is to focus much of our effort on peacetime (or "Phase 0") activities. There are several reasons for this. Peacetime activities can make use of deterrent means that take time to have their desired effects or that require repetition to be effective. They expand the range of deterrence options at our disposal. Conducting activities in peacetime also allows time to assess carefully the impact of our deterrence efforts and to adjust if they are ineffective or have unintended consequences. Most importantly, conducting deterrence activities in peacetime may prevent the crisis from developing in the first place or may reduce the risk of waiting until we are in crisis to take deterrent action. By the time indications and warning of potential competitor activity alert us to the fact that we are in a crisis, some of the decisions we hope to influence may have already been made, the options available to us may have narrowed significantly, and our deterrence messages may not reach the relevant decision makers.

Deterrence campaigns start in peacetime and are intended to preserve the peace, but our campaign planning should enable deterrence activities through all phases of crisis and conflict. A campaign approach to deterrence activities in crisis and conflict is necessary because, as a crisis or conflict unfolds, the content and character of a foreign leadership's decision calculus can change significantly. What mattered to a foreign leadership when its forces were on the offensive will likely be irrelevant when the tide has turned, and wholly new factors will enter its decision making. Without a broad and dynamic deterrence campaign plan, we risk discovering that what deterred successfully early will fail later because the competitor's decision calculus has shifted from under our static deterrence strategy and posture.

Conducting multiple competitor-specific deterrence campaigns simultaneously poses a difficult challenge. Targeting a deterrence activity on a single competitor does not mean that other competitors—and our friends and allies—are not watching and being influenced as well. Thus, we need to deconflict our competitor-specific deterrence campaigns to avoid as best we can undesirable second- and third-order effects. The nature of this task requires new analytic capabilities and new planning and execution processes, while the level of effort required means some additional resources must be allocated to the deterrence campaign.

Finally, there is an opportunity presented by the conduct of multiple competitor-specific deterrence campaigns. We may discover that there is a common set of factors that influence the decision calculus of multiple competitors. If true, this would enable the United States to exercise economy of force and effort, addressing those factors with the greatest influence over multiple actors with a common set of deterrence activities.

The Need to Bring All Elements
of National Power to Bear

The decisions our deterrence activities are meant to influence are primarily political-military decisions, made most often by political rather than military decision makers. The factors influencing those decisions usually extend far beyond purely military considerations to encompass political, ideological, economic, and, in some cases, theological affairs. Clearly, a purely military approach to planning and conducting deterrence campaigns is inadequate. Deterrence is inherently a whole-of-government enterprise.

Interagency collaboration is difficult to do well, particularly in the noncrisis atmosphere of peacetime activities—precisely the time that multiple agencies have the most to offer in a deterrence campaign. So how can we ensure that our deterrence campaigns leverage all the elements of American national power, both "hard" and "soft"?[3]

We must find a practical way to involve relevant government agencies in mission analysis, campaign planning, decision making and execution, and assessment of results. An innovative process is needed to consider and include interagency deterrence courses of action, to make whole-of-government decisions on what courses of action to implement, and to coordinate their execution upon selection.

The Need to Bring Our Friends'
and Allies' Capabilities to Bear

US friends and allies share our interest in deterrence success. Because of their different perspectives, different military capabilities, and different means of communication at their disposal, they offer much that can refine and improve our deterrence strategies and enhance the effectiveness of our deterrence activities. It is to our advantage (and theirs) to involve them more actively in "waging deterrence" in the twenty-first century.

One of the most important contributions that our friends and allies can make to our deterrence campaigns is to provide alternative assessments of competitors' perceptions. Allied insights into how American deterrence activities may be perceived by both intended and unintended audiences can help us formulate more effective plans. Allied suggestions for alternative approaches to achieving key deterrence effects, including actions they would take in support of—or instead of—US actions, may prove invaluable. As in the case of interagency collaboration, we need to develop innovative processes for collaborating with our friends and allies to enhance deterrence.

The Need to "Wage Deterrence" against Emerging Forms of Warfare

At its most fundamental level, deterrence functions in the same way regardless of the kind of action we seek to prevent. Convincing a competitor that the perceived benefits of its attack will be outweighed by the perceived costs and that restraint offers an acceptable outcome remains the way to achieve decisive influence over competitor decision making. Nevertheless, the form of warfare we seek to deter can alter both the nature and the difficulty of the task at hand. Three emerging forms of twenty-first-century warfare pose particularly tough challenges for deterrence strategists, policy makers, and practitioners.

Deterring Transnational Terrorism

The continued application by transnational terrorists of catastrophic attacks on civilians by suicidal attackers suggests that our deterrence concept may have little utility against this form of warfare. How can one successfully deter attackers who see their own death as the ultimate (spiritual) gain, who have little they hold dear that we can threaten retaliation against, and who perceive continued restraint as the violation of what they see as a religious duty to alter an unacceptable status quo

69

through violence? The question is a good one. Answering it requires a closer examination of how the nature of transnational terrorism, and the nonstate actors that practice it, create deterrence challenges not posed by most state actors. While there are many differences between deterring state actors and nonstate actors, the two pose particularly important challenges.

First, the task of identifying the key decision makers we seek to influence is more difficult when deterring nonstate actors. For example, al-Qaeda's shift to a more distributed network of terrorist cells in the wake of Operation Enduring Freedom has made "decision makers" out of regional and local operatives. This distributed nature of transnational terrorist networks complicates the conduct of an effective deterrence campaign, but it also offers additional opportunities. A recent Institute for Defense Analyses report highlighted that there are multiple components of the global terrorist network that we can seek to influence in a deterrence campaign.

> These components include the following: jihadi foot soldiers, terrorist professionals who provide training and other logistical guidance and support, the leaders of al Qaeda, groups affiliated by knowledge and aspiration (so-called franchises), operational enablers (i.e., financiers), moral legitimizers, state sponsors, and passive state enablers.[4]

Thus, deterrence could play an important role in the broader campaign against transnational terrorists if it were able to constrain the participation of key components of a movement and undermine support within a movement for the most catastrophic kinds of attacks.

Second, the nature of transnational terrorist movements results in these adversaries valuing and fearing profoundly different things than their state-actor counterparts. Transnational terrorists need to spread their ideology; raise and distribute funds; motivate, recruit, and train new operatives; and gain public acquiescence to (if not active support for) their presence and operations, all while remaining hidden from their enemies. This creates a potentially rich new set of perceptions to influence through deterrence activities, but affecting those perceptions is likely to require the creative development of new means of doing so.

It is not yet clear how important deterrence may be in countering the threats posed to US vital interests by transnational terrorism. However, given that our conflict with these adversaries is likely a long-term one and that the potential benefits of successfully deterring certain kinds of catastrophic terrorist attacks (e.g., the use of weapons of mass destruction) far exceed the costs of attempting to do so, we should work more aggressively on adding deterrence to our counterterrorism repertoire.

Deterring Space Attack

The importance of military space capabilities to the effective functioning of modern armed forces will continue to increase throughout the twenty-first century. The development of counterspace capabilities is already underway in several nations, making active warfare in the space domain a real possibility. Deterring attacks on US and allied space assets poses several important challenges.

First, we must act overtly and consistently to convince competitors that they will reap little benefit from conducting space attacks against us or our allies. Those who might contemplate such attacks in a future conflict need to understand three things: their efforts to deny us access to our military space assets will likely fail, our military forces are ready and able to fight effectively and decisively without such access if necessary, and we possess the means and the will to ensure that they would pay a price incommensurate with any benefit they seek to attain through such attacks.

As made clear above, the threat of cost imposition is an important aspect of American space deterrence strategy. Our threatened responses to an attack on our space assets need not be limited to a response in kind. Our competitors must clearly understand that we consider our space assets as sovereign and important to our national security interests. Furthermore, the importance of maintaining space as a safe and secure global commons to all nations' future economic development may result in the United States treating the initiation of counterspace activities by a foreign power as a significant escalation of a future conflict. Regardless of our initial level of national interest in a given conflict, such an escalation could dramatically increase the US stake in the outcome. Our increased stake could alter our willingness to escalate the scope and level of violence of our military operations. In other words, an attack on US space assets as part of a regional conflict might be viewed as more than a regional issue by the United States and, therefore, elicit an escalated response.

Deterring Cyberspace Attack

Deterring cyberspace attack presents an even more complex challenge than deterring space attacks. As in the space domain, we must convince our competitors that the United States may see cyberspace attack as a serious escalation of a conflict and that we will respond accordingly (and not necessarily in kind). However, the nature of cyberspace operations poses additional challenges as well.

The most significant deterrence challenge posed by the threat of cyberspace attack is the perceived difficulty of attributing such attacks to a specific attacker, be it a state or nonstate actor. If competitors believe we cannot determine who is attacking us in cyberspace, they may convince themselves that such attacks involve little risk and significant gain. In addressing the attribution issue, US cyberspace deterrence strategy and activities must deal with the inherently thorny trade-off between demonstrating our ability to detect and attribute cyberspace attacks and providing intelligence about our capabilities to competitors that could help them pose a still greater cyberspace threat in the future.

Further complicating the deterrence of cyberspace attack is the lack of a known historical track record of US detection, attribution, and response. This lack of precedent could raise questions about the credibility of deterrent actions and could thus embolden potential attackers, who might convince themselves that the action they contemplate would not elicit a response. Yet establishing adequate precedents is made more difficult because few nations have defined publicly what they consider to be a cyberspace "attack," nor have they communicated to competitors the kinds of responses to such activities they might consider.

Cyberspace attacks involve significant potential for producing unexpected second- and third-order effects that might result in unintended and possibly undesired consequences. The deterrence impacts of such uncertainty over the potential impacts of a cyberspace attack would be a function of the nature of the attacker's goals and objectives. A competitor's concerns about unintended consequences could enhance the effects of our deterrence activities if it wishes to control escalation or fears blowback from its cyberspace operations. However, deterrence of a competitor whose primary goal is to create chaos could be undermined by the potential for unintended consequences. We need to carefully consider how to account for such possibilities in our deterrence strategy.

Secure the Continued Role of US Nuclear Force in Twenty-first-Century Deterrence

We have saved a discussion of the continued role of US nuclear forces in deterrence for the end of this article, not because it is less important than in the past, but because it is best understood in the context of the other aspects of twenty-first-century deterrence strategy and activities addressed above.

Many argue that the only legitimate role of nuclear weapons is to deter the use of nuclear weapons in a catastrophic attack against us or our allies. This is indeed their most important role. However, the deterrence roles of the US nuclear arsenal go well beyond deterrence of nuclear attack alone.

US nuclear forces cast a long shadow over the decision calculations of anyone who would contemplate taking actions that threaten the vital interests of the United States or its allies, making it clear that the ultimate consequences of doing so may be truly disastrous and that the American presidents always have an option for which they have no effective counter. Even in circumstances in which a deliberate American nuclear response seems unlikely or incredible to foreign decision makers, US nuclear forces enhance deterrence by making unintended or uncontrolled catastrophic escalation a serious concern, posing what Thomas Schelling calls "the threat that leaves something to chance."[5] These are deterrence dynamics that only nuclear forces provide.

As a result, US nuclear forces make an important contribution to deterring both symmetric and asymmetric forms of warfare in the twenty-first century. Our nuclear forces provide a hedge against attacks that could cripple our ability to wage conventional war because they would enable the United States to restore the military status quo ante, trump the adversary's escalation in a manner that improves the US position in the conflict, or promptly terminate the conflict.

For US nuclear forces to be effective in playing these vital deterrence roles, they must have certain key attributes. They must be sufficient in number and survivability to hold at risk those things our adversaries value most and to hedge against technical or geopolitical surprise. Both the delivery systems and warheads must be highly reliable, so that no one could ever rationally doubt their effectiveness or our willingness to use them in war. The warheads must be safe and secure, both to prevent accidents and to prevent anyone from ever being able to use an American nuclear weapon should they somehow get their hands on one. And they must be sufficiently diverse and operationally flexible to provide the president with the necessary range of options for their use and to hedge against the technological failure of any particular delivery system or warhead design.

Our forces have these attributes today, but we are rapidly approaching decision points that will determine the extent to which they continue to have them in the future. We are the only acknowledged nuclear weapons state that does not have an active nuclear weapons production program. Our nuclear weapons stockpile is aging, and we will not be able to maintain the reliability of our current nuclear warheads indefinitely. We will need to revitalize our nuclear weapons design and production infrastructure if we are to retain a viable nuclear arsenal in a rapidly changing and uncertain twenty-first-century security environment. Similarly, we face critical decisions regarding the modernization of our nuclear delivery systems, due not to their impending obsolescence—all will remain viable for at least a decade, some for two or three—but rather because of the long lead times involved in designing and building their replacements. If, through negotiations or unilateral decisions, we make a deliberate national decision to forego nuclear weapons in the future, we will have to reconsider our fundamental deterrence strategy, for it will no longer be built on the firm foundation that our nuclear arsenal provides.

Conclusion

Deterrence was an essential element of national security practice long before the Cold War and the introduction of nuclear arsenals into international affairs. For millennia, states have sought to convince one another that going to war with them was ill advised and counterproductive, and they sometimes responded to deterrence failures in a manner intended to send powerful deterrence messages to others to reestablish and enhance deterrence in the future. The advent of nuclear weapons did change the way states viewed warfare, however. The avoidance of nuclear war—or, for that matter, conventional war on the scale of World War I or World War II—rather than its successful prosecution became the military's highest priority. This spurred a tremendous flurry of intellectual activity in the 1950s and 1960s that sought to develop a fully thought-out theory of deterrence as well as a massive national effort to put that theory into practice to deter (and contain) the Soviet Union.

Just as the beginning of the Cold War did not create the utility of deterrence as an element of national security strategy, the end of the Cold War did not eliminate it. As we move forward into the twenty-first century, it will be to the United States' advantage to lay the groundwork necessary to ensure that its deterrence strategies and activities are effective in the future. The concept of deterrence is sound, and we have the means necessary to implement it against the full range of threats that are reasonably susceptible to deterrence. The challenge that remains before us is to allocate the resources and create the processes necessary to proactively and successfully "wage deterrence" in the twenty-first century. It is a task that is nonpartisan in nature—one that can be sustained over the years through the commitment of the highest levels of our government.

Notes

1. *Deterrence Operations Joint Operating Concept Version 2.0*, US Department of Defense, December 2006.

2. Thomas Schelling, *The Strategy of Conflict* (Cambridge, MA: Harvard University Press, 1960), 131–34.

3. Joseph Nye, *Soft Power: The Means to Success in World Politics* (New York: Public Affairs Books, 2004), 5.

4. Brad Roberts, *Deterrence and WMD Terrorism: Calibrating Its Potential Contributions to Risk Reduction* (Alexandria, VA: Institute for Defense Analyses, June 2007), Abstract.

5. Thomas Schelling, *Arms and Influence* (New Haven, CT: Yale University Press, 1966), 121–22.

Chapter 6

On Nuclear Deterrence and Assurance*

Keith B. Payne

Weakness is provocative.

—Donald Rumsfeld

Given the diversity of opponents US leaders must hope to deter and the variety of circumstances in which deterrence and assurance will be important goals, a broad spectrum of US strategic capabilities may be necessary. In some plausible cases, nonmilitary capabilities will suffice, while in others the immense lethality of US nuclear threats is likely to be required. In other cases, *punitive* US threats will not deter because the opponent will accept great risks, but *denying* that opponent a practicable vision of success may deter.

US nonnuclear threats and employment options often are likely to be salient for punitive and denial deterrence. For example, in regional contingencies where US stakes at risk do not appear to involve national survival or the survival of allies, some opponents are likely to view US nuclear threats as incredible regardless of the character of the US arsenal or the tone of US statements. And when US priority goals include post-conflict "nation-building" and the reconstruction of a defeated opponent, US advanced nonnuclear threats may be *more credible* because highly discriminate threats will be more compatible with US stakes, interests, and the goals of post-conflict reconciliation and reconstruction.[1]

Reprinted with courtesy from *The Great American Gamble: Deterrence Theory and Practice from the Cold War to the Twenty-First Century, 409–48*. Copyright © 2008 by National Institute Press, "The Nuclear Posture Review: Setting the Record Straight," *Washington Quarterly* 28, no. 3 (Summer 2005); and "What Are Nuclear Weapons For?" *Forum on Physics and Society*, American Physical Society 36, no. 4 (October 2007).

*Originally published in *Strategic Studies Quarterly* 3, no. 1 (Spring 2009): 43–80.

No Deterrence Value for Nuclear Weapons?

Some contemporary commentators take the plausible cases described above to the extreme and assert that US nuclear weapons now offer little or no added value for deterrence over nonnuclear capabilities. The rationale for this assertion is derived from the old balance of terror formula: predictable deterrent effect is equated to the United States' capability to threaten the destruction of a select set of opponents' tangible, physical targets. Consequently, if nonnuclear weapons now can threaten to destroy most or all of that set of targets, then nuclear weapons supposedly no longer are of value for deterrence. The vulnerability of the designated targets, not the specific US instrument of threat, is expected to determine the deterrent effect.

The first of these propositions—that deterrent effect can be equated to target coverage—is fundamentally flawed. The second also is highly suspect; it certainly is possible to *hope* that US nuclear weapons no longer are critical for deterrence, just as it is possible to hope that all leaders will learn to be responsible and prudent. To assert confidently that US nuclear weapons no longer are valuable for deterrence purposes, however, is to claim knowledge about how varied contemporary and future leaders in diverse and often unpredictable circumstances will interpret and respond to the distinction between nuclear and nonnuclear threats. Those who make such a claim presume knowledge that they do not and cannot have.

In addition, a popular refrain of some commentators is that US nuclear weapons should be considered useful *only for deterring nuclear attack.*[2] This is not, and has not been, US deterrence policy. The only apparent rationale for this assertion is to buttress the claim that the deterrence value of nuclear weapons is narrow in scope and purpose and that the commentators' favored steps toward nuclear disarmament could eliminate even that value; if deterring nuclear threats is the *only purpose for US nuclear weapons,* they will then have *no unique value* if others move away from nuclear weapons.

This proposition is logical but artificially narrow. It misses other severe nonnuclear threats to the United States and allies that may not be deterred reliably absent US nuclear capabilities, such as threats posed by chemical and biological weapons (CBW). Commentators can claim for political reasons that US nuclear capabilities should be considered pertinent for deterring only nuclear threats, but CBW threats are real and growing, and there is no basis to conclude that US nonnuclear capabilities would suffice to deter them. Even if the vision of the complete worldwide elimination of nuclear weapons were to be realized, CBW threats would remain. The most that can be said in this regard is that US nuclear weapons might or might not be necessary for this deterrence goal—hardly a robust basis for making profound policy decisions about the most fundamental security questions.

Thinking through some plausible scenarios may be helpful in this regard. For example, if an opponent were to escalate an intense, ongoing conventional conflict by employing CBW with horrific effect against US forces, civilians, or allies, a high-priority US goal would likely be to deter the opponent's subsequent use of CBW. The US deterrence message to the opponent in this case could be that the opponent would suffer exceedingly if it were to repeat CBW use—that the United States would so raise the risks of the conflict for the opponent that it would *choose not to repeat its use of CBW* (even if its initial employment proved useful militarily or politically). This message could be intended to deter a second CBW attack during the crisis at hand and also to send a message to any hostile third parties that they must never consider CBW use against the United States and its allies.

The question in this scenario is whether US *nonnuclear capabilities* alone would constitute an adequate basis for this deterrence message. As noted above, there is no useful a priori answer to this question. Some plausible circumstances, however, suggest the potential unique value of nuclear threats. For example, if a pitched conventional conflict is in progress and the opponent already has been subjected to an intense US campaign of nonnuclear "shock and awe," could the threat of further US nonnuclear fire in response to an opponent's CBW attack be decisive in the opponent's decision making? The United States could threaten to set aside some targeting limitations on its nonnuclear forces for this deterrence purpose. Would such a nonnuclear threat dominate the opponent's calculation of risk, cost, and gain? Or

79

might it look like "more of the same" and have little prospect of being decisive in the opponent's decision making?

The answers to such questions certainly are not so self-evident as to suggest that US nuclear threats would provide no unique added deterrent value. Nuclear weapons may be so much more lethal and distinguishable from nonnuclear threats that, on occasion, they can deter an opponent who would not otherwise be susceptible to control. Strategic nuclear threats have the potentially important advantages of extreme lethality from afar and a relatively obvious firebreak. These could be important qualities to deter the first or second use of CBWs and to help deter future third-party CBW use. Clinton administration secretary of defense Les Aspin rightly pointed to the prospective value of US nuclear weapons for the deterrence of CBW threats given the proliferation of the latter: "Since the United States has forsworn chemical and biological weapons, the role of US nuclear forces in deterring or responding to such nonnuclear threats must be considered."[3]

How and what might constitute an "adequate" US mode of deterrence will depend on the details of the engagement, including opponents' values, vulnerabilities, risk tolerances, perceptions, access to information, and attention. Confident a priori assertions that nuclear threats *are sure to make the decisive difference* for deterrence purposes or that they *can provide no significant added value* betray only the pretense of knowledge regarding how opponents will calculate and behave in the future. Even with a careful assessment of the pertinent details of opponent and context, precise prediction about the linkage of specific threat to deterrent effect is subject to uncertainties.

Nevertheless, a common proposition, initially expressed soon after the Cold War by Paul Nitze, is that the United States may now consider converting its strategic deterrent from nuclear weapons to "smart conventional weapons" because the latter can carry out many of the same "combat missions."[4] Nuclear weapons are said to be of limited and indeed declining value because there are "no conceivable circumstances in which the United States would need to use or could justify the use of nuclear weapons to fight or terminate a conventional conflict with a nonnuclear adversary."[5] This proposition ignores the potential value of nuclear weapons for the deterrence of CBW; it also misses the fundamental point that deterrence requirements are *not set by what may be necessary to "fight or terminate" a conflict.*

Linking the assertion that there are few, if any, necessary "combat" roles for nuclear weapons to the conclusion that nuclear weapons lack *deterrence* value is a non sequitur, even if true. Nuclear weapons could be deemed to have no value whatsoever for combat missions and remain absolutely key to the deterrence of war and the assurance of allies. Deterrence involves exploiting opponents' fears and sensitivities and may have little or no connection to US preferences for the wartime employment of force for combat missions. Assurance, in turn, requires the easing of allies' fears and sensitivities, which again may have little or nothing to do with how the United States might prefer to terminate a conflict. Whether US nuclear capabilities are regarded as useful or not "to fight or terminate a conventional conflict" may tell us nothing about their potential value for the political/psychological purposes of assurance and punitive deterrence. Deterrence, assurance, and war fighting are different functions with possibly diverse and separate standards for force requirements. The potentially different force standards for these different goals should not be confused.

This most basic confusion was apparent during the congressional discussions of the Robust Nuclear Earth Penetrator (RNEP). The RNEP evolved from studies conducted during the Clinton administration and subsequently was pursued by the Bush administration as *potentially important for deterrence purposes.*[6] Yet, some congressional opponents of the RNEP pointed to the apparent lack of a "specific military requirement" as a basis for their opposition.[7] One prominent member of Congress stated that no "military requirement for a nuclear earth penetrator" has been "articulated to me."[8]

The pertinent questions for the RNEP had less to do with any expressed *military requirement* for this niche capability than whether a persuasive case could be made that it would be important for deterrence of significant threats and the assurance of allies. The uniformed military in general may have limited appreciation for a system that, as discussed by political leaders, would be useful as a *withheld* instrument for deterrence. If I can't use it, what good is it? is an understandable question. That "use" standard, however, may have limited relevance when the value of a nuclear capability is determined more by opponent and allied perceptions of it than by US employment plans.

The Apparent Value of Nuclear Weapons for Deterrence

Whether or not nuclear weapons are considered useful for combat missions or have been asked for by military commanders, a quick review of available evidence points toward their potentially unique value for deterrence and assurance. For example, in the 1991 Gulf War, Iraq launched 88 conventionally armed Scud missiles against targets in Israel and Saudi Arabia; those missile strikes continued until the end of the war. In Israel and the United States, there was concern that Iraq would use chemical weapons.[9] The anticipation of such attacks led Israeli citizens to take shelter in specially sealed rooms and to wear gas masks. Although Iraq did not employ chemical or biological warheads, Scud strikes directly inflicted more than 250 Israeli casualties and were indirectly responsible for a dozen deaths, including children, resulting from the improper use of gas masks.[10] UN officials have stated that Iraqi bombs and missiles contained enough biological agents to kill hundreds of thousands,[11] and US officials have confirmed that *if* Iraq had used available biological weapons, the military and civilian casualty levels could have been horrific.[12]

Saddam Hussein was neither a philanthropist nor particularly humane. Why then did he *not* use the available chemical or biological weapons? Was he deterred by the prospect of *nuclear retaliation?* Israeli commentators frequently suggest that the apparent Israeli nuclear threat deterred Iraqi chemical use. In this regard it should be noted that during a CNN interview on 2 February 1991, US defense secretary Dick Cheney was asked about the potential for Israeli nuclear retaliation to Iraqi chemical strikes. Secretary Cheney observed that this would be a decision that "the Israelis would have to make—but I would think that [Hussein] has to be cautious in terms of how he proceeds in his attacks against Israel." The following day, when asked about Secretary Cheney's statement, Israeli defense minister Moshe Arens replied, "I think he said that Saddam has reasons to worry—yes, he does have reasons to worry."[13] This reply, and Secretary Cheney's original statement—in which he did not object to the premise of the question about the possibility of Israeli nuclear retaliation, at least to Israeli analysts—was key to deterring Iraqi chemical weapons use.[14]

The possible direct US role in nuclear deterrence in this case should be highlighted.[15] On 9 January 1991, Secretary of State James Baker expressed a severe deterrent threat to Iraqi foreign minister Tariq Aziz in Geneva: "Before we cross to the other side—that is, if the conflict starts, God forbid, and chemical or biological weapons are used against our forces—the American people would demand revenge, and we have the means to implement this."[16]

President Bush's strongly worded letter to Saddam Hussein warned against the use of chemical or biological weapons. It spoke of the "strongest possible" US response and warned that "you and your country will pay a terrible price" in the event of "such unconscionable acts."[17]

Secretary Cheney also implicitly linked US nuclear threats to Iraqi use of weapons of mass deastruction (WMD): "The other point that needs to be made, and it's one I have made previously, is that he [Hussein] needs to be made aware that the President will have available the full spectrum of capabilities."[18]

Such statements by ranking US and Israeli officials, while not explicitly threatening nuclear retaliation, certainly implied the possibility. These threats appear to be a plausible explanation for Iraqi restraint with regard to chemical and biological weapons. Following the 1991 Gulf War, authoritative accounts of Iraqi wartime decision making on this issue emerged. In August 1995, Iraqi foreign minister Tariq Aziz reported to Amb. Rolf Ekeus, a UN weapons inspector, that "Iraq was deterred from using its WMD because the Iraqi leadership had interpreted Washington's threats of grievous retaliation as meaning *nuclear* retaliation."[19]

Tariq Aziz's explanation has been corroborated by former senior Iraqi military officials, including Gen Wafic Al Sammarai, then head of Iraqi military intelligence. General Sammarai stated, "Some of the Scud missiles were loaded with chemical warheads, but they were not used. They were kept hidden throughout the war. We didn't use them because the other side had a deterrent force."[20] He added, "I do not think Saddam was capable of making a decision to use chemical weapons or biological weapons, or any other type of weapons against the allied groups, because the warning was quite severe, and quite effective. *The allied troops were certain to use nuclear arms and the price will be too dear and too high*"[21] (emphasis added). Similarly, Iraqi general Hussein Kamal, Saddam Hussein's son-in-law and Iraqi minister of military industries, reportedly stated following his defection from Iraq in 1995 that "during the Gulf War, there was no intention to use chemical weapons as the Allied force was overwhelming . . . there was no decision to use chemical weapons for fear of retaliation. They realized that if chemical weapons were used, *retaliation would be nuclear*"[22] (emphasis added). At the time, the fact that some US naval vessels reportedly were deployed with nuclear capabilities aboard may have contributed to this helpful Iraqi view.[23]

In 1995, Brent Scowcroft, President Bush's national security advisor during the 1991 Gulf War, revealed publicly that US leaders had decided in fact that the United States would *not* respond to Iraqi WMD use with nuclear weapons. Rather, according to Scowcroft, the United States would have expanded its conventional attacks against Iraqi tarqets.[24] And President Bush has stated that "it [nuclear use] was not something that we really contemplated at all."[25] Nevertheless, according to the accounts by Tariq Aziz, Gen Hussein Kamal, and Gen Wafic Al Sammarai, the Iraqi leadership *believed* that the United States would have retaliated with nuclear weapons—and the expectations appear to have deterred—as clearly was intended by US officials.

On this occasion, *implicit US nuclear* threats appear to have deterred as hoped; Schelling's proposition regarding the deterring effect of possible nuclear escalation appears to have been demonstrated. The fact that many in the US senior wartime leadership later explained publicly that the United States would *not* have employed nuclear weapons may help to degrade that deterrent effect for the future. A comment by Bernard Brodie vis-à-vis the Soviet Union in 1963 may be apropos: If the opponent is under the "apparent conviction" that the US nuclear deterrent is credible, "why should we attempt to shake that conviction?"[26] Nevertheless, the point here is that the 1991 Gulf

War appears to offer evidence that *nuclear* deterrence, on occasion, can be uniquely effective. Saddam Hussein appears to have been confident that he could withstand the pressure of conventional war with the United States—perhaps based upon his relatively dismissive view of the US will to fight a bloody conventional war. When Secretary of State James Baker told Tariq Aziz of the "overwhelming" conventional power that would be "brought to bear" against Iraq, Aziz responded, "Mr. Secretary, Iraq is a very ancient nation. We have lived for 6,000 years. I have no doubts that you are a very powerful nation. I have no doubts that you have a very strong military machine and you will inflict on us heavy losses. But Iraq will survive and this leadership will decide the future of Iraq."[27] This prediction proved accurate for a decade.

Of course, the explanations of apparent Iraqi restraint offered by Tariq Aziz, Wafic Al Sammarai, and Hussein Kamal do not close the issue; they do, however, suggest that *nuclear* deterrence was at least part of the answer as to why Saddam Hussein did not use WMD in 1991 when he apparently had the option to do so. These explanations also suggest the profound error of those prominent commentators who asserted with such certainty immediately after the 1991 war that nuclear weapons were "incredible as a deterrent and therefore irrelevant,"[28] and the fragility of similar contemporary claims that US nuclear threats are incredible and thus useless for contemporary regional deterrence purposes.[29]

Prominent American commentators can assert that nuclear weapons are incredible and thus useless in such cases; their speculation about US threat credibility, however, ultimately is irrelevant. For deterrence purposes, it is *the opponent's belief* about US threat credibility that matters, and that cannot be ascertained from the views of American domestic commentators. The 1991 Gulf War appears to demonstrate that Iraqi officials perceived US threats as nuclear and sufficiently credible to deter and that this *perception was more important* to US deterrence strategy than were actual US intentions. Nuclear deterrence appears to have played a significant role despite the fact that US leaders apparently saw no need to employ nuclear weapons and had no intention of doing so.

There is little doubt that US *nuclear* threats have contributed to the deterrence of additional past opponents who otherwise may have been particularly resistant to US nonnuclear threats. This deterrent effect is a matter of adversary perceptions—which can be independent of our preferences or intentions regarding the use of force. However we might prefer to deter or plan to employ force, the actual behavior of adversaries on occasion suggests that there can be a difference between the deterring effects of nuclear and nonnuclear weapons. In some past cases, given the adversary's views and the context, it has been "the reality of nuclear deterrence" that has had the desired "restraining effect."[30] In the future, as in the past, the working of deterrence on such occasions may be extremely important.

There is some additional evidence from countries such as North Korea that opponents continue to attribute unique deterrence value to US nuclear weapons. For example, during a 2005 visit by a US congressional delegation to North Korea, Rep. Curt Weldon, vice-chairman of the House Armed Services Committee, raised with senior North Korean military and political leaders the US interest in a nuclear capability to threaten hardened and deeply buried targets. According to the after-trip report by Congressman Weldon and other members of the bipartisan delegation, this was the only US military capability that appeared to concern the North Korean leadership and "got their attention," suggesting its potential deterrence value.[31] North Korean statements regarding US nuclear "bunker burst" capabilities also appear to reveal an unparalleled concern about the possibility of such US nuclear capabilities, thereby suggesting their potential value for deterrence.[32]

Rogues and potential opponents are expending considerable effort on hard and deeply buried bunkers. Some of these bunkers reportedly can be held at risk of destruction *only via nuclear weapons.*[33] During the 1991 Gulf War, some Iraqi bunkers were "virtually invulnerable to conventional weapons."[34] In 1999, concerted NATO air attacks reportedly could not destroy a deep tunnel complex at the Pristina Airport in Kosovo. As a British inspector on the ground at the time reported, "On June 11, hours after NATO halted its bombing and just before the Serb military began withdrawing, 11 Mig-21 fighters emerged from the tunnels and took off for Yugoslavia."[35] Similarly, in

1996, senior Clinton administration officials observed that *only* nuclear weapons could threaten to destroy the suspected Libyan chemical weapons facility located inside a mountain near Tarhunah.[36] Moreover, the US Cold War "legacy" nuclear arsenal apparently has limitations against some protected targets. "Furthermore, the current [nuclear] inventory only has a limited capability for holding hardened underground facilities at risk. The country's only nuclear earth penetrating weapons . . . cannot survive delivery into certain types of terrain in which such facilities may be located."[37]

Adversaries unsurprisingly seek to protect what they value. And, as Defense Secretary Harold Brown emphasized, US deterrence threats should be capable of holding at risk those assets valued by the opponent.[38] Consequently, to the extent that we hope to apply the "logic of deterrence" to rogue-state decision makers, the US capability to threaten that which they value located within protected bunkers may be important for deterrence; if North Korean and other rogue leaders demonstrate the value they attribute to assets via buried and hardened bunkers, the US capability to hold those types of targets at obvious risk of destruction may be an important deterrent threat to those leaderships. Highlighting the potential value of nuclear capabilities to do so hardly connotes a rejection of deterrence in favor of "war fighting" as often is claimed; to the contrary, it reflects an attempt to find plausible deterrence tools suited to contemporary opponents and conditions. This is precisely the point made with regard to deterring the Soviet leadership in 1989 by R. James Woolsey, who subsequently served as the director of central intelligence in the Clinton administration:

> Successful deterrence requires being able to hold at risk those things that the Soviet leadership most values. The nature of the Soviet state suggests that the Soviet leaders most value themselves. This emphasizes the importance of being able to hold at risk deep underground facilities, such as those at Sharapovo, which can only be done effectively by an earth-penetrating [nuclear] weapon.[39]

A fundamental deterrence question regarding such US capabilities concerns which set of specific conditions is more likely to provide the United States with greater leverage: when opposing leaderships have, or do not have, sanctuaries impervious to US prompt threats. Are opponents likely to feel greater freedom

to provoke the United States severely when they believe themselves to be *more* or *less vulnerable* to US deterrence threats?

There are no a priori answers to such questions that can be
assumed to apply across a spectrum of opponents and circumstances. In contemporary cases, however, as in the past—*if* the
complex variety of conditions necessary for deterrence to work
are present and the challenger is risk- and cost-tolerant—then
nuclear deterrence *may be uniquely decisive* in the challenger's
decision making. Moreover, for deterrence to work on those occasions—whether they are few or many—could be of great importance given the potential lethality of emerging WMD threats
to the United States. To assert otherwise—that US nuclear
weapons now provide *no* unique added value for deterrence—
contradicts available evidence and lays claim to knowledge
about opponent decision making that domestic commentators
do not and cannot have. Such assertions reveal more about
what some commentators *wish* to be true than what available
evidence suggests should be believed.

There should be no presumption that nuclear threats always will make the difference between effective deterrence or
its failure. The capability, however, to threaten an adversary's
valued assets with great lethality and from afar—including
well-protected targets—may be critical for some US deterrence
purposes. Unless future leadership decision making is different from that of the past, in some cases *nuclear* threat options
will contribute to deterrence. Given literally decades of experience, the burden of proof lies with those who now contend that
nuclear weapons are unnecessary for deterrence; considerable
available evidence contradicts such a contention.

The decisions of Britain and France also suggest the continuing
value of nuclear weapons for deterrence. Both have reaffirmed
their long-term commitments to maintaining their nuclear capabilities for deterrence purposes, including deterrence of rogue
states and other possible future unexpected contingencies.[40]

Also indicative of the continuing deterrence value of nuclear
weapons are Russia's and China's decisions to modernize and
expand their nuclear arsenals[41] and the apparent desire of
North Korea, Iran, and possibly Syria to possess nuclear weapons.[42] North Korean officials have pointed to the value of nuclear weapons for deterrence:

Today's reality verifies that the [North Korean] nuclear deterrent constitutes the one and only means that can prevent war on the Korean peninsula and defend peace in this region. . . . We will strengthen our nuclear deterrent in every way to prevent war and defend peace on the Korean peninsula and in Northeast Asia and will take a decisive self-defensive countermeasure at the necessary time.[43]

North Korea's nuclear weapons program is "an all-purpose cost effective instrument of foreign policy . . . the single most important lever in its asymmetric conflicts and negotiations with South Korea, the United States, and Japan."[44] So too, Iranian officials reportedly attribute great deterrence value to nuclear weapons. Following Iran's costly war with Iraq in the 1980s, and the subsequent 1991 Gulf War,

Iranian leaders believed that nuclear weapons were the ultimate instrument of asymmetric warfare. They held that if Iraq had had nuclear weapons [in 1991], the United States would never have attacked it. Hence, in January 1995, Iran signed a contract with Russia for the completion of a nuclear power plant in the city of Bushehr, which . . . provided Iran with a pretext to begin building a complete fuel cycle, with the aim of producing enriched uranium for nuclear weapons.[45]

The material question is not whether commentators believe nuclear weapons "ought" to have value for deterrence in a normative sense; they *have* demonstrated that value. The question is whether we are willing to accept the risk of deterrence failure on those occasions in which the United States could not threaten nuclear escalation, possibly including threats to some adversaries' highly valued/protected targets. The added risk of deterrence failure flowing from such an inability surely cannot be calculated a priori with precision. It may be nonexistent or high, depending on the specific circumstances of the contingency. Even if the risk of deterrence failure for this reason is low, however, the possibility would still deserve serious consideration because the consequences of a single failure to deter WMD attack could be measured in thousands to millions of US and allied casualties. And, of course, that risk may not be low.

The Value of Nuclear Weapons for Assurance

Nuclear weapons also appear to have unique value for assurance. Particularly pertinent in this regard are the views of those allies who consider themselves dependent on the United States' nuclear umbrella for extended deterrence. Former senior military officers from the United States, Germany, Britain, France, and the Netherlands have emphasized the continuing importance of the *nuclear* escalation threat for deterrence: "The first use of nuclear weapons must remain in the quiver of escalation as the ultimate instrument to prevent the use of weapons of mass destruction, in order to avoid truly existential dangers."[46]

Similarly, following the North Korean nuclear test in October 2006, Japanese and South Korean officials emphasized the importance they place on US *nuclear capabilities* for extended deterrence. Former South Korean defense ministers asked that US nuclear weapons removed from South Korea in 1991 be returned, and public sentiment turned strongly in favor of South Korea having a nuclear weapons capability.[47] A South Korean delegation to the United States, led by Defense Minister Yoon Kwang-ung, sought an explicit public declaration that if North Korea employed nuclear weapons against South Korea, the United States would respond in kind as if the United States itself had been attacked.[48]

A 2006 Japanese study headed by former prime minister Yasuhiro Nakasone concluded that "in order to prepare for drastic changes in the international situation in the future, a thorough study of the nuclear issue should be conducted."[49] Nakasone noted that Japanese security is dependent on US nuclear weapons but that the future of the US extended deterrent is unclear. Japanese defense minister Fumio Kyuma was explicit regarding the nuclear requirements of extended deterrence. "The strongest deterrence would be when the United States explicitly says, 'If you drop one nuclear bomb on Japan, the United States will retaliate by dropping 10 on you.'"[50] There could hardly be a stronger allied statement of the perceived value of US *nuclear* weapons for the continued assurance of allies or a more explicit *rejection* of US ambiguity in its extended deterrence commitments.

A Japanese commentary on the subject by Kyoto University professor Terumasa Nakanishi laments the "Chamberlainization" of the US extended nuclear umbrella for Japan and explicitly links related fears to the potential Japanese need for nuclear weapons:

> With America not indicating that it will shore up its nuclear deterrence toward China and North Korea, if Japan is going to try to put an actual lid on the North Korean nuclear problem, private Japanese citizens, as "*sensible and prudent Japanese*," should widen and deepen discussion from now on [about] the issue of how Japan can connect its independent national strategy and Japan's own nuclear weapons and nuclear strategy to its foreign policy.[51] (emphasis added)

The expressed definition here of what is a "sensible and prudent" course for Japan may be far different from the preferred US definition of the same.

The Iranian drive for nuclear weapons similarly appears to be leading some neighboring Arab states to anticipate *their own need for nuclear weapons*: "Just such a reaction is underway already in the Middle East, as over a dozen Muslim nations suddenly declared interest in starting nuclear-power programs. This is not about energy; it is a hedge against Iran. It could lead to a Middle East with not one nuclear-weapons state, Israel, but four or five."[52]

That officials and commentators in key allied countries perceive great value in US nuclear weapons for extended deterrence suggests strongly that these weapons *do have unique assurance value.* There is a direct connection between allied perceptions of the assurance value of US nuclear weapons for extended deterrence and nuclear nonproliferation. There may seem to be an incongruity between the US maintenance of its own nuclear arsenal for deterrence and its simultaneous advocacy of nuclear nonproliferation; a prominent member of Congress has likened this seeming incongruity to a drunkard advocating abstinence. However, given the obvious importance of US nuclear weapons for its extended deterrence responsibilities and the critical role which US extended nuclear deterrence plays in nonproliferation, *there is no incongruity.* Sustaining US capabilities for extended nuclear deterrence is critical for nuclear nonproliferation.

Such allied commentary does not demonstrate directly the value of nuclear weapons for *deterrence*—again, it is US *opponents* who ultimately determine the deterrence value of US nuclear weapons. It is, however, significant evidence of the importance of US nuclear weapons for the assurance of allies via extended deterrence. It also is important to recognize that for North Korea's closest neighbors, including Japan and South

Korea, the question of the value of US nuclear weapons is not an academic or theoretical debate about preferred utopian futures. It is a most serious concern among these Asian leaders who undoubtedly understand North Korea at least as well as US commentators. They believe that US nuclear weapons are critical to the deterrence of North Korea and thus their own assurance. These are only perceptions; their perceptions, however, may be particularly well-informed, and both deterrence and assurance fundamentally are about perceptions.

The apparent importance of US nuclear weapons for extended deterrence, assurance, and thus nonproliferation may distress US commentators who would prefer US deterrence threats to be largely or exclusively nonnuclear. Just as deterrent effect ultimately is determined by opponents, however, what does or does not assure allies is not decided by the preferences of US commentators, but by the allies themselves. The United States can decide what priority it places on the assurance of allies and how it will proceed to support that goal, but only the allies can decide whether they are assured. In the contemporary environment, available evidence suggests strongly that assurance is an important goal and that US *nuclear weapons* are critical to the assurance of key allies to a level they deem adequate.

The United States could decide to withdraw the nuclear umbrella and provide only a nonnuclear commitment. As discussed above, however, it is likely that the US withdrawal of its *nuclear* extended deterrent coverage would create new and powerful incentives for nuclear proliferation among its friends and allies who, to date, have felt sufficiently secure under the US extended nuclear deterrent to remain nonnuclear.[53] This linkage is not speculative; it is voiced by allies who feel increasingly at risk. Extreme care should be exercised before moving in a direction that carries the risk of unleashing a nuclear proliferation "cascade"—such as moving prematurely in the direction of a wholly nonnuclear force structure. As a 2007 report by the Department of State's International Security Advisory Board concludes,

> There is clear evidence in diplomatic channels that US assurances to include the nuclear umbrella have been, and continue to be, the single most important reason many allies have foresworn nuclear weapons. This umbrella is too important to sacrifice on the basis of an unproven ideal that nuclear disarmament in the US would lead to a more secure

world . . . a lessening of the US nuclear umbrella could very well trigger a cascade [of nuclear proliferation] in East Asia and the Middle East.[54]

The Credibility of US Nuclear Threats: Implications for the Arsenal

If we hope to apply the logic of punitive deterrence to an opponent in an acute contingency, then that opponent must attribute *some* credibility to our threats. Whether the intensity of that belief corresponds to Kahn's favored threat that leaves *little* to chance or to Schelling's threat that leaves *something* to chance, the opponent must anticipate that there is *some probability* that the US threat would be executed.

In the past, militarists and dictators have seen in America's Western and democratic scruples license to provoke the United States. These leaders have included Adolf Hitler, Hideki Tojo, Mao Zedong, Saddam Hussein, and Slobodan Milosevic.[55] Adolf Hitler frequently boasted that he was not limited by "bourgeois scruples" in the manner of liberal democracies and that this would help ensure his success. Or, as Slobodan Milosevic proudly declared, "I am ready to walk on corpses, and the West is not. That is why I shall win."[56] Obviously, both Hitler and Milosevic misjudged their situations. However, their expectations that Western democratic norms would provide the basis for their victory likely contributed to their willingness to provoke.

This point has implications for the US nuclear arsenal's value for deterrence. In some instances, low-yield, accurate nuclear weapons may contribute to a US deterrent threat that is *more believable* than otherwise would be the case. The US "legacy" nuclear arsenal's generally high yields and limited precision could threaten to inflict so many innocent casualties that some opponents eager to find a rationale for action may seize on the possibility that a US president would not execute an expressed nuclear deterrent threat. Uncertainty regarding the US threat in such cases could work against the desired deterrent effect.

America's aversion to causing "collateral damage" is well known. Some opponents clearly see proper US concerns about civilian casualties, "nation-building," and winning "hearts and minds" as US vulnerabilities to be exploited. They may view as particularly incredible deterrence threats based on the generally high nuclear yields of the US Cold War arsenal, given the civilian destruction which high yields could cause. The US desire to minimize unintended destruction, inspire post-conflict support from an opponent's liberated populace, and pursue post-conflict reconstruction may be priorities in the contemporary period that reduce the apparent credibility of Cold War–style assured destruction nuclear threats.[57] In these cases, US nonnuclear and very discriminate nuclear capabilities may be important for US deterrence credibility. During the Cold War—when US survival was at stake and the context involved thousands of nuclear weapons on each side—these types of considerations were likely to have been less pertinent to considerations of credibility. Now, however, they point toward the potential value of advanced nonnuclear and highly discriminate nuclear threat options for deterrence credibility. Some studies done late in the Cold War, and looking 20 years into the future, pointed to the same conclusion.[58]

Consequently, reducing nuclear yields and improving the accuracy of US nuclear forces may be important for contingencies in which nuclear deterrence is critical but new, post–Cold War priorities are in play. Again, this suggestion is not, as some commentators charge, a rejection of deterrence in favor of "destabilizing," "war-fighting" nuclear weapons. Such a characterization is to apply loaded Cold War deterrence labels to a context in which they lack *meaning*. The potential value of low-yield, accurate nuclear weapons is fully consistent with their possible deterrent effect.

US strategic policies guided by balance-of-terror and assured-destruction metrics subverted long-standing moral strictures against threatening civilians in favor of the goal of deterrence "stability." In the contemporary era, however, when the stakes at risk for the United States in a regional crisis do not include national survival, and when postconflict reconstruction and minimization of damage to the opponent and its neighbors may be priority goals, the credibility of the US deterrent may rest *not on how much damage can be threatened* à la assured destruction but rather on *how controlled is that threatened damage*. Traditional moral considerations and the efficacy of deterrence may now merge.

In short, as the apparent success of nuclear deterrence during the 1991 Gulf War illustrated, perceptions are key to deterrence. Nuclear threats may be important, but high nuclear yields and limited precision *may not* appear to constitute credible threats to opponents who understand US concerns about inflicting "collateral damage" and expect that US "self-deterrence" would provide them greater freedom of action. We should not want the relatively high yields and modest accuracies of the US Cold War legacy nuclear arsenal to give an opportunity for contemporary opponents to view US deterrence threats with disdain.

It does not require much foresight or imagination to conclude that—*to the extent that the logic of deterrence applies*—under plausible circumstances US threats may more readily serve deterrence purposes when US forces can hold enemy sanctuaries at risk with minimal unintended damage. Leaving uncontested an opponent's potential belief that the United States would be incapable of threatening its sanctuaries, or would be "self-deterred" by enlightened scruples from executing its deterrence threats, may contribute to that opponent's felt freedom to provoke the United States. This is not a far-fetched concern. Contemporary rogue states appear eager to exploit both mechanisms in the hope of escaping US deterrence constraints. In this context, capabilities dubbed "destabilizing" by traditional balance-of-terror categorization—such as precision accuracy and counterforce potential—may be important for deterrence. The old notion that a coherent distinction can be drawn between "stabilizing" forces intended to serve deterrence purposes and "destabilizing" forces for "war fighting" fits the old formula but does not fit these contemporary circumstances.

Finally, some commentators have opposed US development of nuclear weapons intended to limit collateral damage because they claim that US forces designed to do so would be considered by a president to be more "useable," thus "lowering the threshold" to US nuclear employment: "The implication is that, if their resulting collateral damage can be substantially reduced by lowering the explosive power of the warhead, nuclear weapons would be more politically palatable and therefore more 'useable' for attacking deeply buried targets in tactical missions—even in or near urban settings, which can be the preferred locales for such targets."[59]

This critique posits that the United States should forego a capability that may be valuable for deterrence for fear that a president might employ it cavalierly. Such a trade-off is at least questionable, particularly given the absence of any history of such cavalier presidential behavior. In addition, because an opponent might consider a US nuclear deterrent threat to be *credible* does not also mean that it is regarded by presidents as easily employable—*as was demonstrated during the 1991 Gulf War.* A president's decision calculus about the actual employment of nuclear weapons is likely to be affected by many factors, particularly including the severity and circumstances of the provocation, other priority US goals, allied considerations, immediate foreign and domestic political circumstances, and personal moral perspectives. The manifest characteristics of US weapons may be more salient to an opponent's *view* of US credibility than it is to a president's view of their usability. A president's perceptions of *useable* and opponents' views of *credible* need not be conflated.

Can there be confident promises that more "discriminate" US nuclear capabilities would strengthen US deterrence efforts or make the difference between deterrence working or failing on any given occasion? *No, of course not.* In the absence of a specific examination of opponent and context, we are dealing again in speculative generalizations about how deterrence may operate. The particular types of nuclear capabilities necessary to threaten opponents' deeply buried bunkers and other targets, while minimizing the potential for collateral damage, could provide the needed lethality and credibility for deterrence on occasion. However, an opponent also could miss such fine points regarding US nuclear capabilities or be so motivated that the specific character of the US nuclear threat is irrelevant to its decision making. What can be said is that—unless a close examination of opponents suggests otherwise—these types of specialized nuclear capabilities *cannot reasonably be touted* as *ensuring deterrence credibility* or *dismissed a priori* as destabilizing and intended for war fighting vice deterrence purposes. In the contemporary environment, they may be intended for and well suited to the political goals of deterrence and assurance.

The Nuclear
Disarmament Vision

Throughout the Cold War and post–Cold War years, various groups and individuals have put forth initiatives for the long-term elimination of nuclear weapons or their near-term reduction to small numbers. With the end of the Cold War, many thoughtful people understandably question why the United States should continue to maintain nuclear weapons, particularly if most plausible adversaries can be defeated militarily with conventional forces alone. The point here is that, on some occasions, deterrence and assurance will be the priority goals. Numerous countries—including contemporary opponents and allies—give every indication that they perceive unique value in nuclear weapons for those purposes, whether or not US domestic commentators believe it or want it to be true. Those perceptions alone create the potential value of nuclear weapons for deterring opponents and assuring allies.

A common problem with recent and past nuclear disarmament initiatives is that they emphasize the risks of maintaining US nuclear capabilities but are silent or wholly superficial in discussing the risks of their elimination. The postulated benefit from the United States' moving toward giving up nuclear capabilities typically is presented in terms of the contribution such a move supposedly would make to the goal of nuclear non-proliferation.[60] US steps toward global nuclear disarmament supposedly will begin the action-reaction process of eliminating those nuclear threats that justify retaining US nuclear weapons for deterrence: no such threat, no such need. As I have argued elsewhere, the traditional balance-of-terror's simplistic action-reaction process is utterly inadequate for contemporary strategic conditions. Whatever the merit of that metaphor for this application, however, the question of nuclear disarmament must include a net assessment—a review of the value of nuclear weapons and the related downside of losing that value.

The burden of proof is on those who now assert that adversaries would be deterred reliably by US nonnuclear capabilities, that allies similarly would be assured reliably by the same, that opponents dutifully would follow the US example, and that the United States could be confident they had done so. *Considerable evidence points* to *the contrary in each case.* In 2006, British prime minister Tony Blair made this point against those questioning his decision to modernize Britain's nuclear capabilities:

> Those who question this decision need to explain why [nuclear] disarmament by the UK would help our security. They would need to prove that such a gesture would change the minds of hardliners and extremists in countries which are developing these nuclear capabilities. They would need to show that terrorists would be less likely to conspire against us with hostile governments because we had given up our nuclear weapons. They would need to argue that the UK would be safer by giving up the deterrent and that our capacity to act would not be constrained by nuclear blackmail by others.[61]

Blair's critics and their US counterparts who now advocate that the United States embrace the "vision" of nuclear disarmament *have not begun* to offer a plausible net assessment in response to this challenge. Instead, they appear satisfied to assert the old action-reaction/inaction-inaction balance-of-terror adage, along with the equally dubious claim—also derived from the old formula—that deterrence now can be orchestrated to work reliably with nonnuclear forces alone. Both assertions can be described as reflecting hope over considerable evidence.

There are conditions that should be considered critical milestones for any significant US steps toward nuclear disarmament. The realization of some of those conditions would represent a more dramatic restructuring of international relations than has occurred since the 1648 Peace of Westphalia. This should not preclude creative thinking about prudent steps toward greatly reduced reliance on nuclear weapons, but it certainly should make us wary of embracing the vision of nuclear disarmament as a practicable goal in the absence of such dramatic change.

For example, one of the reasons nuclear deterrence has been valuable is that it appears to have disciplined the behavior of some states that otherwise could not be trusted to behave peaceably. Not all states are trustworthy, and it is those untrustworthy states with hostile designs that often pose security challenges; they are called "rogues" for a reason. In the past, such untrustworthy governments included Hitler's Germany and Stalin's Soviet Union; now they include the governments of Iran, North Korea, and Syria. These particular rogue leaderships may come and go, but in the future, there will be comparably untrustworthy leaderships with hostile intent. This is pertinent because there is *no indication* that, in a world of sovereign states, adequate international verification and enforcement measures will be available to backstop nuclear disarmament, much less the elimination of CBW. Most experience points to the contrary.

The Clinton administration's thoughtful undersecretary of defense for policy, Walter Slocombe, observed rightly in this regard that if "somehow" all of the pertinent powers of the world were to accept the vision of nuclear disarmament, its realization would demand "a verification regime of extraordinary rigor and intrusiveness. This would have to go far beyond any currently in existence or even under contemplation."[62] Secretary Slocombe noted that the challenge to establishing the necessary verification regime should be obvious—it would have to include "certain and timely" procedures for "forcible" international action to ensure compliance.[63] In the absence of a trustworthy authority with much of the power and prerogative of a world government, such a verification and enforcement regime cannot exist. The enduring lack of reliable verification and enforcement—combined with the likelihood that some states will be untrustworthy, armed, and aggressive—explains why disarmament visions must remain visions in a world of sovereign states.

There are real risks associated with the possession of nuclear weapons. Great risk also may be expected if the United States and its allies were to give up nuclear weapons in the mistaken belief that untrustworthy, hostile states no longer could pose WMD threats. The same hostility and lack of trust inherent in international relations which create the need for nuclear deterrence prevent the realization of visionary solutions to end that need.[64]

Other than the occasional, unpromising call for world government,[65] the proponents of nuclear disarmament *have not begun* to suggest how this sturdy barrier to the realization of their vision and like visions in past centuries may be breached while maintaining US security and the security of allies. We all would like to hear and to believe, but no plausible answer is offered.

In his final speech to the US Congress, Winston Churchill warned, "Be careful above all things not to let go of the atomic weapon until you are sure and more than sure that other means of preserving peace are in your hands!"[66] There is no known basis for concluding that those "other means" are at hand or that threats to peace will disappear. Until then, embracing nuclear disarmament seriously as the priority US goal *should be recognized as entailing the serious risk of further vilifying those US forces that may be important to deter future war, assure allies, and help contain nuclear proliferation.*

Balance-of-Terror Tenets versus Plausible Deep Nuclear Force Reductions

Not all visions offer a wise path forward. Karl Marx's slogan "from each according to his ability, to each according to his needs" was a beautiful vision borrowed from scripture. Attempts to realize that vision in the Soviet Union instead produced misery for millions and probably set back Russian economic development by half a century.

The vision of zero nuclear weapons appears beautiful.[67] Yet, were the United States to pursue that vision as its priority goal, it could degrade the deterrence of war and the assurance of allies. In contrast, these same risks do not *necessarily* apply to deep reductions in the US strategic nuclear arsenal. Deep nuclear reductions could be consistent with continued support for US strategic goals in a dynamic strategic environment—which is why they could be undertaken prudently in select circumstances.[68]

The continuing undisciplined application of the balance-of-terror tenets to contemporary questions of strategic forces and policy, however, will likely *preclude the opportunity* for *prudent deep nuclear force reductions.* As applied, those tenets *work against* the US policies and capabilities that could otherwise help to mitigate the risks associated with deep nuclear reductions and thus help to make them acceptable to US leaders responsible for "the common defense."

The character and size of the US nuclear arsenal should be paced by numerous factors, including:

- the contemporary, highly dynamic strategic threat environment;
- the relationship of the nuclear arsenal to other national goals (e.g., nonproliferation);
- the goals the nuclear arsenal is to serve;

- the potential contributions to those goals by other nonnuclear and nonmilitary means; and,

- budget and technical realities.

The United States cannot control all of these factors with any predictability, but it can influence some. When the alignment of these conditions presents the opportunity for prudent deep nuclear reductions, that opportunity should be pursued smartly. The Bush administration's 2002 Treaty of Moscow, for example, contained a two-thirds reduction in the permitted number of operationally deployed strategic nuclear weapons— from the 6,000 weapons permitted by the 1991 Strategic Arms Reduction Treaty (START) I to a range of 1,700 to 2,200 weap- ons. At the time of the Moscow treaty, Bush administration officials publicly identified *the new and more cooperative rela- tionship with the Russian Federation* as enabling such dramatic reductions.[69] The then-emerging improvement in political rela- tions with Russia on a broad scale permitted deep reductions in the US strategic nuclear arsenal. This potential for deep reduc- tions was *not the result of negotiations for that purpose* but a ba- sic shift in political relations. US officials at the time also stated explicitly that *deeper reductions were possible in the future* as *conditions permitted.*[70]

What might contribute to the opportunity for further prudent reductions? In 2002, Bush administration officials included the development of US advanced nonnuclear forces and defen- sive capabilities as possibly doing so.[71]

Developments in US nonnuclear offensive weapons and damage-limitation capabilities could plausibly contribute to prudent reductions by helping to mitigate the possible risks of deep reductions and by providing nonnuclear offensive and de- fensive capabilities to perform some duties reserved to nuclear weapons in the past.[72] Significant damage-limitation capabili- ties, for example, could help to reduce a risk particularly as- sociated with very low nuclear force numbers: they could help to make US security *less vulnerable* to dangerous technical and geopolitical surprises, including deception by countries that had ostensibly agreed to deep reductions and thereby contrib- uted to the freedom felt by the United States to do so.

In addition, the responsiveness of the US nuclear and strategic forces production infrastructure in principle could help mitigate another of the primary risks involved in deep reductions—if the conditions permitting deep reductions shift and reestablish the requirement for an increase in the US arsenal's quantity or quality. The risk of being caught short in a dynamic environment may be eased by retaining a stockpiled reserve of nuclear weapons *or via the US capability to respond and adapt with new nuclear weapons in a timely way without relying on an inventory of stockpiled weapons.* This latter possibility follows simply from the principle that the United States may not need to have on hand or stockpiled a redundant reserve of nuclear forces *if* they can be produced reliably in a timely fashion: the more reliably, rapidly, and credibly the United States can reconstitute forces in a shifting threat environment, the lower the need to rely on existing inventories of stockpiled or deployed weapons. Consequently, the freedom to reduce nuclear weapons deeply ironically may benefit from the US capability to restore nuclear forces as flexibly and rapidly as may be required by changes in the factors that pace US requirements.

In short, the pacing factor most under US control—that is, the character of US strategic capabilities and nuclear production infrastructure—may help contribute to the realization of deep nuclear force reductions. This could be accomplished by reducing the demand for deployed or stockpiled nuclear weapons and by mitigating the risks that otherwise could be associated with deep reductions—particularly including risks of surprising behavior by opponents and the need to adjust rapidly to changes in the threat environment.

The continuing, mechanical application of balance-of-terror idioms and tenets to contemporary questions of US deterrence strategy and strategic policies will *undercut US policies and capabilities that could facilitate the opportunity for further prudent deep nuclear reductions.* Why? First, the balance-of-terror formula focuses obsessively on calculating the number and type of deployed nuclear weapons considered adequate for "stable" deterrence. Long-term linear planning around that number—and setting successively lower arms-control limitations—works against the flexibility to shift and adapt strategy and capabilities as necessary per the threat conditions that pace actual need. If history were fixed or proceeding reliably in a straight line toward greater amity and peace, the lack of flexibility embedded in the balance-of-terror formula might be acceptable. There is little evidence, however, of such a happy trajectory.

Second, the contemporary action-reaction proposition that manifests a US capability for "new" nuclear weapons production should be rejected because it will drive nuclear proliferation against having the type of viable nuclear production infrastructure that could help the United States adjust as necessary to changes in the threat environment *without relying on inventories of deployed or stockpiled weapons.* Similarly, the traditional "instability" arguments now leveled against nonnuclear strategic forces may reduce the potential for the development and deployment of nonnuclear strategic weapons that could permit less reliance on nuclear weapons.

Third, the traditional balance-of-terror presumption against supposedly "destabilizing" damage-limitation capabilities could keep US vulnerability to the risk of surprise too high for the prudent implementation of much deeper reductions, even if the environment is so conducive. And at very low numbers, the presumption against discriminate, counterforce offensive forces could preclude strategic capabilities important for effective deterrence in plausible circumstances.

In summary, the balance-of-terror formula and tenets tend to be inconsistent with the flexibility and adaptability of US policy and forces that could contribute to prudent, deep nuclear reductions given a permissive threat environment. Sharp opposition to past US policy initiatives for greater flexibility typically followed the balance-of-terror narrative, including the critiques of the 1974 "Schlesinger Doctrine" National Security Decision Memorandum (NSDM-242) and Secretary Brown's 1980 "Countervailing Strategy" (PD-59). And, as is discussed below, the Bush administration's 2001 Nuclear Posture Review (NPR) endorsed deep nuclear reductions, the possibility for further, deeper nuclear reductions, and *each of the capabilities described briefly above that could facilitate further prudent reductions.* Yet these NPR initiatives ran afoul of the continuing power of the same balance-of-terror narrative and have largely been stymied as a result.

103

The 2001 Nuclear Posture Review:
A Self-Conscious Step toward
Prudent Deep Reductions

The Bush administration's 2001 NPR was mandated by Congress to examine the roles and value of US strategic forces in the post–Cold War strategic environment, particularly including nuclear weapons.[73] It identified several avenues to strengthen deterrence, including the need to understand opponents better so that the United States can "tailor its deterrence strategies to the greatest effect."[74] The NPR correspondingly emphasized the need for a wide spectrum of capabilities—conventional and nuclear, offensive and defensive—to support the tailoring of US deterrence strategies against a diverse set of potential contingencies and opponents.[75]

Senior US officials emphasized that the NPR firmly embraced deterrence as a continuing fundamental US goal[76] and that it focused on deterring post–Cold War threats including, in particular, those posed by WMD proliferation.[77] Secretary of Defense Rumsfeld's unclassified foreword to the *NPR Report* specified that its policy direction was designed to "improve our ability to deter attack" while reducing "our dependence on nuclear weapons" for deterrence and placing greater weight on *nonnuclear* strategic capabilities.[78] Correspondingly, it emphasized the need for flexibility in US strategic force sizing as necessary to meet the needs of a variety of possible future threat conditions and delinked the sizing of US nuclear force levels from those of Russia, which *was not considered an immediate threat.*[79] It concluded that the immediate deterrence role for US nuclear weapons could be met with far fewer deployed nuclear forces and that US nuclear requirements could recede further as advanced nonnuclear weapons and defenses matured.[80]

In addition, Secretary Rumsfeld specified that a potential problem with the extant nuclear arsenal was its combination of relatively modest accuracy and large warhead yields.[81] The NPR pointed to the potential for low-yield, precision nuclear threat options and the ability to hold hard and deeply buried targets at risk to improve US deterrence capability and credibility.[82] Correspondingly, the NPR called for the US capability to "modify, upgrade or replace portions of the extant nuclear force or develop concepts for follow-on nuclear weapons systems better suited to the nation's needs."[83]

Finally, as mentioned above, the NPR concluded that the new relationship with Russia permitted the United States to reduce by approximately two-thirds its deployed strategic nuclear warheads from the START I ceiling of 6,000[84] and that the requirements for nuclear weapons might be reduced further still as US nonnuclear and defensive capabilities advanced.[85] Senior Department of Defense officials specified that the NPR's sizing of strategic nuclear warheads at 1,700–2,200 did *not* include Russia as an immediate threat.[86] As Undersecretary of Defense Douglas Feith said in open testimony, "We can reduce the number of operationally deployed warheads to this level because . . . we excluded from our calculation of nuclear requirements for immediate contingencies the previous, longstanding requirements centered on the Soviet Union and, more recently, Russia. This is a dramatic departure from the Cold War approach to nuclear force sizing."[87] Force sizing instead was calculated to support the *immediate* requirements for deterrence and to contribute to the additional goals of assuring allies, dissuading opponents, and providing a hedge against the possible emergence of more severe future military threats or severe technical problems in the nuclear arsenal.[88]

The NPR intentionally moved beyond the balance-of-terror formula that reduces US strategic nuclear force sizing to the familiar deterrence calculation of US warheads and opponents' targets. This was not unprecedented. Former secretary of defense Schlesinger discussed his 1974 "essential equivalence" metric for strategic forces as intended to contribute to allied and enemy *perceptions* of overall US strength.

The NPR also walked away from the balance-of-terror tenet that societal protection is useless, unnecessary, and "destabilizing." Instead, Secretary Rumsfeld tied ballistic missile defense (BMD) deployment directly to denial deterrence and improved crisis-management options, in addition to providing possible relief against the failure of deterrence: "Active and passive defenses will not be perfect. However, by denying or reducing the effectiveness of limited attacks, defenses can discourage attacks, grant new capabilities for managing crises, and provide insurance against the failure of traditional deterrence."[89] The subsequent formal announcement in December 2002 by Pres. George W. Bush that the United States would deploy strategic BMD against limited offensive missile threats was perhaps the most visible break from long-standing balance-of-terror policy guidelines.

Finally, the NPR endorsed a "responsive" industrial infrastructure to help provide the basis for flexible and timely adjustment of US strategic capabilities to technological and geopolitical developments. Again, a goal was to ease the requirement for deployed or stockpiled nuclear weapons; as increased reliance could be placed on a responsive industrial infrastructure to allow necessary adjustment to shifting technical or political conditions, there could be less reliance on deployed and nondeployed reserve warheads.[90]

In summary, the NPR established force sizing metrics that took into account US national goals in addition to deterrence. It recognized the potential for deep force-level reductions, given the new relationship with Russia, and sought to mitigate the risks of those reductions (and possible future, deeper reductions) by establishing a flexible, adaptable approach to force deployments, promoting strategic nonnuclear forces and defenses, and establishing a responsive industrial infrastructure that could reduce reliance on the maintenance of deployed and stockpiled nuclear weapons.

Another Balance-of-Terror/Assured-Destruction Counterreformation: Two Steps Back

Key commentators and members of Congress from both parties were unsympathetic to the NPR and its recommendations, some decidedly so. Responses to the NPR reflected both misunderstanding of its content and the long-familiar points of opposition to *any* strategic policy initiative departing from balance-of-terror and assured-destruction orthodoxy, whether from Democratic or Republican administrations.

Opposition to the NPR mirrored the sharp criticism of both NSDM-242 and PD-59. In each case, criticism followed from the familiar balance-of-terror/assured-destruction formula: support for multiple US nuclear threat options and the endorsement of modest counterforce strategic capabilities supposedly was the work of nuclear "war-fighting" hawks who rejected deterrence.

Commentators who continued to calculate US strategic force requirements via the Cold War's arithmetic formula dismissed the official claim that Russia was *not included* in the NPR's 1,700–2,200 range of strategic warheads. They simply could not fathom how the standard deterrence formula of counting US warheads and opponents' targets could result in the range of 1,700–2,200 warheads *unless* Russia continued to be included as the immediate threat to be deterred.[91] As noted above, however, that balance-of-terror formula was not the NPR's measure; the old metrics simply could not take into account the requirements stemming from the multiple national goals of assurance, deterrence, and dissuasion that were included in the NPR.[92]

In addition, pointing to uncertainty in the functioning of deterrence and recommending damage-limitation measures as a hedge against that uncertainty challenged the core balance-of-terror tenets. When the NPR recommended a defensive hedge and a spectrum of offensive capabilities—nuclear and non-nuclear—to strengthen deterrence, the old labels of "war-fighting" and "destabilizing" could not be far behind.

Commentators' applications of the familiar Cold War formulas and metrics to the NPR's initiatives led inevitably to the erroneous conclusion that the NPR's recommendations reflected a rejection of deterrence in favor of a "destabilizing," "war-fighting" strategy.[93] One commentator's assessment was typical in this regard: "Throughout the nuclear age, the fundamental goal has been to prevent the use of nuclear weapons. Now the policy has been turned upside down. It is to keep nuclear weapons as a tool of war fighting rather than a tool of deterrence."[94] Precisely the same charge was leveled at NSDM-242 and PD-59, despite the fact that neither they nor the NPR fit such a description.[95]

The NPR's embrace of strategic BMD also predictably brought charges of instability and the action-reaction "law" back into play: "Not only did this action destroy the arms reduction process . . . it made inevitable the next round of arms escalation. Missile defense began as Ronald Reagan's fantasy . . . . The resuscitation of the fantasy of missile defense, and with it the raising from the dead of the arms race, may result in catastrophes in comparison to which [the war in] Iraq is benign."[96]

This narrative on the NPR—derived wholly from the Cold War's balance-of-terror standards and terms of art—reverberated first within the United States and then abroad. With that, critics could cite each other as authoritative validation of their interpretation and critiques of the NPR.

A similar application of Cold War norms to the NPR was seen in most congressional commentary and opposition. Consequently, much of the NPR's recommended strategic force program has *not* been pursued. Former senior Pentagon official Tom Scheber has observed in this regard, "*Little progress* has been made on plans to develop and field prompt, conventional global strike [capabilities] and to modernize the nuclear force. In addition, initiatives to modernize the nuclear warhead research and production infrastructure and restore functionality have not progressed substantially"[97] (emphasis added).

This opposition was made more enduring and salient than might otherwise have been the case by the Bush administration's relatively modest efforts to present and explain the NPR publicly. In comparison to previous major initiatives in strategic policy—including NSDM-242 and PD-59—there was considerably less apparent public effort by the White House and the Department of Defense to make the case that the new realities of the twenty-first century demanded the approaches to deterrence and strategic forces presented in the NPR.

A critique based on the Cold War's balance-of-terror orthodoxy was inevitable, even had there been a vigorous effort on the part of officials to present and explain the NPR. That critique has greeted every attempted policy departure from orthodoxy since the 1960s; it constitutes the baseline of accepted wisdom about deterrence and strategic forces for many in the United States. The combination of decades-long familiarity with the idioms and standards of the "stable" balance-of-terror/assured-destruction model, and a limited public effort by the administration to explain the NPR, virtually ensured that the familiar critique based on past terms and definitions would become the accepted public narrative on the NPR. That narrative, in turn, became the basis for congressional opposition.

In addition, and unsurprisingly, there were extreme-sounding commentaries on the NPR that appeared to be driven by partisan politics. For example, Dr. Helen Caldicott, a cofounder of

Physicians for Social Responsibility, provided the following crude, politically partisan commentary during the lead-up to the 2004 presidential elections: "My prognosis is, if nothing changes and Bush is reelected, within ten or twenty years, there will be no life on the planet, or little."[98] Similarly, a *Los Angeles Times* commentary told of "a hawkish Republican dream of a 'winnable nuclear war'" that threatened a "nuclear road of no return," and that "could put the world on a suicidal course."[99] Another asserted, "With Strangelovian genius" the NPR "puts forth chilling new contingencies for nuclear war."[100] Such descriptions were pure hyperbole, of course, but—presented with the appearance of insight—they were frightening hyperbole.

Leaving such extreme commentary aside, most of the reasoned critique of the NPR was based on standard balance-of-terror/assured-destruction formulas and definitions. This was again apparent during the congressional debate over RNEP. Congressional critics objected to it as being the "action" that would inspire the "reaction" of nuclear proliferation and to RNEP's putative "war-fighting" capability, claiming it to be "destabilizing" and contrary to deterrence.

When Cold War measures of merit are applied in such a fashion to a decidedly post–Cold War strategic policy initiative, that initiative can only be deemed unacceptable; the NPR's recommendations were sure to be described as a rejection of deterrence, by definition, because the NPR did not follow the familiar balance-of-terror formula and related strategic force standards and goals. The critique was understandable on its own terms but correspondingly missed the greater reality. The NPR's departure from balance-of-terror orthodoxy did not reflect a rejection of deterrence; it was, instead, an intentional step away from the definition of deterrence and measures of US strategic force adequacy created during and for increasingly distant Cold War conditions.[101] It sought to identify the minimal level of nuclear capability consistent with multiple US strategic goals in a new and dynamic strategic environment. And, in doing so, it recommended a two-thirds reduction in forces and a series of measures to mitigate the risk of such deep nuclear reductions—leaving open the possibility of further nuclear cuts.

The irony here is that the typical critiques of the NPR charged that it was a throwback to Cold War thinking when, in fact, those very critiques sprang from the vintage balance-of-terror narrative. Commentators responded yet again on the basis of past strategic measures and, unsurprisingly, found the NPR in violation of the definitions, terms, and metrics of that old, favored, Cold War deterrence formula—as if that formula continues to be coherent in conditions so different from those which gave it intellectual life.

The NPR was neither beyond critique nor the final word in "new thinking" about strategic forces and policy. Useful commentary, however, now can be based only on recognition that our thinking about deterrence, defense, and strategic forces must adapt to the new realities of the twenty-first century. The NPR's drive to help create conditions suitable for prudent nuclear reductions instead was challenged by traditional Cold War standards and idioms that now have little meaning or value.

Still Holding the Horses

There is an anecdote, perhaps true, that early in World War II the British, in need of field pieces for coastal defense, hitched to trucks a light artillery piece with a lineage dating back to the Boer War of 1899–1902.[102] When an attempt was made to identify how gun crews could increase its rate of fire for improved defense, those studying the existing procedure for loading, aiming, and firing noticed that two members of the crew stood motionless and at attention throughout part of the procedure. An old artillery colonel was called in to explain why two members of a five-member crew stood motionless during the process, seemingly doing nothing useful. "'Ah,' he said. 'I have it. They are holding the horses.'"[103] There were, of course, no longer any horses to hold, but the crew went through the motions of holding them nonetheless. The author of this anecdote concludes that the story "suggests nicely the pain with which the human being accommodates himself to changing conditions. The tendency is apparently involuntary and immediate to protect oneself against the shock of change by continuing in the presence of altered situations the familiar habits, however incongruous, of the past."[104]

The continued application of the balance-of-terror tenets as guidelines for US strategic policy is akin to holding on to nonexistent horses. The expectation of well-informed, "rational" (i.e., prudent/cautious) opponents and the related expectation that the absence of "suicidal" decision making must lead inevitably to the predictable, mechanical functioning of deterrence are weak reeds upon which to base US policy, as they were during the Cold War. Former defense secretary Robert McNamara has stated that deterrence did not fail catastrophically at the time because "we lucked out."

Today, it is even more dangerous to expect the functioning of deterrence to be predictable, easily understood, achieved, and manipulated. Holding on to such unwarranted expectations virtually ensures that the next failure or irrelevance of deterrence will come as a surprise and that the United States simultaneously will dawdle in pursuing critical defensive/preventive measures and avoid the hard work necessary to strengthen deterrence to the extent feasible.

The NPR reflected a transformation in thinking about deterrence and strategic forces brought about by the dramatic change in conditions from those of the Cold War. Its basic recommendations were reasonable, prudent steps to align better our strategic policies and forces to the realities of the new era:

- broadening the range of US strategic goals that define the adequacy of US strategic forces,

- expanding US deterrent threat options,

- emphasizing the deterrent role for nonnuclear options,

- raising concern about the uncertainty of deterrence and the credibility of the inherited Cold War nuclear arsenal for some contemporary deterrence purposes,

- seeking an improved understanding of opponents and their intentions and the flexibility to tailor deterrence to the specific requirements of foe, time, and place,

- moving beyond the balance of terror as the measure of our deterrence and strategic force requirements, and

- placing a new priority on the US capability to limit damage in the event of deterrence failure or irrelevance.

In due course, the fact that continuing faith in fixed Cold War models, terms, and metrics has stymied the NPR's implementation will be a historical footnote—one with possibly lasting effect. The important question to consider now, however, is not the fate of the 2001 NPR but rather the fate of future reviews and efforts to better align US strategic policy and requirements with the reality of multiple and diverse opponents, WMD proliferation, and dynamic threat conditions. Many of the basic contours of US strategic policy goals taken into account by the NPR are likely to endure—particularly including the need to deter multiple threats, assure understandably nervous allies, and provide protection against various forms and sizes of attack, including limited nuclear and biological attacks. Future reviews of US strategic policy will confront the same questions of how US strategies and strategic forces can help support these goals in an unpredictable, dynamic threat environment. The continued application of Cold War strategic orthodoxy to those questions will prevent any plausibly useful set of answers. The balance-of-terror tenets, as applied, serve largely to buttress a political agenda of stasis that actually works *against* the very steps that could facilitate the realignment of the US nuclear arsenal and policy with contemporary realities—including the potential for prudent, deep nuclear force reductions.

It is time to move on from the enticing convenience and ease of the brilliant and innovative theoretical strategic framework of the Cold War. That framework is traceable to hubris, unwarranted expectations, and the need for convenience and comfort, however false. It is based on hopes that are beyond realization and conditions that no longer exist. Outside of the unique Cold War standoff that gave it a semblance of coherence, the balance-of-terror lodestar will be a continuing source of dangerous and confused policy guidance.

Notes

1. The increased importance that US officials attribute to these goals is elaborated in Sharon Behn and Seth Rosen, "US Urged to Focus More on Nation-Building," *Washington Times*, 28 July 2005, 15.

2. Daryl Kimball, "Of Madmen and Nukes," *Arms Control Today* 35, no. 9 (November 2005): 3, http://www.armscontrol.org/act/2005. See also Wolf-

gang Panofsky, "Nuclear Insecurity: Correcting Washington's Dangerous Posture," *Foreign Affairs* 86, no. 5 (September/October 2007): 109–10.

3. Les Aspin, *Annual Report to the President and the Congress* (Washington, DC: US Government Printing Office [GPO], January 1994), 61.

4. Paul Nitze, "Is It Time to Junk Our Nukes?" *Washington Post*, 16 January 1994, C-1.

5. Kimball, "Of Madmen and Nukes."

6. See statements by Assistant Secretary of Defense J. D. Crouch in Tom Squitieri, "Bush Pushes for Next Generation of Nukes," *USA Today*, 7 July 2003, 1.

7. See, for example, David Ruppe, "Republican Lawmaker Slams Bush Nuclear Plans," *Global Security Newswire*, 4 February 2005, http://www.nti.org/d/newswire/issues/2005_2_4.html. See also Jonathan Medalia, *"Bunker Busters": Robust Nuclear Earth Penetrator Issues, FY 2005–FY 2007*, updated 21 February 2006 (Washington, DC: Congressional Research Service, 2006), 9.

8. Congressman David Hobson, quoted in Jim Woolf, "US Drive for Nuclear 'Bunker Buster' Bomb Boosted," *Reuters.com*, 3 February 2005.

9. Pres. George H. W. Bush stated that "one of my big worries as commander-in-chief, which was shared by our military, was the fact that he might use chemical weapons. . . . We lived in fear of it." President Bush in *A Gulf War Exclusive: President Bush Talking with David Frost*, transcript no. 51, 16 January 1996, 5. Gen H. Norman Schwarzkopf, commander in chief of coalition forces, and Gen Walt Boomer, commander of US Marines, also anticipated Iraqi chemical use. See their statements in "The Gulf War, Part II," *Frontline*, no. 1408, 10 January 1996 transcript, 3–4. See also Youssef M. Ibrahim, "Israel Expecting Missiles from Iraq in Case of a War," *New York Times*, 1 January 1991, 1.

10. See the discussion in Moshe Arens, *Broken Covenant* (New York: Simon and Schuster, 1995), 201. See also Senator Arlen Specter, "Statistics on Missile Scud Attacks on Israel," *Congressional Record—Senate*, 5 March 1991, S2689.

11. R. Jeffrey Smith, "U.N. Says Iraqis Prepared Germ Weapons," *Washington Post*, 26 August 1995, A-1. For a comparison of the lethality of conventional, chemical, biological, and nuclear weapons, see Steve Fetter, "Ballistic Missiles and Weapons of Mass Destruction: What Is the Threat? What Should Be Done?" *International Security* 16, no. 1 (Summer 1992): 27.

12. Presentation by Dr. William Shuler, deputy for counterproliferation, Office of the Assistant to the Secretary of Defense for Atomic Energy, 13 December 1995, Seventh Annual SO/LIC Symposium, Washington, DC.

13. Akiva Eldar, "'Saddam Would Have Reason to Worry,' Says Arens When Asked about Unconventional Weapons," *Haaretz*, 4 February 1991, 1.

14. As discussed by Shai Feldman of Tel Aviv University's Jaffee Center for Strategic Studies and Amatzia Baram of Haifa University in their respective papers presented at the conference, "Regional Stability in the Middle East: Arab and Israeli Concepts of Deterrence and Defense," hosted by the US Institute of Peace, 17–19 June 1991, Washington, DC.

15. See the discussion in Tim Trevan, "Inside Saddam's Death Lab," *Sunday Times* (London), 14 February 1999, www.sunday-times.co.uk/news/pages/sti/99/02/4; Tim Trevan, *Saddam's Secrets: The Hunt for Iraq's Hidden Weapons* (North Pomfret, VT: Harper Collins, 1999), 45; and Keith B. Payne, *Deterrence in the Second Nuclear Age* (Lexington, KY: University Press of Kentucky), 81–87.

16. *Baghdad INA*, 9 January 1991, translated and presented in "INA Reports Minutes of Aziz-Baker Meeting," FBIS-NES-92-009, 14 January 1992, 27.

17. Reprinted in *US Department of State Dispatch, Persian Gulf*, no. 2, 14 January 1991, 25.

18. *Public Statements of Richard B. Cheney, Secretary of Defense*, vol. 4 (Washington, DC: Historical Office, Office of the Secretary of Defense, 1990), 2547.

19. Smith, "U.N. Says Iraqis Prepared Germ Weapons," A-19.

20. Statement by Gen Wafic Al Sammarai, "The Gulf War, Part I," *Frontline* no. 1407, 9 January 1996 transcript, 12.

21. Statements by Gen Al Sammarai, "The Gulf War, Parts I and II," *Frontline no.* 1407, 9–10 January 1996 (emphasis added). Comprehensive background interviews available at www.wgbh.org. See also, Trevan, "Inside Saddam's Death Lab," and Trevan, *Saddam's Secrets*.

22. Quoted in *General Hussein Kamal UNSCOMI/AEA Briefing*, (UNSCOM/IAEA Sensitive) 22 August 1995, Amman, Jordan (emphasis added). Transcript available at http://www.globalsecurity.org/wmd/library/news.iraq/un/unscom-iaea_kamal-brief.htm.

23. See, for example, International Institute for Strategic Studies, *The Military Balance: 1990–1991* (London: Brassey's, 1990), 216–18.

24. See the transcript of statements by Brent Scowcroft, *NBC News Meet the Press*, 27 August 1995, 10.

25. Bush, *Gulf War Exclusive*. Then–secretary of state James Baker also stated that President Bush "had also decided that US forces would not retaliate with chemical or nuclear weapons if the Iraqis attacked with chemical munitions." James Baker, *The Politics of Diplomacy* (New York: Putnam, 1995), 359.

26. Bernard Brodie, "What Price Conventional Capabilities in Europe?" *Reporter* 28 (23 May 1963): 28.

27. Statements by James Baker and Tariq Aziz, "The Gulf War, Part I," *Frontline*, no. 1407, 9 January 1996 transcript, 9, cited in, Payne, *Deterrence in the Second Nuclear Age*, 136.

28. Carl Kaysen, Robert McNamara, and George Rathjens, "Nuclear Weapons after the Cold War," *Foreign Affairs* 70, no. 4 (Fall 1991): 102.

29. Kimball, "Of Madmen and Nukes."

30. As concluded by Richard Ned Lebow and Janice Gross Stein, *We All Lost the Cold War* (Princeton, NJ: Princeton University Press, 1994), 356.

31. Cong. Curt Weldon, "Congressional Delegation to North Korea Trip Report" (Presentation, Nuclear Strategy Forum, cited with permission), Washington, DC, 22 February 2005.

32. See, for example, the review of North Korean statements on the subject in the report by Mark Schneider, *Kim Jong Il and Nuclear Deterrence* (Fairfax, VA: National Institute for Public Policy, 2005), 13–19.

114

33. Medalia, *"Bunker Busters,"* 1. See also the extended discussion of this subject in Kurt Guthe, "Implications of a Dynamic Strategic Environment," in Keith Payne et al., eds, *Rationale and Requirements for US Nuclear Weapons and Arms Control, Volume II* (Fairfax, VA: National Institute for Public Policy, 2001), 64–69.

34. General Accounting Office (GAO), *Operation Desert Storm: Evaluation of the Air Campaign,* GAO/NSIAD-98-134 (Washington, DC: GAO, June 1997), 198.

35. Tim Ripley, "Kosovo: A Bomb Damage Assessment," *Jane's Intelligence Review* 11, no. 9 (September 1999): 11.

36. *Remarks by Dr. Harold Smith before the Defense Writers Group,* 23 April 1996, 1–4 (as transcribed by the Office of the Assistant Secretary of Defense for Public Affairs).

37. Bryan Fearey, Paul White, John St. Ledger, and John Immele, "An Analysis of Reduced Collateral Damage Nuclear Weapons," *Comparative Strategy* 22, no. 4 (October/November 2003): 312. See also the similar statement by Secretary of Defense Donald Rumsfeld in Ann Scott Tyson, "'Bunker Buster' Casualty Risk Cited," *Washington Post,* 28 April 2005, A-7.

38. See the statement by Harold Brown in US Senate, Committee on Armed Services, *MX Missile Basing System and Related Issues,* Hearings, 98th Congress, 1st Session (Washington, DC: GPO, 1983), 6–7.

39. R. James Woolsey, "US Strategic Force Decisions for the 1990s," *Washington Quarterly* 12, no. 1 (Winter 1989): 82.

40. See, for example, *The Future of the United Kingdom's Nuclear Deterrent,* presented to Parliament by the Secretary of State for Defence and the Secretary of State for Foreign and Commonwealth Affairs by Command of Her Majesty, Cm 6994 (London: Her Majesty's Stationery Office, December 2006); and *Speech by French President Jacques Chirac on Nuclear Deterrence,* at the L'Ile Longue submarine base in Finistere on 19 January 2006, available via the French Embassy in the United States at info-france-usa.

41. For reviews of Russian and Chinese post–Cold War nuclear force and policy developments, see respectively, Mark Schneider, *The Nuclear Forces and Doctrine of the Russian Federation,* Nuclear Strategy Forum no. 003 (Fairfax, VA: National Institute Press, 2006); and Schneider, *The Nuclear Doctrine and Forces of the People's Republic of China,* Nuclear Strategy Forum no. 007 (Fairfax, VA: National Institute Press, November 2007).

42. It appears that Syria received North Korean assistance in the attempted covert construction of a nuclear reactor "not intended for peaceful purposes." White House spokeswoman Dana Perino, quoted in "US Details Reactor in Syria," *Washington Post,* 25 April 2008, A-12.

43. Statement by a spokesman of the North Korean Foreign Ministry, 31 March 2004, Korean Central News Agency, 1 April 2004, Open Source Center, Document KPP20040401000030.

44. Samuel S. Kim, *North Korean Foreign Relations in the Post–Cold War World* (Carlisle, PA: US Army War College, Strategic Studies Institute, April 2007), 87.

45. As observed by Kamram Taremi, a researcher at the Center for Graduate International Studies, University of Tehran, in "Beyond the Axis of Evil: Ballistic Missiles in Iran's Military Thinking," *Security Dialogue* 36, no. 1 (March 2005): 102–3.

46. Klaus Naumann, Gen John Shalikashvili, The Lord Inge, Jacques Lanxade, and Henk van den Breeman, *Towards a Grand Strategy for an Uncertain World: Renewing Transatlantic Partnership* (Washington, DC: Center for Strategic and International Studies, 2007), 94, http://www.csis.org/media/csis/events/080110_grand_strategy.pdf.

47. See Dana Linzer and Walter Pincus, "U.S. Detects Signs of Radiation Consistent with Test," *Washington Post,* 14 October 2006, A-14; and Reuters, "S. Koreans Want Nuclear Weapons Due to North-Survey," 12 October 2006, http://asia.news.yahoo.com/061012/3/2r7t9.html.

48. "S. Korea Presses US Over 'Umbrella,'" *Washington Times,* 21 October 2006, A-2.

49. Quoted in "North Korea's Nuclear Threat: Is US Nuclear Umbrella Effective?" *Daily Yomiuri,* 20 March 2007, http://www.opensource.gov/portal/server.pt/gateway. See also "Nakasone Proposes Japan Consider Nuclear Weapons," *Japan Times,* 6 September 2006; and Tim Johnson, "Nuclear Taboo Slowly Giving Way," *Miami Herald,* 24 September 2006, 1.

50. Quoted in "North Korea's Nuclear Threat/Reinforcing Alliance with US Helps Bolster Nuclear Deterrence," *Daily Yomiuri* (Internet version) in English, 23 March 2007.

51. Terumasa Nakanishi, "U.S. North Korea Moving Toward Normalizing Diplomatic Ties; Japan Must Discuss Nuclear Deterrence, Prepare for 'Worst-Case' Scenario," *Seiron,* 1–31 December 2007, 222–33, translated and printed in Open Source Center, *Japan: Pundit Says Japan Should Discuss Nuclear Deterrence, Worst-Case Scenario,* JPP20071106015003, https://www.opensource.gov/portal/server.pt/gateway/PTARGS_0_0_200_51_ 43/htt.

52. Joseph Cirincione, "Cassandra's Conundrum," *National Interest,* no. 92 (November/December 2007): 16–17.

53. See the discussion in International Security Advisory Board, *Report on Discouraging a Cascade of Nuclear Weapons States* (Washington, DC: US Department of State, 19 October 2007), 22–23.

54. Ibid., 23.

55. See the discussion in Keith B. Payne, *The Fallacies of Cold War Deterrence and a New Direction* (Lexington, KY: University Press of Kentucky, 2001), 61–73.

56. Quoted in Josef Joffee, "A Peacenik Goes to War," *New York Times Magazine,* 30 May 1999, *New York Times on the Web,* "Archives," 1.

57. Some former senior officials have concluded that the United States must place greater priority on "nation-building" and post-conflict "reconstruction." See Behn and Rosen, "US Urged to Focus More on Nation-Building." A new US Army field manual reportedly "puts nation-building as a military task alongside combat operations." Sara Carter, "Army Manual Stresses Nation Building," *Washington Times,* 3 March 2008, A-1.

58. See, for example, The Commission on Integrated Long-Term Strategy (chaired by Fred Iklé and Albert Wohlstetter), *Discriminate Deterrence* (Washington, DC: GPO, 1988), 2.

59. Sidney Drell et al., "A Strategic Choice: New Bunker Busters Versus Nonproliferation," *Arms Control Today* 33, no. 2 (March 2003): 9.

60. See, for example, George Shultz, William J. Perry, Henry A. Kissinger, and Sam Nunn, "A World Free of Nuclear Weapons," *Wall Street Journal*, 4 January 2007, 15.

61. *Future of the United Kingdom's Nuclear Deterrent*, 5.

62. See the testimony of Walter B. Slocombe, undersecretary of defense for policy, *The Future of Nuclear Deterrence, Hearing before the Subcommittee on International Security, Proliferation, and Federal Services of the Committee on Governmental Affairs, United States Senate*, 12 February 1997, 6 (prepared text).

63. Ibid.

64. The limitations on the international system created by the inherent lack of trust within the system are an overarching theme in Kenneth N. Waltz, *Man, the State and War* (New York: Columbia University Press, 1954).

65. See, for example, Walter Cronkite, "Cronkite Champions World Government," *Washington Times*, 3 December 1999, A-2; and The United Methodist Church, Council of Bishops, *A Pastoral Letter to All United Methodists In Defense of Creation: The Nuclear Crisis and a Just Peace* (1986), 71.

66. Winston Churchill, quoted in a speech by Prime Minister Margaret Thatcher to a joint meeting of the US Congress, 20 February 1985, http://www.margaretthatcher.org/speeches/displaydocument.

67. See, for example, Shultz et al., "World Free of Nuclear Weapons"; George Shultz, William J. Perry, Henry A. Kissinger, and Sam Nunn, "Toward a Nuclear-Free World," *Wall Street Journal*, 15 January 2008, 13; and Amb. Max Kampelman, "A Serious Look at Our World," *Comparative Strategy* 25, no. 2 (April–June 2006): 153–55.

68. For an aged but still useful examination of the question of deep nuclear reductions, see Francis Hoeber, *How Little Is Enough? SALT and Security in the Long Run* (New York: Crane, Russak & Company, 1981), 20–39.

69. See, for example, US Department of Defense, *Statement on Nuclear Posture Review*, no. 113-02, 9 March 2002, http://www.defenselink.mil/news/Mar2002/b03092002_bt113-02.html.

70. Statement of the Hon. Douglas Feith, undersecretary of defense for policy, Senate Armed Services Committee, *Hearing on the Nuclear Posture Review*, 14 February 2002, 7 (prepared text).

71. Ibid.

72. These points are elaborated in Kurt Guthe, *A Different Path to Nuclear Arms Reduction*, Discussion Paper (Fairfax, VA: National Institute for Public Policy, 27 December 2007), 1–4.

73. See Keith B. Payne, "The Nuclear Posture Review and Deterrence for a New Age," *Comparative Strategy* 23, no. 4/5 (October–December 2004): 411–20; and Payne, "The Nuclear Posture Review: Setting the Record Straight," *Washington Quarterly* 28, no. 3 (Summer 2005): 135–51.

74. Donald H. Rumsfeld, "Adapting US Strategic Forces," *Department of Defense Annual Report to the President and the Congress 2002*, chap. 7, 4, http://www.defenselink.mil/execsec/adr2002.html_files/chap7.htm.

75. Ibid., 2; Statement of the Hon. Douglas Feith, 3, 5, 7; and J. D. Crouch (assistant secretary of defense for international security policy), *Special Briefing on the Nuclear Posture Review*, 9 January 2002, http://www.defenselink. mil/transcripts/2002/t0 1092002_t0109npr.html.

76. Statement of the Hon. Douglas Feith, 3–5; Crouch, *Special Briefing*; and John Gordon, *Statement before the Senate Armed Services Committee*, 14 February 2002, 2–5 (prepared text).

77. Donald H. Rumsfeld, "Foreword," *Nuclear Posture Review Report*, submitted to Congress on 31 December 2001, http://www.defenselink.mil/ news/Jan2002/d20020109npr.pdf.

78. Ibid.; and Statement of the Hon. Douglas Feith, 5.

79. Tom Scheber, Keith Payne, and Kurt Guthe, *The 2001 Nuclear Posture Review: Sizing the Nuclear Force* (Fairfax, VA: National Institute for Public Policy, November 2007), 1.

80. Statement of the Hon. Douglas Feith, 7; Rumsfeld, "Adapting US Strategic Forces," 3; and Keith B. Payne (deputy assistant secretary of defense for forces policy, Office of the Secretary of Defense), *Nuclear Posture Briefing to the Defense Science Board*, 20 February 2003.

81. Quoted in Julian Borger, "Bunker Bomb Will Bust Test Ban," *Guardian*, 11 March 2002, 12. See also Linton F. Brooks, *Statement before the Senate Armed Services Subcommittee on Strategic Forces*, 4 April 2005, 2–3 (prepared text).

82. Tom Scheber, Office of the Secretary of Defense, *The ABCs of the NPR* (unclassified briefing, 2003).

83. Rumsfeld, "Adapting US Strategic Forces," 5; see also Statement of the Hon. Douglas Feith, 4.

84. Statement of the Hon. Douglas Feith, 5–6.

85. Ibid., 7.

86. Ibid., 5–6; and Rumsfeld, "Foreword."

87. Statement of the Hon. Douglas Feith, 6.

88. Rumsfeld, "Adapting US Strategic Forces," 5–6; Statement of the Hon. Douglas Feith, 3, 5; Keith B. Payne, *The Nuclear Posture Review: Key Organizing Principles* (unclassified Department of Defense briefing on the NPR), 30 July 2002, 9; Gordon, *Statement*, 7–8; and Scheber et al., *2001 Nuclear Posture Review*, 3–6.

89. Rumsfeld, "Foreword."

90. Scheber et al., *2001 Nuclear Posture Review*, 6.

91. Richard Sokolsky, "Demystifying the US Nuclear Posture Review," *Survival* 44, no. 3 (Autumn 2002): 141; Morton Halperin, "Parsing the Nuclear Posture Review," *Arms Control Today* 32, no. 2 (March 2002): 19–20; and David McDonough, *The 2002 Nuclear Posture Review: The 'New Triad,' Counterproliferation, and US Grand Strategy*, Centre of International Relations, University of British Columbia, Working Paper no. 38 (August 2003), 35.

92. As described in Scheber et al., *2001 Nuclear Posture Review*, 3–5.

93. See, for example, Roger Speed and Michael May, "Dangerous Doctrine," *Bulletin of the Atomic Scientists* 61, no. 2 (March/April 2005): 38–49; David Mc-Donough, *Nuclear Superiority: The 'New Triad' and the Evolution of Nuclear Strategy*, Adelphi Paper No. 383 (New York: Routledge, 2006), 63–84; and Lawrence Freedman, *Deterrence* (Malden, MA: Polity Press, 2004), 2, 24, 84.

94. Ivo Daalder, quoted in Michael Gordon, "Nuclear Arms: For Deterrence or Fighting?" *New York Times*, 11 March 2002, A-1.

95. See, for example, Seymour Melman, "Limits of Military Power," *New York Times*, 17 October 1980, 31.

96. James Carroll, "The Paradox of Missile Defense," *Boston Globe*, 5 June 2007, A-11; see also David Rupp, "Democratic Senator Says Bush Policies Increase Risk of Nuclear Abyss," *Global Security Newswire*, 29 January 2004, http://www.nti.org/d_newswire/issues/2004_1_29.html#8944A21C.

97. Tom Scheber and Keith Payne, *Examination of U.S. Strategic Forces Policy and Capabilities* (Fairfax, VA: National Institute for Public Policy, February 2008), 4.

98. As quoted in "Nuclear Weapons 'Immoral,' Say Religious, Scientific Leaders," *Los Angeles Times*, 9 March 2004, http://www.oneworld.net.

99. Robert Scheer, "Commentary: A Nuclear Road of No Return: Bush's Bid for New Kinds of Weapons Could Put the World on a Suicidal Course," *Los Angeles Times*, 13 May 2003, B-13.

100. William Arkin, "Secret Plan Outlines the Unthinkable," *Los Angeles Times (latimes.com)*, 10 March 2002, http://www.latimes.com/news/opinion/laop-arkinmar10.story.

101. Crouch, *Special Briefing*.

102. This anecdote is recounted in Elting Morison, *Men, Machines, and Modern Times* (Cambridge, MA: MIT Press, 1966), 17–18.

103. Ibid., 18.

104. Ibid.

Chapter 7—Framing Deterrence for the 21st Century

A Conference Sponsored Jointly by the Royal United Services Institute, King's College, London, and the US Air Force Research Institute
18–19 May 2009

18 May

Time	Scheduled Activity	Speaker	Facilitators	Recorders	OPR
0800–0900	Welcome, Coffee, Admin	N/A	N/A	N/A	RUSI Event Staff
0900–0940	Speaker 1: Deterrence in the 21st Century	Keith Payne	Directors (Clarke, Frost, Shaud)		AFRI
0940–1000	Case Study 1: Estonia and Cyber Attack	TBD	Directors (Clarke, Frost, Shaud)		RUSI/King's
1000–1130	Workshop 1: Deterrence in the 21st Century	N/A	Workshop 1 / Workshop 2 / Workshop 3 / Workshop 4	Workshop 1—Hayden / Workshop 2—Hukill / Workshop 3—Lowther / Workshop 4—Carter	
1130–1230	Lunch		Directors (Clarke, Frost, Shaud)		RUSI Event Staff
1230–1310	Speaker 2: State versus State Actors	TBD	Directors (Clarke, Frost, Shaud)		
1310–1330	Case Study 2: India-Pakistan	TBD	Directors (Clarke, Frost, Shaud)		
1330–1500	Workshop 2: State versus State Actors	N/A	Workshop 1 / Workshop 2 / Workshop 3 / Workshop 4	Workshop 1—Hayden / Workshop 2—Hukill / Workshop 3—Lowther / Workshop 4—Carter	
1500–1530	Tea, Coffee	N/A	N/A	N/A	RUSI Event Staff
1530–1610	Speaker 3: State versus Nonstate Actors		Directors (Clarke, Frost, Shaud)		
1610–1630	Case Study 3: Israel-Hezbollah War, 2006		Directors (Clarke, Frost, Shaud)		
1630–1800	Workshop 3: State versus Nonstate Actors		Workshop 1 / Workshop 2 / Workshop 3 / Workshop 4	Workshop 1—Hayden / Workshop 2—Hukill / Workshop 3—Lowther / Workshop 4—Carter	
1800–1900	Cocktails	N/A	N/A	N/A	RUSI Event Staff

Framing Deterrence for the 21st Century

A Conference Sponsored Jointly by the Royal United Services Institute, King's College, London, and the US Air Force Research Institute
18–19 May 2009

Time	Scheduled Activity	Speaker	Facilitators	Recorders	OPR
0800-0900	Welcome, Coffee, Admin	N/A	N/A	N/A	RUSI Event Staff
0900-0940	Speaker 4: Counterproliferation	Ashton Carter	Directors (Clarke, Frost, Shaud)		AFRI
0940-1000	Case Study 4:Iran	TBD	Directors (Clarke, Frost, Shaud)		RUSI/King's
1000-1130	Workshop 4: Counterproliferation	N/A	Workshop 1 / Workshop 2 / Workshop 3 / Workshop 4	Workshop 1—Hayden / Workshop 2—Hukill / Workshop 3—Lowther / Workshop 4—Carter	
1130-1230	Lunch		Directors (Clarke, Frost, Shaud)		RUSI Event Staff
1230-1310	Speaker 5: Nonstate Actors versus States	TBD	Directors (Clarke, Frost, Shaud)		
1310-1330	Case Study 5: The Madrid Train Bombing—al-Qaeda versus Spain	TBD	Directors (Clarke, Frost, Shaud)		
1330-1500	Workshop 5: Nonstate Actors versus States	N/A	Workshop 1 / Workshop 2 / Workshop 3 / Workshop 4	Workshop 1—Hayden / Workshop 2—Hukill / Workshop 3—Lowther / Workshop 4—Carter	
1500-1530	Tea, Coffee	N/A	N/A	N/A	RUSI Event Staff
1530-1630	Plenary Preparation Workshop		Directors (Clarke, Frost, Shaud)		
1630-1730	Plenary Session and Closing Remarks		Directors (Clarke, Frost, Shaud)		
20 May					
0800-1200	Hotwash		All	All	RUSI, KCL, AFRI

122

Chapter 8

Contemporary Challenges
for Extended Deterrence

Tom Scheber

Nearly 30 countries currently depend on US nuclear guarantees.[1] These countries include the other 25 members of the North Atlantic Treaty Organization (NATO) and such countries as Japan and the Republic of Korea (ROK) that have explicit nuclear security commitments. Other countries, such as Australia, Israel, and possibly Taiwan, have more general security commitments of various forms in which nuclear guarantees are not explicit but are implied in general statements of US protection. In late 2008, media reports stated that the Barack Obama administration would consider making explicit a US nuclear guarantee to Israel in response to the threat from a nuclear-armed Iran.[2]

The world has changed significantly since the United States first provided extended deterrence guarantees to NATO and later to select allies in regions that were deemed critical to US interests. These guarantees were extended to allies who were closely aligned with the West against the Soviet Union and who were in proximity to regional threats from the Soviet Union or other communist states.

Significant changes in the global landscape over the past two decades include the dissolution of the Soviet Union and the Warsaw Pact, expansion of membership in the NATO alliance, and the emergence of new weapons of mass destruction (WMD) threats to the United States and its allies. In this new environment, United States extended deterrence guarantees remain in effect, but changes in contextual factors require a close and fresh look at the contemporary challenges of deterrence to include perspectives of allies who rely on these guarantees. The discussion that follows examines the implications for extended deterrence from three types of challenges in the contemporary environment:

- Continuing proliferation of WMD and delivery systems that directly threaten allies;
- New and emerging direct threats to the United States; and

123

- A newly assertive Russia with a strategy of increased reliance on nuclear weapons.

Challenge #1: Proliferation of WMD and Delivery Systems that Threaten Allies

This challenge results from the continued proliferation of chemical, biological, and nuclear weapons and capabilities for the delivery of these weapons. US allies are increasingly concerned about these threats. Examples include direct threats to Japan and the Republic of Korea from the growing arsenal of North Korea's ballistic missiles that could be armed with nuclear or chemical warheads, the potential nuclear program under way in Iran that—given the range of Iran's ballistic missiles—would pose a threat to numerous friends and allies, and China's nuclear modernization and expansion programs that pose a serious concern to US allies in the Asia-Pacific region, particularly Japan.

These new and growing direct threats may cause some allies to question the ability and resolve of the United States to use its leadership and military to deal with determined proliferators that threaten them. If the United States is unwilling or unable to prevent these countries from acquiring nuclear weapons, why should allies believe the United States will protect them after these states acquire nuclear weapons? Allies carefully note declaratory statements and actions by the United States regarding activities of such proliferators as North Korea and Iran. Recently, the credibility of US resolve has been called into question, in part, by its failure to roll back the nuclear weapons programs of North Korea and Iran. Particularly damaging to US credibility over the past few years have been declaratory statements by senior US officials who cite "redlines"—explicit warnings to North Korea and Iran not to undertake specific actions—that were subsequently ignored by the regimes in Pyongyang and Tehran without apparent consequences. Specific examples are included in the discussion that follows.

Direct Threats to Asian Allies

Japan and the ROK face threats of increasing lethality. North Korean acquisition (and retention) of nuclear weapons and the dynamic, ongoing Chinese military buildup raises questions among allies about US nuclear guarantees and the resolve and capability of the United States to deter aggression in East Asia.

North Korea has repeatedly ignored US-declared redlines regarding aspects of its nuclear weapon and ballistic missile programs, as illustrated in the following examples.

In June 2006, US intelligence reported activities under way in North Korea to prepare to launch a number of ballistic missiles. One of the missiles being prepared for launch was a Taepo Dong-2 that was assessed as being capable of delivering a nuclear weapon–sized payload to the continental United States.[3] On 26 June, Pres. George W. Bush stated, "I have made clear to our partners on this issue [Japan, South Korea, China, and Russia] . . . that we need to send a focused message to the North Koreans in that this [long-range missile] launch is provocative." On 29 June, at a news conference with Japanese prime minister Junichiro Koizumi, Bush again warned, "Launching the missile is unacceptable." On 4 and 5 July, North Korea defied US warnings and launched seven ballistic missiles into the Sea of Japan, including the Taepo Dong-2.

On 3 October 2006, North Korea announced that it was preparing to conduct a nuclear test. Later that same day, Secretary of State Condoleezza Rice responded by stating that

> The United States is seriously concerned about today's announcement by the North Korean government of its intention to undertake a nuclear test. . . . A North Korean test of a nuclear weapon would severely undermine our confidence in North Korea's commitment to denuclearization and to the Six Party Talks and would pose a threat to peace and security in Asia and the world. A provocative action of this nature would only further isolate the North Korean regime. . . .

Furthermore, the next day Assistant Secretary of State Christopher Hill stated that

> [The test is], frankly, rather unthinkable. . . . The DPRK [Democratic People's Republic of Korea], if it wants an economic future, indeed . . . if it wants a future, needs to get rid of these weapons. It can have a future or it can have these weapons. It cannot have both. . . . We are not going to live with a nuclear North Korea. . . . I'm not prepared, at this point, to say what that precisely means, but I'm telling you, we cannot accept a nuclear North Korea. . . . We're not coming to terms with a nuclear North Korea."

North Korea ignored these warnings and conducted an underground nuclear test on 9 October 2006.

Given this record of North Korea flaunting its ability to threaten its neighbors and the apparent lack of response from the United States, it should be no surprise that Asian allies are concerned. One noteworthy example of allied concerns occurred in the fall of 2006, in the immediate wake of the North Korean nuclear test. Noboru Hoshuyama, former director general of the Defense Facilities Administration Agency and managing director of the Research Institute for Peace and Security, issued a report that recent aggressive behavior by North Korea was evidence of a weakening of influence of the United Nations (UN) Security Council and a decline in US influence over international issues. The report went on to say that Japan must consider the dire security environment based on the following factors:

- Political, military, and economic emergence of China;
- Declining US involvement in pending global situations;
- Manifestation of threats emanating from nuclear, biological, chemical, radiological, and missile weapons;
- Posture of surrounding nations towards Japan; and
- North Korean nuclear weapon and missile tests.

The report predicted that "conditions would probably exacerbate further." Of the recommendations that followed, the first recommendation was to study "concerns [for] improving the reliability of the nuclear umbrella and reviewing the 'Three Non-Nuclear Principles' [of abjuring manufacture, possession, and introduction of nuclear weapons]."[4]

Even before the nuclear test by North Korea, Japanese security experts were examining the relative value of US extended deterrence guarantees. Japanese concerns over a growing regional threat and uncertainty over US extended deterrence guarantees were featured in *An Image of Japan in the 21st Century*, a report issued on 5 September 2006 from the Institute for International Policy Studies, headed by former Japanese prime minister Yasuhiro Nakasone. The report noted the potential for tremendous future change in the international situation. It stated, "Japan, maintaining its position as a non-nuclear weapons state and working to strengthen the Nuclear Non-Proliferation Treaty system, should study the nuclear issue to be prepared in the event of tremendous future change in the international situation." Nakasone, when questioned by the press on the report, noted that Japan was currently dependent on US nuclear weapons but that it was uncertain whether US willingness to provide nuclear-related guarantees would continue.

Following the North Korean nuclear test, Japanese officials conducted an internal review of national security needs. One Japanese press report stated that senior defense ministry officials and military experts generally agreed on the following three principles to guide Japan's actions: (1) reinforce the US nuclear and conventional deterrent capability; (2) install missile defense systems in Japan; and (3) possess the capability to attack military bases of an enemy country. The report asserted that "to better ensure the US nuclear arsenal achieves its desired deterrent effect, a clear manifestation of such US intent would have an important meaning." The same article also reported that "Defense Minister Fumio Kyuma spoke in no uncertain terms about strengthening the deterrence of US nuclear weapons. The strongest deterrence would be when the United States explicitly says 'If you drop one nuclear bomb on Japan, the United States will retaliate by dropping 10 on you,' he said."[5]

The Nakasone report and related comments created a stir worldwide. Within a short time, Japanese officials had walked back the comments to reassure others that Japan was not on the brink of a nuclear decision. One analysis of the situation concluded that "neither an increasing security threat nor a fundamental shift in US policy alone will be sufficient to trigger a Japanese nuclear breakout. But the combination of these two factors could drive Japanese domestic shifts and weaken Japan's non-nuclear norm enough so that Japan would adopt a different strategic posture."[6]

In the immediate wake of the North Korean nuclear test and the atmosphere of insecurity that followed, US officials traveled to Tokyo and reaffirmed their continued support for security commitments to the Northeast Asian allies. A few months later, the following joint statement was issued at the conclusion of the 1 May 2007 US-Japan Security Consultative Committee meeting attended by Secretary of State Condoleezza Rice, Secretary of Defense Robert Gates, Minister for Foreign Affairs Taro Aso, and Minister of Defense Fumio Kyuma: "U.S. extended deterrence underpins the defense of Japan and regional security. The United States reaffirmed that the full range of US military capabilities—both nuclear and non-nuclear strike forces and defensive capabilities—form the core of extended deterrence and support US commitments to the defense of Japan."

Direct Threats to Allies in the Middle East and Europe

A second concern with direct threats to allies is associated with the near-term threat to allies in the Middle East and Europe from Iran's nuclear weapon development program. Not all US allies who would be threatened directly by a nuclear-armed Iran are protected explicitly by the US nuclear umbrella. Allies concerned about this potential threat include Turkey (a member of NATO), Israel (Iran's president had threatened to wipe Israel off the map), and the Middle East states populated predominantly by Sunni Muslims (for example, Egypt and Saudi Arabia). The complexity of issues related to the security of these allies is illustrated briefly below.

Turkey shares a border with Iran, and they cooperate on issues ranging from energy resources to combating terrorist activities of the Kurdistan Workers' Party (PKK). As evidenced by Turkey's refusal to grant the United States use of its territory for the invasion of Iraq in 2003, Ankara is increasingly sensitive to the unique challenges resulting from its geography. Ankara is working to build constructive relations with its neighbors, including Russia, Iran, and Syria, while continuing to fulfill its obligations as a long-standing member of NATO. Turkey's proximity to Iran places Turkish cities and facilities within range of even relatively short-range Iranian missiles, and NATO bases in Turkey would likely be targets of a nuclear-armed Iran. Turkey's goal of membership in the European Union has been blocked by some of its NATO partners. If threatened by a nuclear-armed Iran, Turkey may feel the need for its own, independent nuclear deterrent force instead of relying on its NATO allies.

Israel has been extremely vocal over the near-term threat from a nuclear-armed Iran. Reports in the Israeli media often speculate how much longer Israel can wait before launching preventive attacks on known and suspected Iranian nuclear-related sites. The head of the Mossad, Israel's intelligence service, has told the Knesset (parliament) that Iran's nuclear weapons program represents "the biggest threat to Israel's existence since its creation."[7] During the 1991 Persian Gulf War, Saddam Hussein's forces launched Scud missiles at Israeli cities that were capable of delivering chemical warheads. US officials convinced Israeli leaders to withhold a response and to allow the United States to take the lion's share of the responsibility for deterring Iraqi WMD use and disrupting and defending against Scud attacks on Israel. Whether the United States would offer an explicit nuclear guarantee to Israel and whether Israel would allow its security to depend on a US commitment to respond to nuclear strikes from Iran are open questions.

Egypt, Saudi Arabia, and other predominantly Sunni states in the region have expressed a renewed interest in nuclear energy. This interest in nuclear technology by oil-rich states in the Middle East is judged by many to be a thinly veiled hedge against Iran acquiring a nuclear weapon capability. If Shi'a-dominated Iran is unchecked in its development of a nuclear arsenal, Sunni Muslims are likely to anticipate that they will be among the targets of coercion—or worse. On the margins of a UN meeting on 16 December 2008, six Arab states—Bahrain, Egypt, Jordan, Kuwait, Iraq, Saudi Arabia—and the United Arab Emirates met with Secretary of State Rice and expressed their concern about Iran's nuclear policies and its regional ambitions. A news report greatly understated their concern when it said, "These countries have very deep interests in how this issue is resolved."[8] Iran's nuclear weapon aspirations could trigger nuclear proliferation by one or more of these countries that are not currently beneficiaries of US extended nuclear guarantees.

An official of the United Arab Emirates stated that the United States should consider countering an Iranian threat by offering Middle East allies protection under a nuclear umbrella.[9] Saudi officials are reported to have made statements that, in response to an Iranian nuclear threat, they would prefer to rely on a US nuclear umbrella. However, if they believe the "United States lacks the will or capability to defend Saudi Arabia against a nuclear-armed Iran, Saudi Arabia is more likely to pursue a nuclear weapon capability of its own." If needed, they would seek "a nuclear guarantee from Pakistan."[10]

European states are also concerned about the potential nuclear threat from Iran. The most common scenario suggested by Europeans involves an Iranian threat to use ballistic missiles to deter the intervention of external powers in a crisis in the Persian Gulf. As a German observer put it, "Iran might try to blackmail NATO in the course of a crisis in the Middle East. The message would be 'If you get engaged, we can attack your homeland.'"[11]

The recent record of United States declared redlines that have been ignored by Iran is similar to that of North Korea, as discussed earlier. US officials have repeatedly stated that uranium enrichment by Iran, a necessary step as part of a nuclear weapons development capability, is simply unacceptable. On 21 February 2006, Undersecretary of State Nicholas Burns stated that "we cannot allow Iran to achieve that capability." President Bush said that "the international community must come together to make it very clear to Iran that we will not tolerate the construction of a nuclear weapon. Iran would be dangerous if they have a nuclear weapon"[12] and that "[Iran] trying to clandestinely develop a nuclear weapon, or using the guise of a civilian nuclear weapon program to get the know-how to develop a nuclear weapon, is unacceptable."[13] Appearing on *Meet the Press* on 7 December 2008, president-elect Barack Obama repeated the warning that Iran's development of nuclear weapons is "unacceptable."

Iran, ignoring US-stated redlines, has pressed ahead with its uranium enrichment activities and has publicly announced its achievement of milestone events. The credibility of US security guarantees cannot be helped by this record of establishing declaratory redlines and then not taking firm and visible action in response to the crossing of those redlines.

At least five implications for the United States have resulted from these new and growing direct threats to allies.

- The United States needs a deterrence strategy tailored to each state that poses a potential threat to allies. The strategy should be designed to influence the decision making of adversary leaders and convince them that attempts to coerce US allies with WMD-related threats or their use will not result in net gains and could bring devastating losses.

- While deterring adversaries, the United States must also communicate to allies—at least in general terms—how US extended deterrence guarantees are being implemented on their behalf. US regional allies will view each situation from a perspective that is likely to differ significantly from that of the United States itself.

- Defenses and other capabilities that can help limit damage, should deterrence fail, are becoming increasingly important for assuring allies.

- Redlines are important aspects of US declaratory policy. They should be formulated carefully and attended to with equal care. When redlines are crossed, a prompt and appropriate response should follow. US leaders will need to consult with threatened allies in developing declaratory strategy and redlines and in responding appropriately should potential adversaries cross established redlines.

- Should regional security situations worsen, including threatened or actual use of WMD on allies, the United States must be prepared to take action in a manner consistent with the pledges that it has communicated to protected allies if it hopes to sustain credibility.

Challenge #2: New and Emerging Direct Threats to the United States

This challenge results from the increasing number of potential adversaries who can directly threaten the United States with long-range weapons. During much of the Cold War, the Soviet Union was the only adversary that could directly threaten the US homeland. (China had a limited number of intercontinental-range ballistic missiles capable of reaching at least part of the United States.) As described earlier, during the Cold War, the United States developed a sophisticated strategy to underpin its extended deterrence guarantees to allies and to deter Soviet aggression.

In the contemporary environment, Russia continues to modernize and produce new types of nuclear weapons capable of targeting the United States. Many of these weapons are touted by Russian officials as being designed to evade ballistic missile defenses. In addition, China is dramatically increasing its arsenal of nuclear weapons capable of ranging the United States and Asia. When the most recent Nuclear Posture Review was completed in December 2001, China was assessed as having only about 20 DF-5A (CSS-4) intercontinental ballistic missiles (ICBM) capable of ranging the United States with each missile able to deliver a single nuclear warhead.[14] With the recent deployment of the modern DF-31 and DF-31A ICBMs and expected near-term deployment of JL-2 submarine-launched ballistic missiles (SLBM), China's intercontinental nuclear arsenal is projected to increase sharply in the decade ahead. According to several reports, some DF-31As will carry multiple warheads, and China is planning for at least five nuclear-powered fleet ballistic missile submarines (SSBN), each with 12 JL-2 ballistic missiles. Reports originating in China indicate that in the future, JL-2 missiles will be able to carry as many as five and possibly eight warheads.[15]

In addition to the traditional threats from major nuclear powers (Russia and China), two rogue states (North Korea and Iran) are developing long-range ballistic missiles capable of ranging the continental United States. North Korea, long suspected of possessing a rudimentary nuclear weapon capability, conducted an underground nuclear test in October 2006 and has attempted flight tests of long-range Taepo Dong-2 missiles. Iran appears to be making steady progress on its uranium enrichment efforts and continues to demonstrate its ability to field ballistic missiles of increasing range. On 12 November 2008, Iran is reported to have tested a two-stage, solid-fuel missile, and on 3 February 2009, Iran placed a satellite in orbit, thereby demonstrating most of the technical capability necessary for an ICBM.[16] US officials have estimated that Iran could have enough highly enriched uranium for a nuclear weapon by 2009 but that a more likely estimate is in the 2010–2015 time frame.[17]

Adversary capabilities that pose direct threats to the United States could pose problems in the future to the credibility of extended deterrence. These threats could cause allies to question whether the United States would follow through on its commitments when doing so would put at risk the US homeland. Simply put, the vulnerability of the United States to Chinese, North Korean, Iranian, or Russian nuclear attack could fray the US nuclear umbrella. Would allies be confident that the United States would remain committed to their security if US military action were invariably linked to direct threats to the US homeland?

Potential opponents of the United States have recognized the leverage that could be gained from posing such a nuclear threat, particularly in regional conflicts where their stakes would be greater than those of the United States. One Chinese official (Gen Xiong Guangkai), for example, has threatened a nuclear attack on the United States to deter US intervention in a future conflict over Taiwan: "In the 1950s, you three times threatened nuclear strikes on China [i.e., during the Korean war and the 1954 and 1958 Taiwan crises], and you could do that because we couldn't hit back. Now we can. So you are not going to threaten us again because, in the end, you care a lot more about Los Angeles than Taipei."[18]

The implications for the United States from the challenge posed by the growth of direct threats to the United States include the following:

- The increasing need for effective and credible defenses and prompt global strike weapons to provide capabilities to limit damage should deterrence fail, as well as consequence-management capabilities. These will help to devalue direct threats to the United States. With adequate capabilities to limit damage to the United States, allies are more likely to feel confident that it will have the freedom of action needed to carry out commitments to defend its threatened partners.

- The need for a range of effective US response capabilities (including nuclear and nonnuclear strike, nonkinetic offensive options, and space control capabilities) to deter those that might threaten the United States and thereby try to prevent it from intervening in regional affairs.

- Potential adversaries that may consider threats to coerce the United States are likely to try to exploit vulnerabilities in technological advantages of the US military. Therefore,

133

reducing US vulnerabilities to asymmetric attack (e.g., cyber attack, space control) will be important to protect US advantages and assure allies that US strengths are resilient to enemy action.

- Assured second-strike capabilities for the US nuclear force will continue to be valuable to allies as they observe growth in potential threats to the United States and reductions in the size of the US nuclear force.

Challenge #3: A Newly Assertive Russia

This challenge results from Russia's self-declared increased reliance on nuclear weapons for security and as instruments of foreign policy. A newly assertive Russia is not shy about displaying its hostility toward the United States and its allies. This challenge combines aspects of both types of challenges mentioned above—direct threats to allies and direct threats to the United States.

During the tenure of Russian president Vladimir Putin (2000–2008), the Russian policy-making elite developed an elaborate system of exaggerating perceived threats to justify the retention and modernization of a large Russian nuclear arsenal. Moscow claims to be the target of potential threats from other established nuclear powers, saying that "nuclear weapons of all states that possess them are ultimately aimed at Russia."[19] The United States and NATO remain at the top of the list of potential Russian adversaries. The West's advanced weapon programs, ballistic missile defense, and military applications of space are superior to those of Russia and therefore are targets of Russia's aggressive foreign policy.

Russian leaders regard sustaining and demonstrating a robust nuclear potential as the foundation of their country's special role in geopolitics, a paramount precondition for strategic parity with the United States, and a place on the world stage. In 2003 Putin bragged that "Russia and the United States are the biggest nuclear powers. Our economy might be smaller, but Russia's nuclear potential is still comparable to that of the United States. . . . Also important is that we have the years of experience, the technology and the production potential, the technological chains and the specialists. Russia is a great nuclear power."[20]

With his administration marked by the revival of Russian global ambitions, Putin consistently demonstrated his support for Russia's nuclear weapons production and deployment. A typical statement to that effect was made on 9 June 2006 during a meeting with heads of key enterprises for the Russian nuclear complex: "Our country's nuclear potential is of vital importance for our national security interests. The reliability of our 'nuclear shield' and the state of our nuclear weapon complex are a crucial component of Russia's world power status."[21]

New and future members of NATO are increasingly anxious over recent Russian overt nuclear threats. Moscow has attempted to coerce leaders of the Czech Republic and Poland to convince them to reject US proposals to station elements of a ballistic missile defense system in their countries. Russian officials have made numerous, explicit threats that missile defense sites in the Czech Republic and Poland would become targets for Russia's nuclear force. After both countries rejected the Russian bluster and signed agreements with the United States to station missile defense capabilities, Moscow broadened its coercive tactics and threatened to station short-range Iskander missiles in Kaliningrad to target the missile defense sites.

At the NATO summit in the spring of 2008, Ukraine and Georgia hoped to be granted a formal process leading to NATO membership. To bully their former allies and influence NATO decision making, Moscow officials let it be known that such a move would result in these two countries being targeted by Russian nuclear forces. In August 2008, Moscow demonstrated its willingness to use force against its neighbors when it invaded Georgia.

Russian nuclear threats complement other strong-arm tactics being employed by Moscow, such as threatening to cut off energy supplies (oil and natural gas) under their control. These tactics are intended to drive a wedge between alliance members who are not threatened directly by Russia and wish to remain that way and those members being threatened, often because they seek closer and more formal relationships with the West. The newer NATO members are former Warsaw Pact states; they are located closer to Russia than the longer-standing

NATO members, and they do not have a lengthy history of well-established relationships with the United States and Western Europe. In addition, the new members of the alliance note that key NATO institutions and military installations have not been located on the territory of the newer members, and they are not active participants in NATO nuclear burden sharing. For these reasons, they may feel that they are at the edge of the US nuclear umbrella and perhaps perceive themselves as second-class members of the alliance.

Some NATO allies feel that a sense of vulnerability to a newly aggressive Russia increases the incentive for closer ties with the United States. For example, the Polish defense minister, Bogdan Klitch, has cited the need for Poland to have extra protection because Russia is richer and more confident than it was a decade ago. "We have a reduced level of security," Klitch has said. "The lack of the Polish feeling of security is provoked by the tendencies of Russia over the past few years."[22] He also has noted, "The distribution of NATO institutions in Europe is not balanced. The majority of the NATO and EU [European Union] institutions are located in the western part of Europe. That is why we began those talks with the Americans over missile defense."[23]

In December 2008, a Norwegian official addressed a seminar held in Washington, DC, regarding extended deterrence. He explained that Norway closely observes the military activities of Russia and the geopolitical context associated with those activities. Based on recent observations, he concluded that, with respect to Russia, NATO will need effective deterrence in the future.

An Estonian opined that the Russians wish to inspire fear to gain respect:

> The message from NATO has been that there is no threat from Russia and that NATO is not afraid of Russia. That annoys the Russians very much. They just don't understand. It doesn't fit in their paradigm. They interpret it to mean that Russia is not respected or taken seriously. Domestically as well, the government wants respect from the people, and it is trying to gain respect through the complete defeat of its opponents. It has no tolerance of other points of view. They put their critics in jail or shut them up in other ways, as with Khodorkovsky and Kasparov. The Russian leaders are accordingly hostile to democracies on their borders—the Baltic states, Georgia, and Ukraine. . . .[24]

Similarly, a Pole said, "In the Russian mentality respect comes from fear, rather than admiration for positive qualities. The

Russian leaders are trying to gain respect by making others fear them. This is partly sincere, and partly for a manipulative purpose. They are using anti-NATO rhetoric and policies to justify their retention of power."[25]

NATO analyst Michael Rühle has identified several issues related to extended deterrence in an expanded alliance. One issue is the acknowledgement that, as part of an attempt to expand in a way that is nonthreatening to Russia, NATO has limited its ability to expand nuclear burden sharing to its new members. NATO pledged to Russia that its expansion would be done consistently with "three no's": no intention, no plan, and no reason to deploy nuclear weapons on the territory of the new members. This excludes all new NATO allies at the outset from playing a meaningful role in NATO's nuclear burden-sharing arrangements. In addition, while long-time NATO members have participated in nuclear-related debates over the decades and are familiar with statements on the role of nuclear weapons and deterrence in NATO's strategic concept, many of the newer allies, according to Rühle, have little knowledge of "the sophisticated strategic thinking about deterrence and nuclear weapons that has developed in the West, although that is slowly changing through active participation in NATO's nuclear planning group staff group [sic] meetings and an active 'outreach' educational program to new Allies."[26]

The implications for the United States of a Russian Federation that is assertive and highly dependent on its nuclear forces for security, as well as for its foreign policy agenda, include the following:

- A US nuclear force that is "second to none" (e.g., not inferior in size or capability to that of Russia) will continue to be important to allies who distrust Russian leaders and view Russia as a potential threat.

- The expansion of NATO has resulted in US extended deterrence guarantees being provided to additional states. These states are in closer proximity to Russia and in areas that Moscow has long considered within its sphere of influence. These allies are likely to be the target of direct nuclear-related threats from Russia.

137

- US defense planners should anticipate continuing nuclear threats by Moscow in response to foreign policy developments that are not entirely to the liking of the Russian leadership.

- For the foreseeable future, Moscow will continue to possess the ability to threaten directly the United States and US allies with a large, diverse nuclear force. Moscow will continue to rely on its nuclear force, in part, to compensate for the weakness of its general-purpose forces.

- If Moscow continues to brandish its nuclear arsenal as it has over the past several years, it is conceivable that Russia could find itself in a conflict on its borders that it cannot resolve with diplomacy or conventional forces. An overextended Russia that believes its own harsh rhetoric and relies heavily on nuclear weapons should be a serious concern.

- US planners should anticipate such behavior and work with allies to develop a strategy that discourages Russian provocations and assures both older and newer NATO allies.

Sustaining the Credibility of the US Nuclear Force

In addition to the three challenges for extended deterrence in the contemporary environment discussed above, one additional problem is important to consider—uncertainty among allies regarding the long-term US commitment to sustain an effective and credible nuclear force. Both allies and potential adversaries carefully watch developments in the United States. Since the end of the Cold War, the United States has reduced the size of its operationally deployed strategic nuclear force by almost 80 percent and has retired and dismantled most of its nonstrategic nuclear warheads. In sharp contrast with the other nuclear powers recognized by the Non-Proliferation Treaty (Russia, Britain, France, and China), the United States has not implemented a nuclear modernization plan for a nuclear force appropriate for the twenty-first century. Foreign observers of US politics will note the high-profile debates over studies of nuclear weapon concepts and the termination of such recent initiatives as the Robust Nuclear Earth Penetrator and the Reliable Replacement Warhead. Allies and possibly adversaries alike are watching this trend and questioning the long-term viability of the US nuclear force.

This discussion of contemporary challenges for extended deterrence has identified the contextual changes in the global security environment that have occurred and the issues that should be addressed if extended deterrence guarantees are to continue to be effective for deterrence, credible for assurance, and a stabilizing contribution to the US security strategy. Without periodic close examination and appropriate adjustments in extended deterrence relationships, these and future contextual changes are likely to pose significant strains on alliance relationships and may result in the eventual failure of either deterrence, assurance, or both.

Notes

1. Kathleen C. Bailey et al., "White Paper on the Necessity of the US Nuclear Deterrent," 15 August 2007, 3, www.nipp.org.

2. Aluf Benn, "Obama's Atomic Umbrella: US Nuclear Strike if Iran Nukes Israel," *Haaretz*, 11 December 2008. During the 2008 presidential campaign, then candidate and now secretary of state Hillary Clinton warned, "I want the Iranians to know that if I'm the president, we will attack Iran [if Iran attacked Israel with nuclear weapons]. In the next 10 years, during which they might foolishly consider launching an attack on Israel, we would be able to totally obliterate them." Interview on *Good Morning America*, ABC TV broadcast, 22 April 2008.

3. J. Michael McConnell, Director of National Intelligence, "Annual Threat Assessment of the Director of National Intelligence," prepared statement before the Senate Select Committee on Intelligence, 5 February 2008, 15.

4. "Japan: Ex-Defense Official Urges Nuclear Policy Review with Less US Involvement," JPP20061206026003 Tokyo Research Institute for Peace and Security WWW-Text (in Japanese), 1 December 2006.

5. "North Korea's Nuclear Threat: Reinforcing Alliance with US Helps Bolster Nuclear Deterrence," JPP20070323969090, Tokyo, *Daily Yomiuri* in English, 24 March 2007.

6. Mike M. Mochizuki, "Japan Tests the Nuclear Taboo," *Nonproliferation Review* 14, no. 2 (July 2007): 319–20.

7. Quoted in Richard L. Russell, "Arab Security Responses to a Nuclear-Ready Iran," in Henry Sokolski and Patrick Clawson, eds., *Getting Ready for a Nuclear-Ready Iran* (Carlisle, PA: Army War College Strategic Studies Institute, October 2005), 29.

8. "Arab Nations Call for Regular Meetings on Iranian Nuclear Program," Associated Press, 17 December 2008.

9. Indira A. R. Lakshmanan, "Iran Might Be Deterred by US Nuclear Umbrella, Gulf Ally Says," *Bloomberg.com*, 9 April 2009.

10. US Senate, "Chain Reaction: Avoiding a Nuclear Arms Race in the Middle East," Report to the Committee on Foreign Relations, February 2008, 12–17.

11. Interview by National Institute for Public Policy (NIPP) consultant in Brussels, 22 April 2008.

12. Meeting between President Bush and bipartisan senators on Iranian nuclear activities, 18 June 2003.

13. Statement by Pres. George W. Bush during a meeting with German chancellor Angela Merkel, 13 January 2006.

14. Shirley A. Kan, *China: Ballistic and Cruise Missiles*, Report No. 97-391F (Washington, DC: Congressional Research Service, 10 August 2000), 8–9.

15. Mark Schneider, *The Nuclear Doctrine and Forces of the People's Republic of China* (Fairfax, VA: National Institute Press, November 2007).

16. "Iran Tests New More Accurate Missile," *Global Security Newswire*, 12 November 2008; and "Iran Launches Homegrown Satellite," British Broadcasting Company, 3 February 2009.

17. Donald M. Kerr, Principal Deputy Director of National Intelligence, remarks to the Washington Institute for Near East Policy 2008 Soref Symposium, The Ritz Carlton, Washington, DC, 29 May 2008, www.odni.gov/speeches/20080529_speech.pdf.

18. Quoted in Barton Gellman, "Reappraisal Led to New China Policy," *Washington Post*, 22 June 1998, A1, A16. When he issued this warning in late 1995, Xiong was deputy chief of general staff of the People's Liberation Army and its chief of military intelligence.

19. Makhmut Gareev, "New Conditions—New Military Doctrine," *Nezavisimoe Voennoe Obozrenie*, 2 February 2007 (in Russian).

20. Interview with Al Jazeera television, 16 October 2003, www.kremlin.ru/eng/text/speeches/2003/10/16/1648_54238.shtml.

21. "Opening Remarks at Meeting with Heads of the Russian Nuclear Weapons and Nuclear Energy Complexes," Novo-Ogaryovo, 9 June 2006, www.kremlin.ru/eng/text/speeches/2006/06/09/1952_type8291type82913_106757.shtml.

22. Judy Dempsey, "Poland Wants US to Be 3rd Leg of Its Security Plan," *International Herald Tribune*, 22 April 2008.

23. Ibid.

24. Interview by NIPP consultant in Brussels, 23 April 2008.

25. Ibid., 21 April 2008.

26. Michael Rühle, "US Extended Deterrence and NATO," paper presented at the US Nuclear Strategy Forum, 9 June 2008, 5.

Chapter 9

Case Study—The August 2008 War between Russian and Georgia

Denis Corboy

How did it happen that in August 2008 Russia and Georgia fought a nineteenth century war in the twenty-first century? Why was the West caught unawares? And why did all the actors end up as losers? This presentation attempts to answer these and related questions, to look at the background that led to the Five-Day War, and to point to some lessons to be learned.

The principal actors were all affected by the outcome. Moscow launched its first large-scale military operation outside the Russian Federation since the end of the Cold War. Its recognition of the independence of Abkhazia and South Ossetia was the first attempt to revise interstate boundaries on the territory of the former Soviet Union. While in military terms Russia won the war, it left in its wake myriad unforeseen problems leading to greater insecurity in the Caucasus, both North and South. Georgia lost its dream to restore territorial integrity and any illusions that it might have harboured that the United States or the North Atlantic Treaty Organization (NATO) would come to its aid, if attacked. Not only was Georgia humiliated on the battlefield, its military infrastructure was destroyed along with the loss of business confidence and its hopes of rapid economic development. For the United States, the reckoning was equally telling. The Five-Day War exposed the fact that the commitments of the Bush administration to Georgia's territorial integrity were no more than rhetoric and that any belief in Washington that the United States had leverage in Moscow was an illusion. US credibility was seriously undermined, and justifiably Russians said "the emperor has no clothes."

For the European Union (EU), the successful diplomacy of the French presidency in negotiating the cease-fire agreement raised its reputation regionally and its standing internationally. A major result of the conflict has been that the EU increased its involvement in the Caucasus and is now providing a visible presence to support peace and stability. The EU Monitoring Mission (EUMM) is the only international presence in the conflict zone after the Russian veto of both the United Nations and the Organization for Security and Co-operation in Europe observer missions. While the EU is committed to a deeper involvement in the region, it still lacks a coherent strategy for the future and now faces a real moment of truth. An earlier debate regarding whether the EU should do the job alone or go for a transatlantic strategy to include, for example, US and Canadian members in the EUMM appears to have been settled in favour of maintaining a European Security Defence Policy mission only. Do not rule out that for reasons of cost or for more logistical support this could change.

The New Russia

The August 2008 events were a wake-up call that the post–Cold War period of dealing with a Russia that was cooperative, compliant, and aspiring to be another European democracy was over. Putin's Russia aimed to redress the perceived humiliations that followed the breakup of the Soviet Union and the widely held belief that the West disregarded its views and did not show respect for its interests. The Russian sense of grievance was aggravated by Western support for the colour revolutions, proposals to extend NATO to its borders, the whole context of NATO's actions in the Balkans/Serbia, and subsequent granting of independence to Kosovo. This new confidence was based on a revived nationalism, new wealth from resurgent hydrocarbon revenues, and a determination to use energy as a weapon of both economic and foreign policy. A key Russian objective became the reestablishment of primacy over the former Soviet space or that part that remained outside the EU and NATO: Ukraine, Moldova, and the South Caucasus. The most hardened pro-Western country and therefore greatest irritant among these was post–Rose Revolution Georgia, which also had the misfortune to be singled out in a shorthand way to remind the others that a high price had to be paid for steering a path away from Russia. Mikheil Saakashvili had badly miscalculated that in provoking Moscow, he would earn more support for Georgia in Washington, particularly in the Bush White House. In reality Georgia was the most vulnerable of the near-abroad countries, largely due to the unresolved conflicts in Abkhazia and South Ossetia, which had in large part been orchestrated from Moscow.

Bedevilled by History

The fractious and turbulent history of the Caucasus and Russia's role there during the empire, the Soviet years and subsequently, formed the backdrop to the 2008 war. Throughout the nineteenth century, Georgia was part of the Russian empire, during which time the status of Abkhazia and South Ossetia remained ambiguous. When the first Republic of Georgia came into existence, 1918–21, both were included, but Abkhazia never was entirely integrated into the rest of Georgia. Stalin gave them autonomous republic status within Georgia, and furthermore, he granted Abkhazia the right to secede. This became a time-bomb that exploded into the civil war of 1992–93 immediately after the breakup of the Soviet Union. Zviad Gamsakhurdia, the first elected president of the new republic, used military force to counter the Abkhaz attempt to create an independent state. Russia provided forces on the ground and airpower to support the Abkhaz side, which resulted in substantial loss of life on all sides of the conflict, and more than 300,000 refugees were forced to flee to the rest of Georgia. A Commonwealth of Independent States (CIS) peacekeeping mission was established to supervise the 1993 cease-fire, but Russia proved to be the only CIS country able to send peacekeepers at that time. From the beginning, there was an ambiguity in having one of the sides to the conflict being at the same time the peacekeeping force, and that ambiguity was never resolved. The civil war caused the ethnic cleansing of the majority Georgian and ethnic Mingrelian population of Abkhazia. The status quo allowed Russia to maintain a degree of instability, and continuing the so-called frozen conflicts gave leverage over Georgia, a country that always had the potential to become unfriendly to Moscow. During the 10 years preceding the 2003 Rose Revolution, relative peace was maintained, and Georgia had little alternative but to accept the situation.

When President Saakashvili came to power in 2004, his vision was to build Georgia into a modern European democracy that would become an integral part of the Euro-Atlantic community. Even some of the Tbilisi elites saw the future of their country as an Israel in the heart of the Caucasus. Saakashvili became committed to removing every trace of the Soviet legacy and permanently removing the country from the influence of its former masters. From the day he was elected, he stated that his primary objective was the restoration of the national territory, but offering both separatist entities maximized autonomy within a loosely defined united Georgia. The nongovernmental organizations on the ground in Abkhazia and South Ossetia, mostly British, believed a settlement was possible but only following lengthy confidence building, persuasion, and a policy of "hearts and minds." Before the August war, significant progress had been achieved in this regard, and Track 2 dialogue was well advanced. However, one of the key constraints stemmed from an approach to these matters by the Tbilisi leadership that whenever carrots were offered, a stick never was far behind. The impression grew that Saakashvili was prepared to take "hearts and minds" only so far before reverting to the belief that a united Georgia would be achieved by coercion. Another constraint, Russia remained opposed to any meaningful settlement between the separatists and Tbilisi. Moscow was not prepared to see a modern, economically and politically independent Georgia develop on its southern border. As part of its strategy, it sought to maintain the status quo in the conflict zones.

During his first four years, Saakashvili could arguably claim that Georgia was among the leaders in the post-Soviet space in democratic reform and in fighting corruption. That was until the tragic events of November 2007, when there was a violent crackdown on peaceful demonstrators accompanied by the forced closure of the only major independent television station, Imedi. Before this, there had been a rapidly growing economy with high levels of foreign direct investment that won praise from the World Bank and other international institutions. For the Bush administration, Georgia was a success story that featured prominently in its democracy agenda. The relationships that developed among the articulate American-educated Saakashvili, President Bush, Vice President Dick Cheney, and such legislators as Republican senator John McCain were increasingly close and trusting. To some extent, this partly explains why the US administration, particularly the White House, failed to see the danger of Saakashvili's increasingly anti-Russian rhetoric and what turned out to be the disastrous consequences of not ensuring that the attack on the South Tskhinvali did not happen.

Buildup to War

In autumn 2006, Russia started taking measures aimed at bringing Georgia to heel. A series of embargoes were imposed that covered all aspects of relations including trade, transport, finance, visas, and diplomatic contacts. In Russia, Georgian citizens were subjected to harassment: children were expelled from schools and remittances home banned. The stated objective was to bring the Georgian economy to its knees and in the process alienate the population from Saakashvili and his government. The strategy not only failed but had the opposite result. The government gained in popular support; trade, which had been largely dependent on the Russian market, became diversified; and international support for Georgia increased. For example, Russia had been the traditional market for Georgian wine, and following the embargo, producers were obliged to find new markets. For the first time, producers focused on quality and marketing, which they did with some success.

Some evidence suggests that by early 2006 Russia had started preparations for a military intervention. The strategy was the same as had been successfully employed in Transnistria and Moldova in July 1992. Local militias were employed to create small-scale incidents with the potential for escalation on both sides. As intended, this triggered a Moldovan response followed by Russian retaliation. Once Moldovan positions were overrun, then president Mircea Snegur had to choose between abandoning territory and taking military action. His selection of the military option allowed the Moscow public relations machine to paint Moldova as the aggressor. When the latter launched a wider defensive operation, it was met with overwhelming Russian military force. Similarly, the 2008 Georgian conflict began with small-scale incidents that escalated to shelling of Georgian populated villages and harassment of Georgians on both sides of the border. In the first week of August, the Ossetian militias, augmented by Chechen fighters from the North Caucasus, intensified their attacks. What followed was an ill-considered Georgian decision to shell Tskhinvali, including civilian-populated parts of the city. Georgian troops entered South Ossetia and killed some Russian peacekeepers. The Georgian action provided Russia with its justification for a massive military attack and the occupation of South Ossetia and most of the northern part of Georgia itself, including the strategic port of Poti. The evidence is clear that Georgia had not planned to take back South Ossetia in an August coup. Why were 2,000 of its best-trained troops still in Iraq? Why was its government—from the prime minister down—on holiday leave and unaware that anything was happening? And why, above all, was there no attempt to close the Roki tunnel, the only land entry point from Russia? Russian troops met little resistance from a Georgian army quickly put in disarray. Russian troops then advanced to within 10 kilometres of the capital, Tbilisi, where they stopped. One can only speculate whether this was the result of President Sarkozy's negotiations in Moscow, a diplomatic intervention from Washington, or a realisation that an occupation by Russia of Georgia and putting in power a pro-Russian president would have been a step too far.

It is too early for a full assessment of the Russia-Georgia war because there is no prospect of a settlement between the parties, and a tense situation continues on the new borders that now comprise territory never previously occupied by the separatists but currently manned by Russian border troops. For some in the Kremlin, Georgia remains unfinished business. Saakashvili continues to hold power in Tbilisi, Georgia's aspirations for NATO and EU membership are undiminished (even if it is more unlikely to be achieved in the foreseeable future), the southern route for oil and gas pipelines from the Caspian Sea to Europe remains outside Russian control, and as for the rest of the near abroad, far from being intimidated, they have become increasingly wary of their large former master. What has not been fully understood is that the war was neither about territory nor the independence of Abkhazia or South Ossetia but was fought, more than any other reason, to prevent Georgia from going West and bringing NATO to Russia's backyard. Russia's failure to gain control over Georgia has wider consequences for Putin's stated designs for the near abroad. An independent, successful Georgian state, not friendly to Russia

146

and strutting the international stage, would be a nightmare for Moscow and could well encourage others to follow.

In retrospect, the relevant question is not who started the war, but why it was not adequately foreseen and made subject to more concerted efforts of preventative diplomacy. Conflicts in the Caucasus have always seemed inevitable, and history teaches that once launched, they spiral out of control, if not checked. The responsibility rests not only with the two protagonists but equally with the international community for its failure to see the storm clouds gathering over the Caucasus, to read properly the signals emanating from Moscow and Tbilisi, and to act accordingly. One year later, Russia pauses to assess the cost of its next move. The United States, which has reluctantly had to recognise limits to its power, proposes to recalibrate relations with Russia and policy towards Georgia and Ukraine. As already mentioned, the EU has as a consequence been handed a key role and challenge to craft a united strategy towards the region. Can the EU, which is largely dysfunctional in regard to Russia, rise to the occasion? Georgia will find it difficult to come to terms with the reality that the separatist regions are irretrievably lost for the foreseeable future, that it is inevitable some accommodation has to be reached as quickly as possible with Russia, and above all, that it will only be after regional and political stability has been restored that the Georgian economy can hope to return to its past short-lived success.

Denouement

The immediate challenge for the United States and Europe is to find a strategy to engage with Russia on the major global issues while at the same time providing adequate security for the newly independent states, particularly Georgia and Ukraine. The objective should be the training of troops not solely to fight wars in Iraq or Afghanistan but to defend their own countries. One lesson of the August 2008 war was that the United States' highly trained Georgian troops did not have the capacity to counter a traditional old-style 1940s invasion. In its aggressive behaviour towards the near abroad, Russia has made a major miscalculation in believing that fear and distrust can provide a basis for good relations in the modern world. At the beginning of this case study, I referred to the nineteenth-century paradigm. The lasting impression of the 2008 war, if I could paraphrase James Sherr, was seeing a twenty-first-century Russian power use nineteenth-century military methods to achieve a result that in all probability will cause fatal damage to its long-term interests in both the North and the South Caucasus.

Chapter 10

Deterrence and Counterproliferation

Malcolm Chalmers

When dealing with deterrence and nuclear weapons, and counterproliferation specifically, theory is pretty important because thankfully there are not very many concrete case studies. We need to be particularly careful in not reading too much from the lack of major-power war since 1945. Certainly, that particular experience seems to suggest that nuclear weapons added to the restraint on war, more generally, and also to nuclear war. But the continuing tension throughout the Cold War and the close shaves that there were—together with the heavy investments in nuclear and conventional weapons throughout the Cold War—suggest that there was never a very high level of confidence during that period that nuclear deterrence *alone* could provide a decisive and error-free method of war prevention. Most of all, it taught us that the very characteristic that makes the nuclear threat effective in helping deter war—the awful destructive power of these weapons—also means that the room for error is very low indeed. If we did learn anything from the end of the Cold War, in 1989, it is the radical unpredictability of international affairs.

So strong has become the norm of the nonuse of nuclear weapons since 1945 that any use of nuclear weapons now or in the next couple of decades could bring about as profound a change in the international system as the end of the Cold War itself. But the nature of these radical consequences would depend very much on the specifics of the crisis and the specific lessons that people learned from that crisis. Even if nuclear weapons were not used against the United States or a European state, it would constitute an international crisis of a magnitude significantly greater than that generated by 9/11. It could trigger massive changes in the world and possibly very much for the worse.

When we talk of counterproliferation as our objective, we should remember that it is only a means to the end of preventing war—especially to the end of preventing nuclear war. In turn, deterrence can and should be seen only as one of several

149

tools for the prevention of war and indeed for the management of war, as well as one of only several tools for the prevention and management of proliferation.

What are the major risks of war and nuclear war in particular in relation to which deterrence might play a role? First, the problem of preventing war, nuclear war, and indeed the problem of proliferation, should not be confined to those states that have not yet acquired nuclear weapons—like Iran or Syria. There are also very real concerns with states which have already acquired nuclear weapons. In 2009 Pakistan is probably at the top of that list, and North Korea is probably not very far behind. In a discussion of deterrence, the distinction between states which have nuclear weapons and those which don't is perhaps artificial. Even in discussing international law (e.g., arms control or the NPT), deterrence is of critical importance whether or not countries are signatories of international instruments and in particular the NPT.

Second, and perhaps my most substantive point, is that students of history and of conflict often suggest that war may be especially likely at times when the leaders of one state believe there is a window of opportunity to launch a strike against another state before that state closes a perceived gap and gains superiority (or loses inferiority) in military capability, particularly when there is a perception that the window may be closing. Scholars have argued that this may have played a role in German motivations for going to war with Russia in 1914. There was a live debate in the late 1940s and early 1950s about whether a preemptive strike against the Soviet Union before the Soviets acquired a substantial nuclear capability was an option. There was certainly a discussion about preemptive strikes against China by the United States and/or the Soviet Union in the 1960s. There was of course the Israeli attack on Osirak in Iraq, and today there is a discussion about Israel and Iran.

But at the same time, in parallel to that discussion about whether these windows of opportunity might exist, there is also an argument that, at least in principle, the incentives for preemption decline as the forces of different nuclear weapons states come into more of a balance, particularly when states acquire assured second-strike capabilities, however those capabilities are defined. Certainly, the latter part of the Cold War is seen as an example of that alleged stability.

Here, I think it is useful to think about this question in terms of a window of opportunity debate between what one might term *window optimists* and *window pessimists*. Window optimists argue both that (a) the transitional period between a time of crisis instability and high-perceived incentives for preemption and a subsequent period of relative stability is relatively short and that (b) the window itself is relatively lacking in severity, so the incentives for preemption are in practice relatively low. Window optimists argue that the destructive power of nuclear weapons is so great and most states so risk averse that mutual deterrence between states can be quickly established once any nuclear capability is obtained.

Window pessimists, by contrast, argue that the window can be prolonged and that there may well be repeated particular circumstances and points in time at which preemption could be seriously contemplated or feared. Window pessimists are sceptical that stability can be easily created and worry (for example) about the impact of missile defences and conventional strike capabilities in preventing, or indeed undermining, stable nuclear relationships.

Where one stands on the relationship between optimists and pessimists makes a real difference, for example, as to how relaxed one is about the prospects of further proliferation to countries like Iran. Unfortunately, we don't have enough experience to know who is right, and it could be too late once we find out—a reality that certainly might incline us to work on the assumption that the pessimists might be right.

Third is the role of conventional deterrence in the prevention of the use of nuclear weapons. In circumstances where we have states which are strong in conventional terms confronting states which are weak, conventional forces can and indeed should play a central role in making deterrence credible. As long as nuclear weapons exist in the arsenal of an opponent, the user of any WMD must take into account the possibility that there will be a nuclear response. But the scale of damage is so difficult to calibrate and likely to be so antithetical to the values of our own states that where possible it will be much better to focus on conventional responses to nuclear first use, including regime change where that is a feasible alternative. In-deed, the more that timely conventional responses to nuclear use are seen to be a credible deterrent to that use, the more that this will strengthen deterrence rather than weaken it.

Fourth is the issue of extended deterrence and the extent to which one country, the United States in particular, might be willing to risk its own vital interests, at least to some extent, to provide guarantees to others against the use of nuclear weap-ons. Extended deterrence is about perception, and many of the policy issues we will face in the future relate to perceptions of whether past commitments to extended deterrence can be sus-tained. There is an argument around the North Atlantic Treaty Organization (NATO) strategic concept in this regard, but there is also an argument about the extent to which extended deter-rence will play an enhanced role in the Middle East were Iran to acquire a nuclear capability, even if this were a latent capability. The presence of conventional forces and possibly nuclear forces can play an important role here as a tripwire and as an indica-tion of resolve. But one should never underestimate, whatever the force deployments, the critical importance of the demonstra-tion of political will, the political processes of consultation, and the general foreign policy orientation on key issues which will be necessary to lend political credibility to those guarantees.

We should also be aware that the need for deterrence is bal-anced by the need not to provoke. A good example of this was a recent suggestion—perhaps not seriously floated, but never-theless floated in a recent article by a US Air Force officer—that nuclear-capable aircraft based in Aviano, Italy, should be rede-ployed to Poland. In pure deterrence terms, this indeed might make some sense in enhancing NATO deterrence against the possibility of a Russian advance westwards. It would also be entirely compatible with the spirit of equality within NATO. But there are many people who would argue that there would also be some likely negative impact in terms of the likely response from Russia, and it would be at the very least premature to take such a course given the currently very low probability of Russian aggression in such member states as Poland.

Fifth and finally, in relation to arms control, arms control has now returned in a big way into the debate about nuclear weapons, most of all as a result of the initiatives by the US president but initiatives also strongly supported by the United Kingdom government. In relation to our discussion, the next steps, a Comprehensive Test Ban Treaty and a new START, may not have profound implications, though the process of reconfiguring force structures for a new strategic agreement may well be more significant. As we proceed down that road, there will be harder and harder discussions and decisions to make, particularly if we move towards a world that is more multipolar in nuclear terms than at present.

The window optimists, those who think that deterrence is pretty stable with wide margins in relative capabilities, will worry less about the exact nuclear balances as we come down in numbers between the United States and Russia and as other states are brought in and as people start looking at various nuclear balances, including the concerns over hidden stockpiles and the role of missile defences. There are also questions as to how the strategic arms control process will be affected if there was further overt proliferation, especially in the case of Iran. It depends exactly on what form that proliferation might take and the reaction of Iran's neighbours to such steps. It is likely that it would lead to an arms control process which is even more zigzag than the straight linear path to a global zero which some suggest is possible.

Even if it is not a linear process, however, the quest for arms control is as old as nuclear weapons themselves. It will not go away, however many nuclear weapons states there are, even if the form that it takes may change quite radically. So we will need to continue to reflect on how arms control can flexibly respond to the problems we face. And our concepts of deterrence will need to continue to be developed in close synergy with those for arms control and indeed with our war prevention strategy as a whole.

Chapter 11

Deterrence and Saddam Hussein
A Case Study of the 1990–1991 Gulf War

Barry R. Schneider

War and deterrence begin in the minds of men. Deterrence is a psychological phenomenon that begins between the ears of the adversary you are trying to influence. When you seek to deter a rival from doing something you do not wish him or her to do, you must find a way to influence his perceptions of situations, for people act not necessarily on reality but on their perception of it. As Henry Kissinger once said, "A bluff taken seriously is more useful than a serious threat interpreted as a bluff."[1]

To deter, you need to influence the rival's cost/gain evaluations. The rival needs to understand that he or she has far more to lose by initiating conflict or by escalating it to unacceptable levels than by not doing so.

In this study, we look at Pres. Saddam Hussein of Iraq and Pres. George H. W. Bush of the United States and their respective governments' attempts to deter one another just before Iraq invaded Kuwait in August 1990 and through the subsequent gulf conflict that ended in February 1991. On the United States' side of this deterrence effort, one must also include the deterrent effect of US coalition partners in the crisis and war.

In this analysis, we look at the following series of deterrence questions:

1. What are the limits of deterrence theory? Are the clearly stronger military powers able to deter significantly weaker powers all or most of the time?

2. What are the elements of deterrence strategy that Western strategists developed during the Cold War confrontation with the Soviet Union?

3. Why was Saddam Hussein not deterred from ordering the Iraqi invasion of Kuwait in August 1990?

4. Why was Saddam Hussein not deterred from facing vastly superior coalition forces assembled to force him out of Kuwait between August 1990 and January 1991?

5. Why were the United States and the coalition forces not deterred by Iraq from initiating combat in January 1991?

6. Why did Saddam Hussein not resort to use of his chemical and biological weapons in the war as an equalizer against more powerful coalition forces?

7. Why during this conflict was he not deterred from attacking Israel, a state with a nuclear arsenal?

8. Why did the United States and the coalition not pursue Iraqi forces into their country and end the Saddam Hussein regime in Baghdad? Was the United States deterred from pursuing the war all the way to Baghdad by the residual Iraqi military capability?

9. Was the United States deterred from the use of nuclear weapons in the war by the threat of Iraqi retaliation with chemical and/or biological weapons?

10. What conclusions and lessons can be extracted from this conflict regarding deterrence as a strategy for future crises?

The Limits of Deterrence

Deterrence is based on deductive reasoning, not evidence from history. It is a rational deduction that a weaker power should not be willing to risk almost certain defeat if it starts a war with a much more powerful rival. Also, it is a logical assumption that leaders of countries should not enter into conflicts where it appears to them that they would be incurring catastrophic losses or would likely lose things the leadership values most.

On the face of it, this seems rational and almost indisputable. The problem is that deterrence does not work so often and so clearly in the real world. An inductive approach that looks at the empirical evidence from past international conflicts shows a mixed picture.

Surprisingly, reviews of case studies show that history is full of occasions when demonstrably weaker opponents have initiated what appear to be absolutely irrational attacks on much stronger opponents.[2] According to one RAND study, in 22 percent (17 of 76) of conflicts that occurred from 1816 to 1974, weaker military powers initiated wars with stronger states. This obviously can have disastrous results in some cases. For example, in the 1864–1870 War of the Triple Alliance, Paraguay's dictator, Francisco Solano Lopez, invaded Brazil. He also attacked Argentina when that state did not allow his forces free passage through its territory. Uruguay then joined these two giants in the conflict against Paraguay. By the end of this ill-advised aggression by Paraguay, that small country had 85 percent of its population killed, reduced from 1.4 million in 1864 to just 0.22 million by 1870. By the war's end, Paraguay had just 29,000 adult males left alive.[3]

Such wars can be caused by crazy rulers. They can also be initiated by those simply unwilling to live under the heel of the enemy, thereby putting honor and their cause above survival. Think, for example, of Patrick Henry's famous words in the American Revolution, "Give me liberty or give me death." The signers of the American Declaration of Independence in 1776 all were willing to risk their lives in their cause. Indeed, "five signers were captured by the British and brutally tortured as traitors. Nine fought in the War for Independence and died from wounds or from hardships they suffered. Two lost their sons in the Continental Army. Another two had sons captured. At least a dozen of the fifty-six had their homes pillaged and burned . . . Seventeen of them lost everything that they owned."[4]

Weaker states also start ill-advised wars due to wishful thinking, misperception, group think, illogic born of stress, or a stubborn refusal to confront the facts.[5] In some historical cases, decision makers have chosen to focus primarily on their aims and own resources and have discounted those of the adversary, despite clear evidence that they will lose if they push further into the crisis.

Another situation that pushes weaker powers to attack much stronger states is where time is considered not to be on their side. Saddam Hussein in 1980 is thought to have attacked Iran, a larger country with more resources and three times the population of Iraq, because he feared that Iran would attack in a year or so when it was better organized. Leaders sometimes feel forced to start a war immediately when their chances of success, while slim, would be even poorer at a later time.

Weaker indigenous groups often launch wars against stronger opponents out of nationalist sentiment and a desire to remove foreign or rival group influences. This is an old story repeated many times, as revolutions opposed colonial regimes or the domination of other ethnic groups. In many cases, these revolutionaries are pitting their superior zeal and a greater stake in the outcome against superior rival military forces that often do not have the same commitment to victory over time. Many times these revolutions and insurgencies fail. Sometimes, however, the fortunes of the sides reverse over time, such as happened in China when communist guerrilla forces challenged initially superior nationalist Chinese forces and eventually became the stronger side in winning a protracted civil war.

Others may decide to fight an enemy with superior potential rather than give up long-standing goals or a way of life. They may bet that their willingness to absorb casualties is greater than their rival's and that he or she will tire of the war and be willing to sue for peace short of total victory, leaving the smaller state that initiated the war in possession of their goals. This appears to be the Japanese leadership before Pearl Harbor and of Saddam Hussein after the coalition buildup in Saudi Arabia had put a powerful army in Saudi Arabia in 1990 after his invasion of Kuwait. It also appears to have been the mind-set of the Confederate leaders when they challenged the much more populous and industrialized North in the American Civil War.

Moreover, deterrence assumes that state leaders can control their subordinates. Leaders of weaker states might not authorize an attack on a stronger power, but it may take place anyway because some subordinates do not follow orders.

Others might decide to strike out and start a war if they believed their regime is about to fall. Some might initiate or escalate a conflict against a hated enemy for highly emotional reasons or if it might marshal more domestic support for their leadership at home. This is the inside-outside theory of war causation—a conflict started for internal domestic reasons. This appears to have been a partial cause of the 1982 Argentine-United Kingdom war in the Falklands, where for largely domestic political reasons, the ruling junta challenged British control of the islands.

Still other leaders might be religious, cultural, or ideological zealots who will stop at nothing to destroy some hated adversary, leaving the consequences to chance. For example, at the height of the Cuban missile crisis, the Castro brothers, in a fit of revolutionary zeal, were urging the Soviet leadership to fire at the United States their nuclear-tipped missiles stationed in Cuba, even though it meant their own likely deaths and the wholesale destruction of their country. Some initiators of combat may care more about their place in history than about the immediate consequences for themselves and their people.

However, this is not to say that deterrence cannot or should not work in the majority of cases. Rather, remember that deterrence of war or escalation still can fail when a much stronger power confronts a weaker one or even where both sides would suffer catastrophic warfare losses if they entered into a conflict.

Cold War Deterrence Theory

Luckily this did not happen during the Cold War when a central nuclear war could have caused hundreds of millions of deaths. By 1949 both the United States and Soviet Union had nuclear weapons, and both sides held the life or death of the rival society in their hands. The peace was secured by the dual-hostage situation described as mutual assured destruction.[6] If the system failed, it would have been deadly.

Deterrence theory developed as US and allied policy makers and strategists worked to understand the implications of nuclear weapons and how they might be used to keep the peace and advance US and allied security. Several elements were eventually recognized as fundamentally important to strategic deterrence.

First, it was deemed crucial that the United States and its allies maintain a nuclear retaliatory force that could inflict what an aggressor leadership would consider unacceptable damage to itself and its vital interests.[7] Aggressors must be made to believe that the risks of attacking the United States and its allies were clearly and significantly greater than any conceivable rewards they might gain from such action.

Second, a potential aggressor must be made to realize that the US and allied leaders not only must have such lethal capabilities but must also be willing to use such retaliatory power, if challenged. Adversary risk-taking leaders must be convinced, by word and deed, that our leaders are willing, not simply to threaten to use force in response to aggression, but also to act should the line be crossed. Without both the physical capability to inflict unacceptable levels of damage on an aggressor party and the evident will to use such force, the US and allied deterrent would lack credibility and might risk war where an adversary adventurer misperceived the situation. For example, this might have been the cause of the October 1962 Cuban missile crisis.[8]

Third, the origin of the attack must be known, if the real aggressor is to be deterred. If an adversary leader thought he or she could disguise the origin of the attack, perhaps making it seem as if it came from another state, the attacker might feel he or she could strike and escape the consequences. This is the problem discussed by the late Herman Kahn when he talked about the possibility of what he termed *catalytic war*.[9] Party A might strike Party B, making it look like it came from Party C, causing B and C to fight. Thus, a vigilant early warning and tracking system and an effective forensics capability should be a fundamental part of any successful deterrent posture. Deterrence requires a return address.

Fourth, the US and allied retaliatory forces must be able to ride out an adversary surprise attack and still retaliate with overwhelming and accurate force, holding hostage what the rival leaders value most. This has led the United States to rely on a mix of forces in a strategic triad of nuclear-armed ICBMs deployed on US soil; strategic bombers, deployed worldwide, carrying both nuclear standoff missiles; nuclear gravity bombs; and nuclear-tipped submarine-launched ballistic missiles carried on ballistic missile submarines that roam the world's oceans. Even the former Soviet Union, with its extensive nuclear forces, could not have hoped to preemptively destroy so much of the United States and allied nuclear forces to escape nuclear annihilation in return. It was seen as impossible for anyone to destroy all retaliatory elements of the US alliances and strategic triad to escape assured destruction in return. Maintaining this second-strike capability was deemed an essential component of a classical deterrence posture.

Fifth, deterrence is based on assuming an opponent has complete knowledge of the situation and will act rationally. This sounds plausible, but how do you define rationality? Are suicide bombers rational? Further, if adversary leaders are willing to die or see most of their followers die to inflict terrible wounds on the United States and/or its allies, then deterrence may fail even if you can "take them with you."

In an era of multiple personalities guiding rogue states, some of them being high-risk takers, deterrence could fail. If deterrence fails, the United States and its coalition partners will need capable counterforce units and excellent missile and air defenses all the more to limit casualties and preserve the chance for a military victory. In a crisis that has not yet escalated to war, the presence of such capable offensive strike forces and effective defenses may help to deter war.

If an adversary knows there is a good chance his or her deployment of chemical, biological, radiological, and/or nuclear (CBRN) weapons may attract US counterforce strikes that could destroy his or her weapons before they can be employed, he or she might be deterred from acquisition or the attempted use of them. The same logic pertains to a situation where his use of weapons of mass destruction (WMD) in wartime would be nullified by active and passive defenses. Either way, through offense or defense, if United States and allied forces were to rob him of a potent threat, he may be more reluctant to incur the costs of building and deploying such weapons. Thus, a rogue state regime may be deterred by the threat of retaliation or by the threat of having his attack neutralized by effective defenses. He might be deterred either by the sword or the shield or by a combination. Deterrence produced by possessing effective military countermeasures (i.e., deterrence by denial) and deterrence produced by the threat of an overwhelming retaliation should be mutually reinforcing.

On the other hand, we can never be absolutely sure when deterrence has worked, but it is obvious when it has failed to work. When it fails, a war begins or a conflict escalates. When a deterrence policy and posture are successful, this is a nonevent, since no war starts or no escalation takes place. However, correlation is not necessarily causation. Just because

161

A precedes B does not prove A caused B. Indeed, B might have another cause altogether.[10]

How does one prove without a certain deterrence policy that something otherwise might have happened? Unless one were able to step out of the present and rerun history to see what would have happened differently without a given deterrence policy or posture, one cannot prove that the deterrence stance caused the outcome. So deterrence is far from an exact science. Deterrence is an art, and we can only infer when it is successful, since we have not yet found a way to read an adversary's mind or re-run historical events with one or more of the variables changed.

The Faceoff: George H. W. Bush versus Saddam Hussein

The 1990–1991 Gulf War involved 34 coalition governments and leaderships all pitted against Iraq. It was not simply crisis bargaining and warfare directed by two men. Thirty-four coalition leaderships had to be coordinated, and military personnel from 34 militaries had to be made into one effective fighting force with a unity of command.

Things were simpler on the other side. In Iraq, important military and diplomatic decisions were those of Saddam Hussein acting essentially alone. This was far less true of Pres. George H. W. Bush. But in the end, he mobilized and led the coalition to war. He also made the final decision about when to attack the Iraqi Army in Kuwait, and, after 40 days of air bombardment and 100 hours of a ground war later, it was his decision to declare and negotiate a cease-fire with Iraq that stopped short of going on to Baghdad.

It would be difficult to find two more different men facing each other in a crisis or a war. They were separated widely in their education, exposure to the wider world, family upbringing, values, culture, language, regional, and political systems. Moreover, the leader of each country inherited a different set of world, regional, and domestic problems and pressures. Both inherited a different set of commitments and policies from their predecessors and had a different public to deal with. Saddam

Hussein and George Bush, therefore, came to this 1990–1991 conflict with different backgrounds and perspectives.

Simply put, George Herbert Walker Bush was born to privilege and power. His father was a US senator. Saddam Hussein was born in a poor Iraqi village, and his father died before he was born. Bush attended Andover Preparatory School and Yale University. Hussein dropped out of school in his teenage years and did not finish high school until he was 24. At the time, he was being sought in Iraq for an attempted killing of the Iraqi president and was a fugitive living in Cairo, Egypt. Saddam never earned a college degree, although he attended several law classes while in Egypt.

The two also differed in other ways. Bush served as a pilot in the US Navy in World War II, engaged in 58 air combat missions, and won the Navy Cross for bravery. Saddam Hussein never served in the Iraqi military, and, when he applied as a young man, he was denied entry into the Iraq military academy, one of the few paths available for poor Iraqis attempting upward mobility.

Bush was widely traveled and had served overseas as US ambassador to China and later as chief US ambassador to the United Nations. Hussein never traveled outside the Middle East. Bush was knowledgeable about the international system and worldwide threats. He served as director of the Central Intelligence Agency. Saddam worked exclusively within the Ba'ath Party, where he first served as an organizer, as a hit man, and later as the feared head of party security responsible for thousands of executions.

Bush served in elective politics in the United States, first as a congressman from Texas, later as chairman of the Republican Party National Committee, and finally as vice president and president of the United States. By 1990 Bush already had won five elections on his way to the top of the US political system. On the other hand, Saddam Hussein had murdered and terrorized his way to the top of the Iraqi political system. He had never won an election until after he seized the presidency in 1978. All political contests thereafter probably were rigged, as he built a terrorist police state.

His was a fearful and feared regime, and Saddam Hussein essentially was the sole foreign policy and defense policy decision

163

maker in Iraq. It could be said that "Saddam was Iraq and Iraq was Saddam" from the standpoint of policy decisions. As Charles Duelfer later concluded in a 2004 report to the director of the Central Intelligence Agency, "Saddam Hussein so dominated the Iraqi regime that its strategic intent was his alone."[11]

It is instructive to realize how little knowledge Saddam Hussein had of the United States or its leaders. While President Bush was no Middle East expert, he was far better informed than Saddam about the other side's capabilities. However, both leaders lacked a clear knowledge of the other. FBI interrogator George Piro, assigned the task of interrogating Saddam after his capture in 2003, concluded from months of interviews that "one striking theme that emerged was just how little we knew about Saddam and how little he knew about us."[12]

These two leaders came from opposite ends of the earth. One is reminded of the Kipling verse when considering these two when he said "East is East, and West is West, and never the twain should meet." Their cultures were as different as were their life experiences. Saddam was a thug and mafia-like Iraqi leader, born in poverty, who maneuvered and eventually killed his way into power in Iraq. In 1991 two of his biographers concluded that "in the permanently beleaguered mind of Saddam Hussein, politics is a ceaseless struggle for survival. The ultimate goal of staying alive and in power justifies all means. Plots lurk around every corner. Nobody is trustworthy. Everyone is an actual or potential enemy."[13]

Bush was an American blue blood who started from a favored position and then achieved his way to the top of the US political system. When he and Hussein confronted each other over Kuwait, President Bush was leader of the richest country in the world and the head of the most powerful military force ever deployed. Confronting him was Pres. Saddam Hussein, with his million man army, the fourth largest in the world, now sitting astride 19 percent of the world's oil supplies after his occupation of Kuwait.

The Invasion of Kuwait

After the Iran-Iraq war, badly needing funds to rebuild and protect his regime, Saddam Hussein ordered his forces to seize oil-rich Kuwait to repay his creditors, recoup his wealth, and re-equip his security and armed forces.[14] At that time, "Iraq had approximately $80 B in debts stemming from the war with Iran, compared with a GNP of about $35 B, with a hard-currency income of about $14 B."[15]

If his biographers are to be believed, Saddam Hussein probably invaded Kuwait only after long and careful thought. In previous critical decisions, he was a careful planner. For example, when deciding whether to nationalize the nation's oil wells in 1972, Saddam exhibited a blend of caution and boldness. His chief biographers say that "the nationalization affords yet another vivid example of Saddam's calculated risk-taking style of operation. He proved himself a cautious, yet daring decision maker who did not flinch before a challenge. Weighing his options carefully and taking the necessary precautions, he did not rush into a hasty decision. But once he made up his mind, he moved swiftly and resolutely toward his target."[16]

After the invasion when his aggression against Kuwait was challenged by the United States and most of the rest of the world, Saddam refused to back down as the United States–led coalition poured military personnel, equipment, and supplies into nearby Saudi Arabia starting in August 1990 and continuing until the end of hostilities in February 1991. Early in this military buildup, tensions were high at the White House because it took months to get enough firepower transferred to the theater to offset an initial Iraqi Army advantage in the theater. Meanwhile, Saudi Arabia and its oil reserves seemed at the mercy of Iraq's Army if Saddam chose to continue its operations and invade the Saudi kingdom.

Clearly, at this point the United States leadership had spelled out its determination to defend Saudi Arabia and its desire to compel Iraq to withdraw from Kuwait. To bolster this deterrence posture, the United States had the potential military might to defeat Iraq, and this might was augmented by the verbal and nonverbal signaling of US and allied intentions. The United States was engaged in a continuing military mobilization in the gulf and was engaged in a worldwide diplomatic campaign to enlist allies into a coalition and to condemn Iraq's invasion at the United Nations.

165

Why didn't Saddam Hussein realize the catastrophe he was about to suffer and withdraw his forces back to Iraq before the coalition juggernaut destroyed his armed forces in the field? There are several hypotheses. First, he might not have had the situational awareness, and he may have believed the US president and coalition leaders were simply bluffing. Second, Saddam might have engaged in wishful thinking and not faced the unpleasant possibilities he had not foreseen. Third, he might not have understood the total mismatch his forces were facing and how few casualties they could inflict on a technologically superior force. Fourth, Saddam might have feared that a military withdrawal would undermine his leadership and status in Iraq and lead to his replacement. Fifth, Saddam may have calculated that he simply could not do without Kuwait's oil revenue to finance his own depleted treasury and to rebuild his security forces and army, and, thus, perhaps he was gambling on being able somehow to keep his Kuwaiti prize.[17]

As the crisis deepened and war was about to begin again, the United States sought to persuade Iraq to withdraw from Kuwait without a fight, or, if a war was inevitable, at least try to persuade the Iraqi leader not to order the use of chemical or biological weapons by warning that he would face dire consequences if he did.

Saddam Hussein, on the other hand, may have sought to deter a coalition attack or a US-UK-French use of nuclear weapons by threatening retaliation with his chemical and/or biological weapons. Once the war began, the United States hoped in vain to deter Saddam from attacking Israel, and, once that failed, acted to influence the Israelis to let the US and coalition troops do the retaliating for them rather than have Israel enter the war and split the coalition.

Saddam, facing a superior foe, misunderstood what a mismatch it was for his army and air forces to try to compete with the coalition forces and felt that high US casualty rates would buy him a compromise peace that would have left his regime intact. He badly miscalculated how many casualties his forces could inflict, but his residual chemical and biological weapons, unused in the conflict, might have helped deter a US invasion and occupation of Iraq after Saddam's forces had been driven from Kuwait.

Sometimes, an adversary leader may operate in a world of his or her own, surrounded by yes-men and cut off from realistic intelligence about the United States, its allies, and their intentions. This appears to be the case with Saddam Hussein at the time of Desert Storm. Such an enemy leader may disregard the messages and intelligence reports he or she receives, preferring instead to follow his or her own thinking and adhering to previous stereotypes or misinformation.

US Attempts to Deter Iraq from Invading Kuwait (July–August 1990)

When trouble brewed over rights in the Rumaila oil fields, a disputed area along the Iraq-Kuwait border, President Bush sent his ambassador, April Glaspie, to see if the dispute could be settled peacefully. Her meeting with Saddam Hussein appeared to be cordial and gave no hint of his inclination to take military action against Kuwait nor did it say much about the US interest in backing Kuwait in the dispute. Indeed, according to reports, "US Ambassador April Glaspie told Saddam that 'We have no opinion on the Arab-Arab conflicts, like your border disagreement with Kuwait.'"[18] Later, the US State Department followed with another message that said that Washington had "no special defense or security commitments to Kuwait." Saddam must have seen this as an indication that he would have little to fear from the United States if he intervened in Kuwait.

Although it is likely that Saddam Hussein had already decided on the invasion of Kuwait at that time, Ambassador Glaspie reported that he seemed inclined to negotiate. This was communicated to President Bush, who then had the US State Department transmit the message to the Iraqi leader stating that "I am pleased to learn of the agreement between Iraq and Kuwait to begin negotiations in Jeddah to find a peaceful solution to the current tensions between you. The United States and Iraq both have a strong interest in preserving the peace and stability of the Middle East. For this reason we believe these responsibilities are best resolved by peaceful means and not by threats involving military force or conflict."[19]

If this letter had included a stronger tone, one that emphasized a threat to use military power to block any move by Iraq
to settle the dispute by means of the Iraqi Army taking over
Kuwait, Saddam might have put the invasion plan on hold. Using 20-20 hindsight, it is easy now to conclude that President
Bush's letter, though reasonable on its face, was evidently not
the warning shot across the bow that the situation required.
The US response was too mild to influence a dictator who did
not play by any agreed-upon international rules and who was
bent on seizing a prize that could solve most of his financial
and security problems if his aggression went unopposed.

Saddam Hussein might have interpreted the mild US response
as a green light to do what he wanted to do. Certainly, it was not
a stern warning to cease and desist. He might well have calculated that the United States was distracted elsewhere and that
it would not respond forcefully to a fait accompli. Kuwait might
have looked like a prize that could easily be taken, an immediate benefit that could be realized with only a distant, intangible,
and uncertain risk being run in undertaking to occupy it. This
would fit with the pattern of Saddam Hussein's operational code
at home and abroad: plan carefully, conceal your moves, and
then strike decisively and violently to achieve your ends. Also,
preemptively attack against your unprepared, unsuspecting, mis-
led opponent. Moreover, Saddam did not think the US leadership had much of an appetite for combat or battle casualties, as
it had withdrawn when it had had its fill of casualties in
previous conflicts in Vietnam and Lebanon.

As former secretary of state James Baker notes in his memoir,
"With his flagrant move into Kuwait, Saddam Hussein's ambitions revealed themselves in all their grandiosity."[20] The question that comes to mind regarding this scenario is why the
United States did not do more to deter his attack on Kuwait. The
answer was that the Bush administration's leadership was distracted and simply did not anticipate such a violent move from
Saddam Hussein. James Baker further explained this point,
saying,

> With the benefit of hindsight, it's easy to argue that we should have rec-
> ognized earlier that we weren't going to moderate Saddam's behavior,
> and shifted our policy approach sooner to a greater degree than we did.
> At the least, we should have given Iraqi policy a more prominent place on

our radar screen at an earlier date. I believe the reasons we didn't change our policy approach earlier and to a greater extent are myriad and complex. And while I wish we'd focused more attention on Iraq earlier, given what happened, I remain unpersuaded that anything we might have done, short of actually moving armed forces to the region, would have deterred Iraq's invasion of Kuwait.[21]

Furthermore, Baker believes that there was little support at first for blocking Saddam's ambitions in Kuwait. In his "view the only realistic chance to deter Saddam would have been to introduce US forces into the region—and neither the Kuwaitis, the Saudis, the Soviets, nor the Congress would have supported that course before August 2. Indeed, it was only the shock of the invasion that allowed us to intervene militarily at all."[22]

In addition, the United States was fully occupied with events happening inside the Soviet bloc as the Berlin Wall came down, and Eastern Europe began to revolt against communist party control in Czechoslovakia, Poland, Hungary, and East Germany. Also, Soviet leader Mikhail Gorbachev was unwilling to implement the Breshnev doctrine and to use the Red Army to terrorize the Eastern Europeans back into submission. The US foreign policy leadership was primarily focused on these events and too little attention was paid to the local squabble between Iraq and Kuwait over oil rights along their border.

Saddam acted when the US focus was directed elsewhere. His invasion caught everyone unprepared. As James Baker recalls,

Without exception, our friends in the region consistently argued that Saddam was only posturing and that confrontation would simply make matters worse. Simply put, the reason why nobody believed Saddam would attack is because no realistic calculation of his interests could have foreseen a full-scale invasion of Kuwait. Shevardnadze had put it correctly in Moscow on the third day following the invasion: "This was an irrational act that made no sense."[23]

Baker also recalls that

[E]ven the Israelis believed that Saddam was bluffing to bully the Kuwaitis into economic concessions. Israel's intelligence service, the Mossad, told US intelligence counterparts that Saddam's rhetoric was designed to deter an Israeli attack, not threaten one of his own. As late as July 31, King Hussein and President Mubarak reassured us that Saddam was engaged in verbal bluster, not literal threats. Ironically, most of our allies privately worried throughout the spring and summer of 1990 that the United States might overreact to Saddam's new aggressiveness![24]

169

However, no one who understood Saddam Hussein's volatile nature, his extreme ambition, and his lifelong tendency toward violence should have been surprised. Just the fact that a strong military under his command resided next door to a poorly defended neighbor in Kuwait that was oil rich should have suggested vigilance in any crisis brewing between the two. One has the image of a lion contemplating a lamb with the latter about to become dinner, or in Kuwait's case, an oil prize that represented 8 percent of the world's proven oil reserves, sitting next to Saudi Arabia, another relatively defenseless state that owned another 25 percent of the world oil reserves. Coupled with Iraq's estimated 11 percent, Saddam Hussein would control much of the Middle East oil supply. However, the United States and the rest of the world were caught by surprise and were unprepared to take the deterrence steps that might have persuaded Saddam to stop short of an invasion of Kuwait.

Saddam Hussein's first name translated into Arabic means "one who confronts." He had lived up to that throughout his entire violent lifetime. The "butcher of Baghdad" had a career that was filled with blood and violence. He was thought to have killed his first victim when only a teenage boy. He was a hit man for the Ba'athist Party and tried to assassinate the leader of Iraq. Later, when his cousin ruled Iraq, he served as the head of a lethal and brutal security service that killed opponents without remorse. He ruled with fear and his models were Stalin and Hitler whose biographies he had read with admiration. In 1978 he forced his cousin from power and took over as leader of Iraq. The bloodbath in Iraq escalated, as he exterminated tens of thousands of domestic adversaries. In one of his first acts as Iraq's supreme leader, he called a meeting of hundreds of top Ba'ath Party leaders, singled out many of them for so-called acts of disloyalty, arrested and read them their death sentences on the spot, and forced the remainder of his party leaders to serve in firing squads that shot their doomed colleagues the next day.

Not satisfied with violence against possible domestic opponents, Saddam Hussein almost immediately went to war with his neighbors. In 1980, less than two years after the coup that brought him to power, he ordered his army to attack Iran. The result was an eight-year war that bled both states and featured the extensive use of chemical weapons and ballistic missile attacks, both initiated by Saddam's commands. In retrospect, the United States and other states concerned with the security of the region and its important oil reserves should have anticipated possible violence from a dictator whose entire career was marked with a resort to violence in solving his problems or acquiring his goals.

Coalition Deterrence of Iraq from Invading Saudi Arabia, 1990–1991

During the initial phases of the 1990–1991 Gulf War, both sides attempted to deter the other from certain actions. Saddam sought to deter US intervention into the conflict by the threat of heavy US and coalition casualties. From August 1990 until January 1991, the United States and the other coalition partners sought to deter Saddam from ordering his forces, then in Kuwait, to invade Saudi Arabia before it could be adequately defended. Iraq already had 11 percent of the world's proven oil reserves when Saddam Hussein ordered his forces into Kuwait. Had he held on in Kuwait, he would have gained another 8 percent of the world's oil reserves or 19 percent overall. Had he continued on and conquered Saudi Arabia, a country that owns 25 percent of the world's oil reserves, Saddam would have controlled 44 percent of the world's oil reserves. Clearly, he had to be stopped or US and allied vital interests in the region would have been threatened.

However, it is not at all clear whether Saddam Hussein ever seriously considered invading Saudi Arabia after consolidating his hold on Kuwait. Thus, we do not know if deterrence worked or was not needed in this case.

Certainly the thin Saudi and US forces there in August and September 1990 could not have offered much resistance. However, to invade Saudi Arabia would have shed US and Arab blood, and the few US forces sent immediately to the Saudi kingdom would have served as a trip wire, a down payment on further US fighters to come and give battle to the Iraqi Army should they be attacked. Thus, an Iraqi attack on Saudi Arabia almost certainly would have triggered a war with the United

171

States, something the Iraqi dictator almost certainly should have wanted to avoid, if possible. Thus, the US forces trip-wire force quite likely served to halt the Iraqi force at the Saudi border until a military buildup there would permit coalition offensive action in January 1991.

Saddam's Failure to Hold the Coalition at Bay

Once the United States began to move its own forces into the region after the Iraqi seizure of Kuwait, Saddam Hussein had one of two moves available. First, he could order his forces to attack and occupy much of Saudi Arabia just as they had in Kuwait. If he were to do this, he would have had to act immediately, for time was not on his side. A seizure of the Saudi kingdom would have greatly complicated the United States' task of introducing large forces into the region. He could have inflicted far more casualties and been much harder to dislodge from Kuwait if he had continued his offensive in August or September 1990 on into Saudi Arabia. In retrospect, the best defense he could mount was a good offense early before Operation Desert Shield could establish a significant force in the region to oppose his forces.

His second option was to do nothing except build up his defenses along the Saudi-Kuwait border and watch as the coalition troops poured into the theater opposite his army in Kuwait. Saddam selected the second option and relied upon his large army in Kuwait to deter an attack by threatening large coalition casualties should they attack. This was a contest of wills with the US president and his allies, and ultimately Saddam Hussein lost. The coalition was not deterred from war, and the result was a catastrophic defeat for the Iraqi military.

Why was the coalition not deterred from attacking Saddam's forces in Kuwait? First, Iraq was dealing with states and forces much greater than his own. President Bush and his advisers and the other coalition leaders had a much greater appreciation of the qualitative superiority of their forces than did Saddam. Operation Desert Shield had put an impressive, well-equipped army of 543,000 US troops and thousands of other coalition military personnel at the disposal of Gen Norman Schwarzkopf and President Bush by January 1991.

It was clear to most military experts that the coalition would have control of the air and sea around Kuwait. Further, coalition ground forces had superior armor, superior artillery, superior mobility, superior training, superior protective gear against chemical and biological weapons, and superior intelligence.

Still further, the United States, United Kingdom, and France were states with nuclear weapons, and Iraq had been warned that any use of chemical and biological weapons would possibly be met with overwhelming responses. The bottom line was that it was not likely that Iraq could win a war with the coalition.

Beyond this, most of the states in the region and the West would not allow Iraq to pose such a threat to their oil supplies and economies. Kuwait controlled 8 percent of the known world oil reserves and its neighbor, Saudi Arabia, 25 percent. Add to this Iraq's control of 11 percent, and Saddam Hussein would either have or directly threaten up to 44 percent of world oil supplies. It was deemed in no one's best interest to allow this to happen. Therefore, if Iraq did not willingly quit Kuwait, it must be expelled, and the coalition had the military means to make this happen. Saddam had weak deterrent cards to play in this scenario, and he was unable to deter the coalition attack that began on 17 January 1991.

Saddam's Fallback Position
Deterring a Coalition March to Baghdad

Why did Saddam Hussein refuse to withdraw from Kuwait as the coalition military buildup continued opposite his forces in Kuwait from August 1990 until January 1991? At some point, one would have thought that he would have realized that a military superpower and its allies would easily defeat his forces and bring catastrophic consequences to his armed forces and regime. What kept him from retreating in the face of overwhelming force before the coalition military hammer struck?

It is possible that Saddam Hussein believed his own rhetoric and believed either that the coalition, despite the buildup of forces in Saudi Arabia, was bluffing or that his army could hold its own in combat with the United States. It is also likely that Saddam felt that he needed the resources from Kuwait to rebuild his regime and its security forces to remain in power. He might also have reasoned that a forced retreat from Kuwait, coupled with the disastrous war he had just concluded with Iran, would so weaken him at home that rivals might take encouragement from his weakened position and reputation to overthrow his regime and execute him. He might have calculated that it was better to fight and rally the Iraqi people against a foreign foe than to capitulate and face their censure.

Saddam Hussein appeared to believe that even if Iraq failed to deter a coalition attack on his forces and country, he nevertheless calculated that he could deter the United States–led coalition from horizontal escalation of the conflict into Iraq.[25] He believed that he could mount a stout enough defense so that the coalition could not overrun his forces and occupy Iraq. He felt that the US leadership would stop short of attempting a total victory once US forces absorbed very high casualty rates. He might also have retained hopes that he could hang on to some of the Kuwait oil fields if the fighting led to a stalemate.

Saddam Hussein also thought the United States was less formidable than many others believed. Six months before his invasion of Kuwait, Saddam addressed the fourth summit of the Arab Cooperation Council in Jordan and stated that

> Brothers, the weakness of a big body lies in its bulkiness. All strong men have their Achilles heel. Therefore . . . we saw that the United States departed Lebanon immediately when some Marines were killed. . . . The whole US Administration would have been called into question had the forces that conquered Panama continued to be engaged by the Panamanian Armed Forces. The United States has been defeated in some combat arenas for all the forces it possesses, and it has displayed signs of fatigue, frustration, and hesitation when committing aggression on other people's rights and acting from motives of arrogance and hegemony.[26]

As one analyst has written, "Saddam was hoping for a political not [a] military victory in the Gulf War. He believed that he would triumph if, in the course of the ground war, Iraq inflicted substantial casualties on the Americans. On one occasion he even mentioned a casualty figure that [he] believed would break America's will to fight: 'We are sure that if President Bush pushes things toward war and wages war against us—his war of aggression which he is planning—once five thousand of his troops die, he will not be able to continue this war.'"[27]

As a result of this conclusion, Saddam Hussein issued orders to his generals to direct their forces so as to "inflict 'maximum casualties' on US soldiers when the fighting started."[28] He believed that US leaders would face mounting domestic pressure to halt their war efforts as the killing continued and the numbers of US dead increased.

Former secretary of state Baker recalls that "in retrospect, the war may seem to have been a clinical and relatively straightforward affair. At the time, however, we were confronted with very sobering casualty figures, estimated by the Pentagon to be in the thousands; the specter of possible chemical and biological attacks; and a war expected to last for months not days."[29]

Baker summarized that "moreover, Saddam may have misread history. He apparently was fixated by our experience in Vietnam and, like Hafez al-Assad, thought the our pullout from Lebanon after the Beirut barracks bombing in October 1983 showed Americans were 'short of breath.' Unlike Assad, however, Saddam was willing to test that proposition in a high-profile, high-risk way."[30]

As one analyst put it, Saddam Hussein was "a great believer in the eventual victory of the side willing to suffer the most."[31] To win the war politically, if not militarily, Saddam was willing to lose thousands more of Iraqi dead to inflict the requisite number of American dead to achieve his ends.

General Schwarzkopf was worried that Iraqi chemical weapons might cause major coalition casualties. In his memoir he wrote,

> You can take the most beat-up army in the world, and if they choose to stand and fight, we are going to take casualties: if they choose to dump chemicals on you, they might even win. . . . My nightmare was that our units would reach the barriers in the first hours of the attack, be unable to get through, and then be hit with a chemical barrage. The possibilities of mass casualties from chemical weapons were the main reason we had sixty-three hospitals, two hospital ships, and eighteen thousand beds in the war zone.[32] Schwarzkopf was also worried that Saddam Hussein was prepared to use chemical weapons on the coalition army if it tried to go around the Iraqi flanks.[33]

Indeed, Saddam Hussein was perhaps both right and wrong in his deterrence estimates in late 1990. He was mistaken about his army's ability to inflict 5,000 or more coalition casualties in that war. The US personnel killed in action were 148 battle-related deaths and 145 out-of-combat deaths.[34] In addition, the United Kingdom suffered 47 deaths, 38 from Iraqi fire. France suffered two deaths, and the Arab countries, not including Kuwait, suffered 37 deaths.[35] On the other hand, it is clear that Pres. George H.W. Bush was seeking to minimize both coalition and Iraqi casualties, and one reason he halted the war after only 100 hours of fighting was to stop the slaughter on both sides—even at the price of not directly toppling Saddam's regime in Baghdad, despite having that possibility well within his grasp when he ordered the cease-fire.[36]

Colin Powell, then chairman of the Joint Chiefs of Staff, worried also about the downwind effects of targeting Iraqi biological warfare laboratories and facilities. He feared for civilians and coalition military personnel operating downwind, yet he felt that these sites still needed to be neutralized in the air campaign, if possible. Powell was even more concerned about the effects of possible biological weapons attacks on allied troops than he was about those of chemical attacks.[37]

And who can say if the Iraqi military had been able to fight a much more protracted war that the Bush administration might not have called a cease-fire and settled on a compromise peace as the US casualty toll reached Saddam's estimate of 5,000 dead Americans? Note that in the present war in Iraq, in mid-2009, US casualties have yet to reach 5,000 killed, but the United States is withdrawing without having completely defeated the Iraqi insurgency, as the cost of continuing indefinitely is perceived as unacceptable.[38]

Once the shock and awe of the coalition combined arms attack sent the Iraqi forces into precipitate retreat, there was little to stand between the United States–led forces and Baghdad. However, President Bush was deterred from going beyond the Kuwait borders with Iraq for several reasons.

1. The United States did not want Iraq to dissolve, but rather wanted it to serve as a balancer to Iranian power in the region.

2. President Bush wished to stay within the limits of the UN mandate given him and feared he would lose the unity of

the coalition if he widened the war beyond such legal limits. UN resolutions limited coalition actions to expelling Iraq from Kuwait.

3. The United States did not want the war to be perceived as a war of conquest for oil.

4. Pres. George H.W. Bush did not want to incur the costs of occupying, pacifying, and rebuilding Iraq.

5. President Bush wished to limit the economic and human costs of the war, not only to the coalition but to Iraq as well. He believed that entering Iraq would increase the will of the Iraqi Army to fight, since they would be defending the homeland rather than Kuwait. President Bush and his advisers also felt that they did not want to get into an urban house-to-house war, or a chemical or biological weapons war, with increased US casualties.

6. The US leaders did not expect Saddam Hussein to stay in power once the dimensions of his defeat were felt in his country. Carrying the war into Iraq might have made him a national hero in Iraq, rather than a defeated adventurer. As James Baker wrote in his memoirs, "Strategically, the real objective was to eject Iraq from Kuwait in a manner that would destroy Saddam's offensive military capabilities and make his fall from power likely."[39]

7. US leaders wanted to prevent Israel from intervening in the conflict and thereby undermining the Arab ally participation in the war. Also, had Saddam ordered chemical and/or biological attacks on Israel as the war continued, the Israeli leadership might have responded with a nuclear attack on Baghdad. What might have occurred after such an exchange would have been uncertain, but it was not a problem the Bush administration wished to risk.

8. An invasion of Iraq might have backfired politically in the United States and triggered major political opposition to the president. Halting at the border left the United States and the Bush administration with ultra-high approval ratings.

US Deterrence of Iraqi Chemical
and Biological Weapons Use

On the other hand, the United States and its coalition partners were trying to compel the retreat of Iraqi forces from Kuwait short of war from August 1990 until January 1991. Failing to deter war, President Bush, at least, was intent on deterring Saddam Hussein from ordering chemical and biological attacks on coalition forces and from burning the Kuwaiti oil fields. He warned the Iraqi dictator in clear and forceful terms that this would be a catastrophic step if enacted.

Note that the 5 January 1991 letter addressed to Saddam Hussein that President Bush wrote and had Secretary of State James Baker deliver to the Iraqi government via the Iraqi foreign minister, Tariq Aziz, in mid-January 1991, "Let me state, too that the United States will not tolerate the use of chemical or biological weapons or the destruction of Kuwait's oil fields and installations. Further, you will be held directly responsible for terrorist actions against any member of the coalition. The American people would demand the strongest possible response. You and your country will pay a terrible price if you order unconscionable acts of this sort."[40]

To augment Bush's warning, Baker restated to Iraqi foreign minister Aziz the consequences for Iraq if they were not to leave Kuwait:

> Our objective is for you to leave Kuwait. That's the only solution we will accept. And if you do not do that, then we'll find ourselves at war, and if you do go to war with the coalition, you will surely lose. This will not be a war of attrition like you fought with Iran. It will be fought with the means and weapons that play to our strengths, not to yours. We have the means to define how the battle will be fought, and yours do not.

> This is not to threaten but to inform. You may choose to reject it, or not to believe what we say, but we have the responsibility to tell you that we have tremendous technological advantages in forces, and our view is that if conflict comes, your forces will face devastatingly superior firepower. In our view—and you may reject this and disagree—our forces will really destroy your ability to command your own forces.

> We owe it to you to tell you there will be no stalemate, no UN cease-fire or breathing space for negotiations. If conflict begins, it will be decisive. This will not be another Vietnam. Should war begin, God forbid, it will be fought to a swift, decisive conclusion.

> If the conflict involves your use of chemical or biological weapons against our forces, the American people will demand vengeance. We have the means to exact it. With regard to this part of my presentation, this is not a threat, it is a promise. If there is any use of weapons like that, an objective won't just be the liberation of Kuwait, but the liberation of the current Iraqi regime and anyone responsible for using those weapons will be held accountable.[41]

To reinforce the idea that WMD might be met with WMD, Secretary of Defense Dick Cheney also stated publicly that "were Saddam Hussein foolish enough to use weapons of mass destruction, the US response would be absolutely overwhelming and it would be devastating."[42]

In cases like the Gulf War, there are certain possible advantages in dealing with an enemy leader like Saddam Hussein, who has seldom hesitated to use maximum violence to achieve his aims and solve his problems. Such a leader, in his own mind, may project his own ruthlessness upon his opponent, in this case the president of the United States.

If a Saddam-type killer would not hesitate to use all his available weapons against a previous foe, he might expect a stronger adversary to do the same against him if he escalated to WMD use against it.[43] In such cases the ruthlessness of a rogue chief might become the ally of US ability to deter his chemical or biological weapons employment against the United States or its allies.

Since Saddam Hussein did not use chemical or biological weapons in the subsequent fighting in Kuwait, despite the fact that he had previously shown no hesitation about using them against Iran in their eight-year war or against his own Kurdish populations when they opposed him, it might fairly be concluded that US threats deterred his chemical and biological use. Of course, with deterrence one can never prove one hundred percent that it worked. Saddam might not have wanted to use them for other reasons.[44] The US threat of retaliation did not stop him from setting fire to Kuwait's oil fields as his forces evacuated that country. That US deterrent message obviously did not work.

In 1998, seven years after Operation Desert Storm, ex-president George H. W. Bush and his former national security adviser, Brent Scowcroft, published a memoir of their times in power

179

titled, *A World Transformed*. Although Saddam Hussein was still in power in Iraq at the time of the memoir and was still considered a threat to United States and its regional allies, Scowcroft nevertheless wrote that the Bush administration had only been bluffing about using nuclear weapons should Saddam Hussein order the Iraqi army to use chemical or biological weapons. Indeed, Scowcroft wrote that "no one advanced the notion of using nuclear weapons, and the President rejected it even in retaliation for chemical and biological attacks. We deliberately avoided spoken or unspoken threats to use them on the grounds that it is bad practice to threaten something you have no intention of carrying out. Publicly, we left the matter ambiguous. There was no point in undermining the deterrence it might be offering."[45]

James Baker's memoir tells the same story:

> The President had decided, at Camp David in December that the best deterrent of the use of weapons of mass destruction by Iraq would be a threat to go after the Ba'ath regime itself. He had also decided that US forces would not retaliate with chemical or nuclear weapons if the Iraqis attacked with chemical munitions, there was obviously no reason to inform the Iraqis of this. In hopes of persuading them to consider more soberly the folly of war, I purposely left the impression that the use of chemical or biological agents by Iraq could invite tactical nuclear retaliations.[46]

Saddam might have believed this threat simply because he was not a person given to moral limits and had previously always used all weapons at his command. Witness the merciless Iraqi chemical attacks during the Iran-Iraq War against both military and civilian personnel. He might have viewed President Bush as like himself—willing to use everything for victory.[47]

However, it could not have helped subsequent deterrence efforts to publicize that the United States had been bluffing and never seriously considered using its nuclear advantages in the 1990–1991 Gulf War. After all, when the various memoirs of Bush, Scowcroft, Baker, and Powell were being published, Saddam Hussein was still in power in Iraq and might have needed to be deterred from future adventures by succeeding US presidents. Also, it should be noted that other adversary leaders in other states like North Korea, Syria, and Iran can also read, and, as a result, might conclude in future crises that they, too, were relatively safe from any US nuclear retaliations.

In any case, it is not clear that Saddam Hussein believed his biological weapons in particular would be effective, because it later became clear, in the mid-1990s, that Iraq had not made great progress at the time of the 1990–1991 gulf campaign in mating their experimental biological weapons program to an effective delivery system. However, chemical weapons were another thing entirely. His regime had manufactured tens of thousands of chemical weapons and had used them to deadly and strategic effect against Iran. As the CIA later concluded, "In Saddam's view, WMD helped save the regime multiple times. He believed that during the Iran-Iraq War chemical weapons had halted Iranian ground offensives and that ballistic missile attacks on Tehran had broken its political will. Similarly during Desert Storm, Saddam believed WMD had deterred Coalition Forces from pressing their attack beyond the goal of freeing Kuwait."[48]

Indeed, Iraq's military had the most experience delivering chemical weapons in actual battle conditions of any other military in the world at the time of the 1990–1991 Gulf War. On the other hand, it is not clear that Saddam and his commanders believed his forces were superior to US forces on a toxic battlefield where US forces, unlike most of his Iraqi military, were well trained and relatively better equipped than the Iraqi forces to fight in a chemical environment. US and NATO preparations against the possible onslaught of the Warsaw Pact chemical threat had equipped US forces to fight better than the Iraq Army in this realm. Thus, it might have been that US forces' passive defenses played a major part in Iraq's decision not to use chemical arms, perhaps as great a role as President Bush's implied nuclear threat. At any rate, it is likely that the combination of the implied US nuclear retaliatory threat, the superiority of US training, and better protective gear against chemical effects combined to keep the Iraqi chemical weapons out of play.

Iraqi Chemical and Biological Capability Deterrent to US Nuclear Weapons?

What confidence did Saddam Hussein have that the United States would not use its superiority in nuclear arms to destroy

181

his army in Kuwait? First, the Iraqi dictator hoped to deter President Bush and other coalition leaders from attacking because he believed that the Iraqi military, at the time the fourth largest in the world in terms of numbers in uniform, could inflict substantial casualties on what he perceived as a casualty-adverse opponent.

Second, even President Bush's direct warning letter communicated to Saddam Hussein via Secretary Baker in a meeting with Tariq Aziz on 5 January 1991 could be read that the United States would not use its nuclear superiority so long as Iraqi chemical and biological weapons were not used (see appendix B). Thus, there is the question of who was deterring whom? Was George Bush deterring Saddam Hussein's use of chemical and biological weapons? Or was he also indicating that Iraqi chemical and biological warfare capabilities would deter the US use of nuclear weapons on Iraq?[49]

Saddam Hussein put out warnings that Iraqi chemical and biological weapons would be used in the contingency of a US or UK use of nuclear arms. For example, in a meeting with former British prime minister Edward Heath in October 1990, Saddam said, "If the going gets hard then the British and Americans will use atomic weapons against me, and the chances are that Israel will as well, and the only thing I've got are chemical and biological weapons, and I shall have to use them. I have no alternative."[50] President Bush also was under no illusions on this, as he had noted on more than one occasion that Saddam "has never possessed a weapon he did not use."[51]

Saddam possibly felt his biological and chemical weapons were his ace in the hole. Saddam's poison gases had played a key role in holding the stronger Iranian military at bay and had brought the Iranians to the peace table. According to one Middle East analyst, "Saddam took the experience of the war with Iran, in which gas eventually caused the Iranian military to lose its most potent weapon—its will to fight—to mean that Iraq possessed an absolute weapon capable of stopping modernized armies as well."[52]

US leadership had serious concerns about such chemical and biological weapons use or the president would not have made it a central issue in his warning letter to Saddam Hussein. Further, the combatant commander, General Schwarzkopf, was especially concerned that the Iraqi Army might ruin the left hook flanking movement by his ground forces with a devastating chemical barrage. Gen Colin Powell, then chairman of the Joint Chiefs of Staff, was particularly focused on the potential casualties that might come from an Iraqi biological warfare strike.

James Baker also admitted that the casualties that might flow from urban warfare and from Iraqis who would fight harder to protect their homeland would cause many more American deaths. Thus, it is plausible that the chemical and biological threats and anything that had the potential to greatly escalate US casualties impacted US thinking and helped serve as an Iraqi deterrent to an invasion of Iraq.[53] Therefore, it is possible that Saddam's WMD threat, in the form of chemical and biological weapons, might have been responsible for saving his regime.

US and Israeli Failure to Deter Iraq from attacking Israel

The coalition air campaign began on 17 January 1991. The next day, Saddam Hussein ordered the first of 48 Scud missile attacks on Israel and the first of 41 such attacks against the coalition forces in Saudi Arabia. Apparently, the threat of possible Israeli nuclear retaliation did not deter such a decision. This was risky, for clearly Israel had enough nuclear firepower to utterly destroy Iraq. Saddam was playing a dangerous game.

On the other hand, Saddam was attempting to split the coalition by attacking Israel. Would the coalition's Arab allies fight on the same side as Israel against another Arab state? This was considered highly unlikely in Washington, DC.[54] For this reason, US leaders were concerned that an Israeli counterattack would undermine the support of the Arab partners in the US coalition against Iraq.

Thus, US leaders rushed Patriot theater missile defenses to help defend Israel from Iraqi missiles and devoted over 2,000 air sorties against the Iraqi Scud missile launchers to suppress them and prevent Israel from getting into the conflict. Ultimately, the swift and decisive air-land-sea war unleashed by the coalition made short work of the Iraqi military forces, and the combination of theater missile defenses and US diplomacy all helped dissuade Israel from participating with its armed forces.

Conclusions and Lessons Learned

Lesson 1: What deterred the Soviet Union in the Cold War will not apply to all cases.

Deterrence is a rational strategy and theory of how to prevent war or escalation of a war. However, the evidence of history is that deterrence often fails. Deterrence is inexact, an art not a science. What works perfectly in one case may fail wholly in another. Indeed, it is the weaker party that attacks the stronger party in about one of every five wars. So deterrence is not a given even when your government or coalition has overwhelming military superiority over an opposing state.

The Cold War strategy that the West adopted to deter a Soviet nuclear or conventional attack seems to have worked, although one can never be absolutely sure what kept the peace. Was it because the West had a retaliatory capability to destroy the Union of Soviet Socialist Republics (USSR) and Warsaw Pact? Was it because in crises, Soviet leaders believed US leaders had the will to use their nuclear weapons if necessary? Was it because the United States and its allies had a second-strike force, one not vulnerable to a surprise disarming attack? Or was it because the West faced rational leaders in Moscow who understood the logic of mutual-assured destruction? Or were we simply lucky? Would war have occurred if all these factors had not been put in place? Or would both sides have maintained the peace anyway? And how much retaliatory force was enough to deter a war with the USSR? Did we need thousands of nuclear weapons or just a few? How much was enough to deter war and the escalation of crises?[55] We can never know for sure. We are only certain that we did not have a central nuclear war with the Soviet Union and its Warsaw Pact and other allies.

One thing that is clear from the Gulf War example is that despite all the destructive power in the US, United Kingdom, and French nuclear arsenals, and for all the coalition's conventional

184

might, they could not deter Saddam Hussein from seizing Kuwait, and they could not compel him to withdraw his forces without first resorting to war. One reason for this is that the United States and other coalition forces did not develop a firm response to Iraq prior to Saddam's decision to invade Kuwait. Had the United States delivered a strong warning and deployed forces to back this up before Saddam's final decision to invade Kuwait, he might have been deterred. The tardiness of the deterrence signals ruined the chances for success.

This strategy calls into question whether the Cold War calculus of what it takes to deter a conflict was working in the Gulf War. Apparently, the possession of nuclear weapons by his opponents did not deter Saddam Hussein, compel him to leave Kuwait, or end the conflict until his forces were routed in Kuwait. He was willing to strike US, United Kingdom, French, and Israeli targets, risking possible nuclear annihilation. He was willing to fight a coalition of 34 states in Kuwait rather than withdraw peacefully.

Lesson 2: States that possess WMD or other extra-ordinary military power may feel they can afford to start a conflict and keep it within tolerable levels of escalation so they can achieve their aims.

Perhaps Saddam Hussein believed that the threat of his chemical and biological (CB) weapons would deter nuclear use by the coalition forces, and perhaps he even believed that, under his chemical and biological deterrent umbrella, his forces in Kuwait were formidable enough to deter a coalition attack or to prevent a complete and utter defeat.

Saddam Hussein may have relied on his CB capability first to deter any coalition attack on his forces in Kuwait. This failed on 17 January 1991, when the coalition air attack began. Second, he may have relied on his CB threat to prevent the US, United Kingdom, French, and Israeli nuclear attacks. There is no evidence that such weapons use had ever been seriously considered by any of the four states. Indeed, memoirs of US decision makers—Bush, Scowcroft, Baker, and Powell—indicate this was never seriously considered, although Secretary of

185

Defense Cheney asked the Joint Chiefs to look into the utility of nuclear strikes if the president changed his mind later.

Finally, Saddam Hussein may have assumed that his CB arsenal would have made it costly for the coalition to march to Baghdad, occupy Iraqi territory, and replace his regime. He might have been tempted to use such weapons and risk further coalition escalation to nuclear weapons as his situation became more and more desperate. Even if he resisted the impulse to use CB weapons as the invasion of Iraq began, it is likely that if it became clear to him that his regime was about to fall, the CB gloves would have come off, and the coalition might have been struck with a last-minute chemical and biological revenge strike.[56] Saddam Hussein probably realized that coalition leaders would also understand the perils from Iraq's CB weapons of trying to achieve a total defeat of his regime. It is likely he is correct that this possibility weighed heavily in the US and coalition decision not to press for a total defeat of his forces and regime in Iraq.

Lesson 3: Saddam felt he was willing to sustain deeper casualties than the United States and this would give him a political if not a military victory. States willing to suffer more than their opponents may count on their adversary halting the war effort when causalities reach a certain painful threshold that tempers their war aims.

It appears that Saddam was willing to gamble that the United States was so casualty averse that we would halt our military operations after suffering the first 5,000 deaths from the clash with Iraq. Of course, he was badly mistaken in how his forces matched up with the coalition. Since his forces were able to kill only about 200 US fighters in the battles that ensued, not 5,000, his theory of deterrence of US and coalition escalation, estimated at a threshold of 5,000 killed in action, was never tested.

It should be noted that President Bush and his field commander, General Schwarzkopf, were preparing for possible heavy coalition causalities. Note that the United States and the coalition had transported 63 mobile field hospitals to the region before launching Operation Desert Storm, as well as two hospital ships and 18,000 hospital beds.[57]

On the other hand, while Saddam Hussein thought the US leaders were averse to suffering casualties; nevertheless, he still underestimated President Bush's regard for human life—Iraqi lives as well as those of Americans and the rest of the coalition. Indeed, unlike Bush, it may never have occurred to Saddam Hussein to limit his military actions to prevent enemy combatant deaths as well as those of his own forces.

Lesson 4: If the rival leadership does not understand when it faces extreme military disadvantages, deterrence of the weaker by the stronger side is more likely to fail. Situational awareness and rationality must be joined together in the rival leadership for the deterrent effect to work.

If the Cold War deterrence requirement of having a situationally aware and rational opponent was not met fully in the Gulf War, Saddam Hussein may have been logical in his thinking but ignorant of important facts. He was not situationally aware of the magnitude of military forces arrayed against him, nor was he cognizant of much of the movement on the battlefield due to faulty intelligence. For example, he did not have satellites for intelligence, surveillance, and reconnaissance of the coalition forces, and much of the Iraqi air force had fled by the time the coalition ground forces attacked. Saddam never detected the left hook flanking attack that General Schwarzkopf put into motion at the beginning of the land battle.

Lesson 5: Dictators who kill the messenger seldom get good intelligence and are far less effective in countering adverse possibilities.

Saddam Hussein had a decision style that produced yes men only, robbing him of much important information on which to base his decisions. To disagree with him was literally to risk your life, if you were in his circle. His extreme brutality gave him unrivaled power. It also gave him information that conformed only to what his advisers thought he wanted to hear. Saddam did not welcome negative news or views and thus became the prisoner of his own perceptions of reality. He rarely had those views challenged or supported by facts or interpretations that went counter to his preconceptions such as (1) the United States would not respond to an attack on Kuwait, (2) the coalition would not attack him in Kuwait because he had chemical and biological weapons, (3) the Iraqi force could hold its own with that of the coalition, or (4) his forces could at least inflict 5,000 US casualties and save him from absolute defeat.

Lesson 6: Many variables go into whether deterrence will work: time, place, culture, politics, leadership, and the personalities that make the decisions. The greater the divergence between the personalities, worldviews of the adversary leaders, and the leadership stakes in the outcome, the greater the chances for deterrence to fail.

In the 1990–1991 Gulf War, there were two kinds of deterrence to consider: (1) deterrence of the Iraqi invasion of Kuwait and (2) deterrence of an escalation of that war once it had begun. This was a war with many players, but it is fair to begin with the two key players in this drama, Pres. Saddam Hussein and Pres. George H. W. Bush. On the Iraqi side, the unquestioned chief decision maker was Saddam Hussein. Saddam was Iraq, and Iraq was Saddam in this case. He was the unrivaled Iraqi decision maker in foreign and defense policy.[58]

Things were a bit more complicated on the US and coalition side. Pres. George H. W. Bush was the ultimate decision maker.[59] The United States was the key state in the formation of the coalition, since it was and is the world's most powerful military superpower. However, others like United Kingdom prime minister Margaret Thatcher were influential in collaborating with US leadership. Mrs. Thatcher was considered particularly instrumental in advising President Bush to take an uncompromising policy requiring Iraq to abandon Kuwait or face war. The instruments of power were provided by all the coalition members as they mobilized for war, sent their armed forces to Saudi Arabia, and participated in Operation Desert Storm that succeeded brilliantly in routing the Iraqi army in Kuwait.

The frequent insensitivity of enemies to each other's stakes and signals and the all-too-often misperceptions they have of each other's aims and motives are at the core of why deterrence theory so often fails to explain interstate behavior in conflict situations.

188

Lesson 7: Deterrence fails frequently, and what works in one case will fail in another. Governments run largely by a single dominant individual are rare, and thus deterring Saddam Hussein and Iraq will be different from most cases where power is shared. Lessons learned from this case study should be applied cautiously to other cases.

One must also be careful in drawing deterrence lessons from a particular case. In the 1990–1991 Gulf War, Saddam Hussein ruled Iraq with an iron fist and did not have to negotiate with others in forming his decisions. Thus, Iraq was a unitary actor. This will not always be the case. In most states, power and decisions are shared by a group at the top. Power is often dispersed. Deterrence becomes a group affair. One must persuade a group of decision makers and power holders before deterrence can succeed. Thus, on the Iraqi side at least, this is a special case where one man, Saddam Hussein, could speak for the entire country, and his will became Iraq's path.

On the opposing side, although he was by far the most influential decision maker on his side of the conflict, President Bush could not have acted nearly as freely as Saddam Hussein did in Iraq. Bush and his able team first had to mobilize a diverse coalition of 34 allied states, secure the backing of the US Congress, seek the support of the United Nations, and influence US public opinion prior to kicking off the January 1991 counterattack against Iraq. Even so, once such efforts to mobilize support had succeeded, it took additional time to deploy and equip a sufficient military force in the region to repel the Iraqi invaders from Kuwait. Nearly six months elapsed before the coalition was ready to go to war to reclaim Kuwait.

In other cases where a government is attempting to deter a war or launch one, the power to make such decisions may be shared, and policy may be a product of multiple factors that combine to take the decision or policy in a certain direction. This becomes even more complicated the more power is shared on both sides. Thus, the 1990–1991 Gulf War may be a special case, and one must be careful about drawing general conclusions about deterrence from it.

Lesson 8: When dealing with an adversary bent on achieving a fait accompli, quick reaction time is absolutely required. Be alert and ready to act at the outset or fail to deter leaders like Saddam Hussein. When still considering the opening move, a rival leadership can be more easily turned away from an act of aggression. After a decision has been made and a plan set in motion, deterrence can be far more difficult or impossible.

Timing of the US and coalition deterrence campaign was too late against Saddam to prevent Iraq's invasion of Kuwait. Right from the start, the US leadership needed to use unambiguous language with a violence-prone leader like Saddam Hussein. All he respected was superior force and will. Anything less was not going to keep him from seizing his prize, particularly since it represented, in his mind, the path to financial solvency and subsequent physical security. It would be wise for the United States and other allies to first inventory their absolute vital interests, including things like preventing the Middle East's oil reserves from falling under the control of a hostile dictator whose interests were opposed to peace and security in the region and whose grip on world energy supplies could not be trusted. After that, a continuous defense and deterrence policy and posture would be needed in the region to keep these vital interests secure.

Where these types of leaders and regimes are positioned to adversely impact US and allied vital interests, particular high-level attention needs to be paid to them. When such a potential challenger is positioned to threaten a vital interest or vital ally, contingency plans need to be preformulated for deterring them from any power grabs or hostile interventions. These plans need to have forces attached to them so that once a crisis begins, these forces can be rapidly mobilized and sent to the region to signal the seriousness of US and allied intentions and to undergird the tough talk and warnings that US and allied leaders must be prepared to give potential aggressors.

Beyond that, it would be wise to profile and pay extra close attention to all foreign leaders like Saddam Hussein who have a track record of violence and aggression and who have shown repeated lawless behavior against domestic rivals and their international neighbors. Interdisciplinary teams of profilers who have read every word and observed every action of that aggressive leadership should help inform US decision makers about the motives, situation, and operational codes of these potential troublemakers. Such teams of profilers should stay with the observation of these particular leaders over years and decades rather than be rotated into other assignments and succeeded by uninformed and inexperienced intelligence officers. Moreover, it would be wise to have at least two parallel teams of profilers to compete in their assessments and provide decision makers with alternative evaluations. It would also be useful if representatives of these competitive Red Team groups would give their interpretations of likely next moves and motives of that particular rival leader or leadership team.

Lesson 9: Beware of the enemy whose modus operandi is to preemptively attack and who has a track record of extreme violence and risk taking.

Saddam Hussein believed in careful plotting and swift and violent preemptive moves against his domestic and foreign foes. He came from a background that made him see enemies everywhere, and he may have been seen as, or even actually been, paranoid. However, as the saying goes, just because he was paranoid does not mean people were not out to get him, especially after he had killed his way to the top of the Iraqi political system. He had actually made so many thousands of enemies by that time that it was probably completely rational to act like a paranoid ruler. First, he had killed the enemies of the Ba'ath Party in Iraq and anyone who stood in their way to power.[60] After that was secure, he killed anyone who he thought might become a rival, even if that was not yet the case. He killed anyone who was growing in popularity like some of the more successful Iraqi generals who fought well in the Iran-Iraq War.

He killed to maintain Sunni power over the majority Shia sect in Iraq. He killed Kurdish leaders who represented an independent power source. Once at the pinnacle of power after 1978, he launched wars against his neighbors in Iran[61] and Kuwait and sent his forces to the doorstep of Saudi Arabia. Tens of thousands of Iraqis, Iranians, and Kuwaitis therefore died as a result of his aggressions.

191

Hussein constantly analyzed who might possibly become his rivals inside Iraq and planned brutal elimination campaigns to remove them by lethal means. In the summer of 1979, Saddam admitted to a colleague that "I know that there are scores of people plotting to kill me, and this is not difficult to understand. After all, did we not seize power by plotting against our predecessors? However, I am far cleverer than they are. I know they are conspiring to kill me long before they actually start planning to do it. This enables me to do it before they have the faintest chance of striking at me."[62]

Saddam's violent and ceaseless domestic purges follow the pattern of the terror campaigns of Stalin's rule in the Soviet Union. Stalin's bloody methods deeply impressed him. Saddam's endless warring foreign policy also reminds one of Adolph Hitler's ceaseless wars against all neighbors and all other ethnic groups.

Saddam Hussein never felt secure, and his prophylactic arrests and executions no doubt kept him in power longer than previous Iraqi leaders who were all removed by coups. Indeed, the five previous rulers of Iraq all lost power in this way. Hussein also felt that the Islamic Republic of Iran posed a potential lethal threat to his rule. Not only were they hostile, they were Shiite Muslims like nearly 60 percent of his Iraqi countrymen. Their revolution had targeted him. He felt he had to preemptively destroy them or see his regime destroyed by them; hence, he decided to attack Iran in 1979 while they were still getting organized. Like his domestic purges, he struck before his enemies realized his lethal intent.

Lesson 10: Understand the situation and perspective of adversary leaders to anticipate when and where they might decide to initiate hostilities. Plan to deter and counter them with contingency plans and quick reaction forces in anticipation of such contingencies.

After the Iran-Iraq war ended in a cease-fire in 1988, Saddam was desperate to rebuild his armed forces and security forces before Iran regrouped and attacked again. Iran had come dangerously close to defeating him in the previous conflict and was a country with three times the population of Iraq and four times the land area. Yet his forces were spent, and because of his adventures, he was out of credit and deeply in debt. This led him to attack Kuwait to recoup his fortunes and prepare for what he feared was the inevitable Iranian resumption of the war. The Bush administration in 1990 did not have its focus on the Iraq-Kuwait dispute, nor did it appreciate Saddam Hussein's dilemma and his modus operandi enough to anticipate his attack and occupation of Kuwait. Bush and his advisers were surprised and unprepared for the event, although the threat could have been anticipated with better intelligence and forethought.

Lesson 11: Understand what motivates the adversary leadership in terms of retention of its personal power and survival to predict your chances of success or failure in attempting to deter further acts of war or escalation. Put yourselves in the adversary's shoes. See the world from his perspective when planning to counter them.

Saddam Hussein may have felt that a retreat from Kuwait would have weakened him in the eyes of the Iraqi military and people and made him more vulnerable to being overthrown. Already he was in a weakened position. He had just concluded a disastrous eight-year war with Iran that cost hundreds of thousands of lives and billions of dollars. He may have reasoned that this, coupled with the forced humiliating retreat from Kuwait, might have given strong encouragement to his domestic and international rivals to try to remove him from power. Better, he might have thought, to take on a foreign force and rally the Iraqi people once more behind his rule against an external enemy than to slink back to Iraq in defeat without putting up a fight. That posture could get him deposed and killed.

Saddam likely reasoned that it was better to fight in Kuwait, try to get a compromise peace, keep some of the fruits of his invasion, and stay in power and stay alive. Thus, Saddam appears to have concluded that what was best for him personally was to put his people and his military through yet another war, however painful. He was willing to lose thousands more Iraqis to preserve his own regime and his own life. Thus, Saddam was not to be compelled to leave Kuwait without a fight.

Lesson 12: While it certainly helps if you are trying to deter a rational opponent rather than an irrational one, rational leaders without a situational awareness can still fail to understand the likely consequences of their actions and may fail to be deterred.

Deterrence can be especially difficult when the opponent is severely lacking in situational awareness. Saddam Hussein was unfamiliar with the United States and its leadership. He had only a weak grasp of our political system. Moreover, he was an untutored military leader who appears not to have grasped the power and capability of the United States and coalition forces arrayed against him once they were mobilized and deployed to the region. Saddam did not trust his own military. He launched the invasion of Iran division by division through personal calls to his commanders because he did not trust them to coordinate operations in a joint fashion. Allowing them to meet and plan operations jointly might have also given them an opportunity to conspire against him. As a result of his separating commands and forcing them to communicate only through him, when that eight-year war began, there were several days before some of his military leaders were even informed that they were at war with Iran.[63]

Gen Chuck Horner, the joint forces air commander during Operation Desert Storm, observed that it was probably not the wisest coalition strategy to try to target Saddam Hussein during the war. He noted that "killing Saddam may have turned out to be a serious mistake. . . . In his paranoia; Saddam often had his top generals executed. The threat of execution sometimes concentrates the mind, but more often, it leads to paralysis. This weakening of his military leadership could only benefit the coalition. And finally, as General Schwarzkopf pointed out after the war, Saddam was a lousy strategist, and thus a good man to have in charge of Iraqi armed forces, under the circumstances."[64]

In retrospect, it is difficult to imagine how Saddam Hussein expected to fight a war effectively against the coalition when his air forces were cleaned from the skies; when his armor and artillery were out-ranged; when he did not have any air and space intelligence, surveillance, or reconnaissance capabilities;

when his forces were poorly trained; and when he lacked adequate command and control of his own forces. He did not appreciate the caliber of US and allied forces he was facing and assumed his large army could inflict thousands of casualties on the coalition, This, he planned, would win him a compromise peace and the chance to survive and fight another day after the immediate conflict had ended. He was lucky to have survived and did not do so because his forces executed his plan or because his strategy worked.

Saddam Hussein's leadership and lack of situational awareness led the Iraqi military into a catastrophic defeat. According to one summary of the war,

> Iraqi military casualties, killed or wounded, totaled an estimated 25,000 to 65,000 and the United Nations destroyed some 3,200 Iraqi tanks, over 900 other armored vehicles, and over 2,000 artillery weapons. Some 86,000 Iraqi soldiers surrendered. In contrast, the UN forces suffered combat losses of some 200 from hostile fire, plus losses of 4 tanks, 9 other armored vehicles, and 1 artillery weapon. . . . Although coalition aircraft flew a total of 109,876 sorties, the allies lost only 38 aircraft versus over 300 for Iraq. . . . The terms of the cease-fire were designed to enable UN inspectors to destroy most of Iraq's remaining missiles, chemical weapons and nuclear weapons facilities.[65]

Lesson 13: Beware of situations where a potential adversary sees great immediate and easy gains to be achieved by taking military action and where his risks are seen as remote, abstract, and distant. It will be important to try to reverse these perceptions of limited and distant risk, and to do so emphatically early in a crisis situation, to improve the chances for deterrence to work.

Saddam Hussein saw an immediate prize in Kuwait where he could add 8 percent of the world's oil supply to his resources, find a way out of his massive debt situation, gain the purchasing power to re-equip his armed forces, protect his regime and his life, and fund future extensions of his power and influence. He got a mild disclaimer from the United States that it had no particular interest in the outcome of his dispute with Kuwait over the Rumailia oil fields. There appeared to be no immediate strong opposition to his unspoken aspiration to add Kuwait to his realm. This could have been foreseen if the United States and other interested regional powers had been more alert and perceived the danger sooner. In mid-1990 a violent and ambitious Saddam Hussein was considering seizing a rich trophy, one that could be had for the taking, without any immediate or significant costs.

Richard Ned Lebow and Janet Gross Stein have examined over 20 cases of deterrence failures and believe that their studies "support the conclusion that policy makers who risk or actually start wars pay more attention to their own strategic and domestic political interests than they do to the interests and military capabilities of their adversaries."[66] Indeed, such aggressors "may discount an adversary's resolve even when the state in question has gone to considerable lengths to demonstrate that resolve and to develop the military capabilities needed to defend its commitment."[67] Thus, a government can do everything right to deter an adversary and still fail because the rival does not estimate the outcome the same way.

Lesson 14: Until a sizeable deterrent force can be sent to a region of potential conflict, it is a useful stopgap to send a trip-wire force to signal US intent to fight any attempt at aggression from the beginning.

Such a US trip-wire force was sent early to Saudi Arabia in the fall of 1990 to show Saddam Hussein that an attack on Saudi Arabia would spill US blood and draw the United States into a conflict with Iraq. This action may have saved Saudi Arabia from an invasion in the period between the August 1990 invasion and occupation of Kuwait, the initiation of the coalition air war in January 1991, and the ground war in February 1991. Like US Army forces stationed in Berlin, Germany, during the Cold War, these trip-wire forces would not have been able to stop the enemy forces from seizing that territory immediately, but it would have been a down payment on a future US military escalation and counterattack. Being drawn into a war with the world's military superpower should serve as a considerable reason for rethinking an aggressive move.

Lesson 15: In cases where both sides possess some form of mass casualty weapons, deterrence can work in both directions. Both can be deterred from use of the chemical, biological, radiological, or nuclear (CBRN) weapons by the threat of the other. On the other hand, both may still feel free to prosecute an extensive conventional war, feeling secure that their CBRN deterrent will shield them from a similar enemy attack.

Saddam Hussein attacked the forces of the coalition that included three nuclear weapons states: the United States, United Kingdom, and France. Moreover, he ordered his force to launch ballistic missile attacks against Israel, reputed to be another nuclear weapons state. This probably would not have happened if Saddam Hussein had not possessed chemical or biological weapons to deter possible nuclear responses.

Further, it is reasonable to assume that Iraq's possession of chemical and biological weapons may have been one of several factors that persuaded President Bush and other coalition members not to follow up their rout of Iraqi forces in Kuwait with a march all the way to Baghdad. The US military and political leaders were fully aware of the potential harm that might have come to US and coalition personnel from a massive chemical or biological attack by Iraq. Indeed, it is possible that massive medical problems were simply generated by allied bombing of chemical weapons storage and production facilities. Some 183,000 US military personnel were victims of symptoms referred to as the Gulf War syndrome in which more than a quarter of the US men and women sent to fight in the war were declared permanently disabled, and some speculate these casualties resulted from coalition air attacks on Iraqi chemical warfare (CW) facilities that caused downwind fallout and contamination.[68]

In summary, it is not possible to prove without doubt that deterrence works, since it is not feasible to prove war would have occurred in the absence of deterrence signals. On the other hand, it is clear when deterrence actions fail. War and conflict escalation are clear signals of a degree of deterrence failure. Even here, it is not possible to know how much further up the escalation ladder the conflict would have climbed if deterrent actions had been taken and signals had not been sent.

In the 1990–1991 Gulf War, no one successfully deterred the Iraqi invasion of Kuwait or successfully compelled the Iraqi Army to leave peacefully. US deterrent signals were too weak at the beginning and too late to stop Saddam Hussein. US tripwire forces sent too early to Saudi Arabia in the late summer and fall of 1990 possibly deterred Saddam Hussein from sending his army through Kuwait and into Saudi Arabia, although it is not clear whether he was willing to risk such a gamble had US reinforcements not been sent to assist the Saudi kingdom.

It seems likely that Saddam Hussein was deterred from using chemical and biological weapons in the stern warning communicated to the Iraqi leadership by President Bush and the nuclear forces at his command. Saddam could not be sure that the United States would not use nuclear weapons in response to a CB attack, especially if the United States and its allies suffered mass casualties from such attacks.

We now know that there was no serious consideration of employing US or allied nuclear weapons during the conflict. The Bush policy team felt that US nuclear superiority should deter Iraqi chemical and biological weapons use and that coalition conventional superiority was so pronounced as to make victory very likely.

Saddam Hussein was willing to let his forces and population bleed to whatever degree to inflict the level of losses that might make his opponents limit their war aims. Indeed, Saddam might have been correct. The potential threat of mass casualties may partly account for President Bush's decision to end the war 100 hours after the ground campaign had routed the Iraqi army in Kuwait. Saddam may have considered Bush's actions as an exercise in "snatching defeat from the jaws of victory," since he survived and retained power after the cease-fire took place.

The 5,000-death threshold that Saddam Hussein predicted would cause the coalition leaders to sue for peace talks never was reached, and his theory of deterrence was therefore untested. However, it appears that the coalition forces were prepared to suffer large losses to achieve their war aims, but since this threshold was never even approached, it is impossible to say when the allies would have considered discussing peace terms due to mounting casualties. The Iraqi dictator took risks far beyond what Soviet leaders were willing to risk in the Cold War when confronted with overwhelming US military power and a dedicated deterrent posture. The risk-taking and violent personality of the Iraqi leader, coupled with the mild deterrent signals that the US sent at the beginning of the Iraq-Kuwait confrontation, led Saddam Hussein to gamble on seizing an oil-rich treasure that could bail him out of the financial problems caused by the huge costs of the Iran-Iraq war. He sought to recoup his losses in Kuwait.

Thus, every crisis and conflict has different elements and players. Deterrence lessons from one case study may or may not apply to another. Deterrence is clearly an art and can fail despite the best practices of the state attempting it, since it takes two sides stepping to the same tune to have it work. Unfortunately, deterrence is a two-sided affair. Ultimately, it will work only if the potential aggressor concludes that the outcome will likely result in a price he is unwilling to risk. Those attempting to deter them can do everything possible to signal why a war would be too costly, but the ultimate decision is up to the Saddam Husseins of the world.

Appendix A

Desert Shield/Desert Storm Timeline[69]

August 1990

   2 Iraq invades Kuwait.

   6 US forces gain permission to base operations in Saudi Arabia.

   7 F-15s depart for Persian Gulf.

   7 USS *Independence* battle group arrives in south of Persian Gulf.

   8 First Tactical Fighter Wing and the 82d Airborne arrive in Persian Gulf.

November 1990

   8 United States sends an additional 200,000 troops.

  29 United Nations (UN) authorizes force against Iraq.

January 1991

   9 US secretary of state Baker delivers Bush warning letter to Saddam Hussein through Iraq foreign minister Aziz.

  12 Congress approves offensive use of US troops.

  15 UN withdrawal deadline passes.

  17 D-day: Coalition launches airborne assault.

  18 Iraq launches Scud missiles at Israel and Saudi Arabia.

  25 Air Force begins attacking Iraqi aircraft shelters.

  26 Iraqi aircraft begin fleeing to Iran.

  29 Battle of Khafji begins. Airpower destroys Iraqi force.

February 1991

  24 Ground war begins. Start of 100-hour battle.

  26 Fleeing Iraqi forces destroyed along "Highway of Death."

  28 Cease-fire becomes effective at 0800 Kuwait time.

Appendix B

A Warning Letter to Saddam Hussein from Pres. George H. W. Bush

Mr. President,

We stand today at the brink of war between Iraq and the world. This is a war that began with your invasion of Kuwait; this is a war that can be ended only by the Iraqi's full and unconditional compliance with U.N. Security Council Resolution 678.

I am writing you now, directly, because what is at stake demands that no opportunity be lost to avoid what would be a certain calamity for the people of Iraq. I am writing, as well, because it is said by some that you do not understand just how isolated Iraq is and what Iraq faces as a result. I am not in a position to judge whether this impression is correct: what I can do, though, is try in this letter to reinforce what Secretary of State Baker told your Foreign Minister and eliminate any uncertainty or ambiguity that might exist in your mind about where we stand and what we are prepared to do.

The international community is united in its call for Iraq to leave all of Kuwait without condition and without further delay. This is not simply the policy of the United States: it is the position of the world community as expressed in no less than twelve Security Council resolutions.

We prefer a peaceful outcome. However, anything less than full compliance with UN Security Council Resolution 678 and its predecessors are unacceptable. There can be no reward for aggression. Nor will there be any negotiation. Principle cannot be compromised. However, by its full compliance Iraq will gain the opportunity to rejoin the international community. More immediately, the Iraqi military establishment will escape destruction. But unless you withdraw from Kuwait completely and without condition, you will lose more than Kuwait. What is at issue here is not the future of Kuwait—it will be free, its government will be restored—but rather the future of Iraq. The choice is yours to make.

The United States will not be separated from its coalition partners. Twelve Security Council resolutions, 28 countries providing military units to enforce them, more than one hundred governments complying with sanctions—all highlight the fact that it is not Iraq against the United States but Iraq against the world. That most Arab and Muslim countries are arrayed against you as well should reinforce what I am saying. Iraq cannot and will not be able to hold on to Kuwait or exact a price for leaving.

You may be tempted to find solace in the diversity of opinion that is American democracy. You should resist any such temptation. Diversity ought not to be confused with division. Nor should you underestimate, as others have before you, America's will.

Iraq is already feeling the effects of the sanctions mandated by the United Nations. Should war come, it will be far greater tragedy for you and your country. Let me state, too, that the United States will not tolerate the use of chemical or biological weapons or the destruction of Kuwait's oil fields and installations. Further, you will be held directly responsible for terrorist actions against any member of the coalition. The American people would demand the strongest possible response. You and your country will pay a terrible price if you order unconscionable acts of this sort.

I write this letter not to threaten, but to inform. I do so with no sense of satisfaction, for the people of the United States have no quarrel with the people of Iraq. Mr. President, UN Security Council Resolution 678 establishes the period before January 15 of this year as a "pause of good will" so that this crisis may end without further violence. Whether this pause is used as intended, or merely becomes a prelude to further violence, is in your hands, and yours alone. I hope you weigh your choice carefully and choose wisely, for much will depend upon it.[70]

George Bush

Iraq launches missile strikes

If Iraq was to be forced to obey UN resolutions, the Iraqi government made it no secret that it would respond by attacking Israel. Before the war started, Tariq Aziz, Iraqi Foreign Minister and Deputy Prime Minister, was asked, "If war starts . . . will you attack Israel?" His response was, "Yes, absolutely, yes."[71] The Iraqis hoped that attacking Israel would draw it into the war. It was expected that this would then lead to the withdrawal of the US Arab allies, who would be reluctant to fight alongside Israel. Israel did not join the coalition, and all Arab states stayed in the coalition. The Scud missiles generally caused fairly light damage, although their potency was felt on 25 February when 28 US soldiers were killed when a Scud destroyed their barracks in Dhahran. The Scuds targeting Israel were ineffective due to the fact that increasing the range of the Scud resulted in a dramatic reduction in accuracy and payload. Nevertheless, the total of 39 missiles that landed on Israel caused extensive property damage and two direct deaths and caused the United States to deploy two Patriot missile battalions in Israel and the Netherlands to send one Patriot Squadron in an attempt to deflect the attacks. Allied air forces were also extensively exercised in "Scud hunts" in the Iraqi desert, trying to locate the camouflaged trucks before they fired their missiles at Israel or Saudi Arabia. Three Scud missiles, along with a coalition Patriot that malfunctioned, hit Ramat Gan in Israel on 22 January 1991, injuring 96 people, and indirectly causing the deaths of three elderly people who died of heart attacks. Israeli policy for the previous 40 years had always been retaliation, but at the urging of the United States and other commanders, the Israeli government decided that discretion was the better part of valour in this instance. After initial hits by Scud missiles, Israeli prime minister Yitzhak Shamir hesitantly refused any retaliating measures against Iraq, due to increasing pressure from the United States to remain out of the conflict.[72] The US government was concerned that any Israeli action would cost it allies and escalate the conflict, and an air strike by the IAF would have required overflying hostile Jordan or Syria, which could have provoked them to enter the war on Iraq's side or to attack Israel.[73]

Notes

1. Quoted in Admiral Mullen, "It's Time for a New Deterrence Model," 2.

2. See Wolf, *When the Weak Attack the Strong.*

3. Original source was Dupuy and Dupuy, *The Encyclopedia of Military History*, 910–11. See also Schneider, *Future War and Counterproliferation*, chapter 4.

4. See Wikipedia, Constitution and Founding Fathers, "What Ever Happened to the Founding Fathers?" This was their promise: "For the support of this declaration, with a firm reliance on the protection of the Divine Providence, we mutually pledge to each other, our lives, our fortunes and our sacred honor."

5. For another good discussion, see Lebow, "Conclusions," chapter 9.

6. Mutual assured destruction went by the acronym MAD. Dr. Warner Schilling later added another acronym for those who wanted to develop offensive nuclear options to disarm the other side with a counterforce strike in this heavily armed nuclear environment. He called this option capable of firing first if necessary (COFFIN).

7. Of course this still begs the question of how much US and allied nuclear capability was enough to inflict that unacceptable level of damage, and what did the adversary think was an unacceptable level of damage? Further, how could we know that for sure? What metrics could we use to determine this? This information or estimation of what was needed, of course, would be used to guide our deterrence strategy, our targeting policy (SIOP), our nuclear force composition, our DOD and DOE acquisition, and budget strategies.

8. For example, during the year leading up to the Cuban missile crisis, it appears that Nikita Khrushchev, general secretary of the Communist Party and leader of the Soviet Union, had concluded that Pres. John F. Kennedy was a weak leader who would not act to thwart a Soviet fait accompli that put Soviet missiles into Cuba. Khrushchev had seen Kennedy's administration fail in the Bay of Pigs crisis to respond to a communist invasion of Laos and fail to respond to Soviet pressure on Berlin. Khrushchev had also engaged in bullying Kennedy at a Paris summit conference where the young president seemed not to acquit himself forcefully. The relative youth and inexperience of Kennedy compared to Khrushchev may have also played a part in the Kremlin's risky decision to place missiles into Cuba.

9. Kahn, *On Thermonuclear War.*

10. Here is an example of the logical problem. If almost all war began in the spring of the year, and the US baseball season starts in the spring, does this then mean that the inception of the baseball season triggers war? No, obviously not. Just because A precedes B does not mean it causes B. Both might be caused by factor C. Correlation (e.g., A then B) is not causation. It is likely that another factor leads to fewer wars starting in the winter—the weather (factor C). Military campaigns are far easier to launch in moderate weather than in the dead of winter when roads are clogged with ice and snow, and army movements are much more difficult. Spring is the opening of campaigning season (and baseball) in parts of the world with severe winters.

11. Duelfer, "Regime Strategic Intent," 1.

12. See *60 Minutes*, "Interrogator Shares Saddam's Confessions." Diane Sawyer of ABC News interviewed Saddam on 24 June 1990 and discovered that he did not know there were no US laws against joking about or criticizing the US president. Nor did he fathom the working of checks and balances in the US political system, where power is shared among the executive, legislative, and judicial systems. Saddam asked, "Who, then, am I supposed to deal with?" See Efraim Karsh and Inari Rautsi, *Saddam Hussein*, 178–79.

13. Karsh and Rautsi, *Saddam Hussein*, 2.

14. See Davis and Arquilla, *Deterring or Coercing Opponents in Crisis*, 7. In 1990 Saddam was trying to re-arm Iraq before Iran could resume the war they had just fought to a draw. He was spending $5 billion annually on modernizing his military. As a result, Saddam Hussein had run out of credit and was facing a mounting financial crisis. He feared that this financial crisis would then result in a security crisis. To add injury, Kuwait and the United Arab Emirates were producing and selling more oil than the limits they had agreed upon at the previous OPEC meetings. This reduced the profit margins for Iraqi oil and infuriated Saddam, who saw these declining oil prices as frustrating his expansionist dreams and as putting his regime in jeopardy. Much like the Japanese, who before Pearl Harbor were reacting to the US-imposed oil embargo that threatened their aspirations for a Japanese co-prosperity sphere in Asia, Saddam had felt the financial noose closing on his dreams when he hit upon the idea of invading oil-rich Kuwait to solve his troubles. Thus, he was adamant about keeping the Kuwaiti prize he had just seized, the prize that was going to solve his financial and security dilemma.

15. Ibid.

16. Karsh and Rautsi, *Saddam Hussein*, 78.

17. Some analysts of previous deterrence failures conclude that "policy makers who risk or actually start wars pay more attention to their own strategic and domestic political interests than they do to the interests and military capabilities needed to defend its commitment. Their strategic and political needs appear to constitute the principal motivation for a resort to force." This observation was based on 20 cases of failed deterrence. See Lebow, "Conclusions," 216.

18. Mearsheimer and Walt, "Can Saddam Be Contained?"

19. Baker, *The Politics of Diplomacy*, 358–59.

20. Ibid., 276.

21. Ibid., 273.

22. Ibid.

23. Ibid., 273–74.

24. Ibid.

25. Herman Kahn wrote about two kinds of escalation of a conflict, vertical and horizontal. Vertical escalation involves walking up the rungs of the escalation ladder to higher and higher levels of conflict. In a war between nuclear armed states, this might begin with low-level conventional conflict and escalate into higher-level nuclear exchanges. Horizontal escalation occurs when the theater of a conflict is widened by involving adjacent territories or other

countries in the conflict, perhaps even extending the conflict to a different theater or region of warfare altogether. See Kahn, *On Escalation*.

26. From a speech given by Hussein at the fourth summit of the Arab Cooperation Council, Amman, Jordan, 24 February 1990. See FBIS NESAS, 27 February 1990, 1–5. Found by this author in Davis and Arquilla, *Deterring or Coercing Opponents in Crisis*, 56.

27. Haselkorn, *The Continuing Storm*, 52. This estimate by the Iraqi dictator was made in an interview on German television and was released by INA, FBIS (NES), 22.

28. Ibid.

29. Baker, *The Politics of Diplomacy*, 303–4.

30. Ibid., 349. Amb April Glaspie "recounted a very telling story about being invited along with other diplomats to a dam construction site in northern Iraq. Saddam had made disparaging remarks about the Vietnamese laborers who were building the dam, dismissing them as sub humans. 'And these are the people who beat the Americans,' he marveled. . . . Iraq's leader thought that Vietnam had so traumatized the American psyche that we would never fight again." See Baker, *The Politics of Diplomacy*, 355.

31. Ibid. Haselkorn's research lists as his source an article in the *Wall Street Journal*, 17 February 1991, written by RADM Mike McConnell, then director of intelligence for the US Joint Chiefs of Staff. McConnell indicated that US forces found such a written order in Kuwait.

32. Schwarzkopf with Peter Petre, *Autobiography*, 439.

33. Ibid. He wrote, "I was worried about the great empty area of southern Iraq where the (coalition) army would launch its attack. I kept asking myself, 'what does Saddam know about that flank that I don't? Why doesn't he have any forces out there?' The intelligence people suggested offhandedly, 'Maybe he plans to pop a nuke out there.' They then nicknamed the sector the 'chemical killing sack.' I flinched every time I heard it."

34. "Gulf War," 39.

35. Ibid.

36. Ibid. The quote is from Rubin, *Cauldron of Turmoil*, 144.

37. Powell with Persico, *My American Journey*, 490–91. He said that "the biological worried me, and the impact on the public the first time the first casualty keeled over to germ warfare would be terrifying."

38. US deaths among military personnel in Operation Iraqi Freedom as of April 2009 were just over 4,200 killed over a period of six years of fighting.

39. Baker, *The Politics of Diplomacy*, 437.

40. For the full text of this letter, see appendix B.

41. Baker, *The Politics of Diplomacy*, 358–59.

42. Cheney, *Conduct of the Persian Gulf War*, 25.

43. On the other hand, if a rogue state leader always expects the strong to use all its weapons against him, why not use his nuclear, biological, and chemical weapons first when they could inflict maximum damage?

44. As James Baker concluded in his book, *The Politics of Diplomacy*, "We do not really know this was the reason there appears to have been no confirmed use by Iraq of chemical weapons during the war. My own view is that

the calculated ambiguity regarding how we might respond has to be part of the reason." See Baker, *The Politics of Diplomacy*, 359.

45. Bush and Scowcroft, *A World Transformed*, 463.

46. Baker, *The Politics of Diplomacy*, 359.

47. On the other hand, it could be argued that Saddam may have believed earlier US pledges not to use nuclear weapons, even in wartime, against those nonnuclear parties in good standing with the nuclear nonproliferation treaty (NPT) regime. In 1978 Secretary of State Cyrus Vance made a unilateral and nonbinding US pledge prior to an NPT review conference to persuade more nonnuclear states to back the treaty extension. This was a policy statement of the Carter administration but not a treaty or legally binding commitment. However, by 1990 the United States had adopted a legal interpretation and doctrine called belligerent reprisal that got the United States out of that legal box. It announced that the US government interpreted its NPT pledge not to use nuclear arms against nonnuclear parties to the treaty as null and void if these states were to initiate the use of either chemical or biological weapons. It is more likely that Saddam did not believe the earlier US pledge not to use nuclear weapons if war began simply because he would not keep such a pledge Baker if he were in the place of the US president.

48. Baker, *The Politics of Diplomacy*, 1.

49. Again, review President Bush's letter of warning to Saddam Hussein. See appendix B.

50. Haselkorn, *The Continuing Storm*. 57. The original citation is CNN, cited in AFMIC Weekly Wire 02-91 (u), File 970613_mno2_91_0_txt_0001.txt (Washington, DC: DIA, 1991). This plan of strategic reciprocity was confirmed in 1995 by Tariq Aziz, who said that the Iraqi military had been authorized to use its biological weapons if Baghdad was attacked with nuclear weapons. See Haselkorn, *The Continuing Storm*, 53.

51. Ibid., 93.

52. Ibid., 31.

53. How seriously the US leadership took the Iraqi chemical and biological warfare threat is testified to by the fact that during the run-up to the war until its conclusion, Pres. George H. W. Bush was accompanied by a military officer who carried a gas mask for emergency use.

54. However, the Syrian chief of staff later stated in a question and answer session, when an Air War College group visited Damascus, that Syria would have stayed in the coalition despite Israeli participation to remove Saddam Hussein's forces from Kuwait.

55. McGeorge Bundy, national security adviser to Presidents John Kennedy and Lyndon Johnson, has written that "there has been literally no chance at all that any sane political authority, in either the United States or the Soviet Union, would consciously choose to start a nuclear war. This proposition is true for the past, the present and the foreseeable future. . . . In the real world of real political leaders . . . a decision that would bring even one hydrogen bomb on one city of one's own country would be recognized in advance as a catastrophic blunder; ten bombs on ten cities would be a disaster beyond history; and a hundred bombs on a hundred cities are unthinkable."

Bundy's analysis would suggest that the United States and any other state should be content with a minimum deterrence posture. On the other hand, some US strategists like former secretary of defense James Schlesinger once enunciated a doctrine of essential equivalence, saying the United States would be safest if it matched the numbers of strategic weapons on the Soviet side no matter their number or overkill capability. This was at a time when both sides had tens of thousands of nuclear weapons. Still others have attempted to strike a balance between the retaliatory power needed and the level of damage that could be inflicted on the adversary. Two RAND analysts calculated the optimal US retaliatory capability for destruction against the Soviet population and industry at a given time. They sought to find a posture that gave "the most bang for the defense buck," yet suggested ways to put rational limits on the size of the nuclear forces required. For example, see Alain Enthoven and K. Wayne Smith, *How Much Is Enough? Shaping the Defense Program, 1961-1969* (New York: Harper and Row, 1971). A reading of their analysis would lead one to conclude that the optimal size of the US nuclear retaliatory force was 400 equivalent megatons of explosive power. In 1971, this would, for example, give the US the capability to kill 39 percent of the Soviet population and 77 percent of Soviet industry. Their calculations also indicated that this would put US destructive power on the "flat of the curve." Even a doubling of the US equivalent mega tonnage to 800 EMT would "only" kill 5 percent more of their population and only 1 percent more of their industry. Thus, some might conclude that the "optimal" solution would be to deploy enough nuclear weapons in such a fashion that, in all likely scenarios, 400 EMT worth of US nuclear weapons would make it through Soviet attacks and defenses to hit their targets in the USSR were the Kremlin leaders ever to launch a nuclear attack. See Enthoven and Smith, *How Much Is Enough?*, 207.

56. Note that Saddam Hussein plotted an assassination attempt against George H. W. Bush on 13 April 1993, when the retired US president visited Kuwait. This revenge strike failed but revealed much about the Iraqi dictator's predilections. He was willing to risk the wrath of the United States just to kill the US leader that had so soundly defeated and humiliated him in the Gulf War of 1990–1991. If he was willing to risk a renewed war and his grip on power to exact revenge, it is not hard to imagine how much more willing he would have been to use all means at hand to deal a last chemical or biological death blow if he thought his regime was about to be destroyed.

57. Schwarzkopf, *Autobiography*, 439.

58. See Duelfer, *Comprehensive Revised Report*.

59. Decisions may be influenced by key decision makers, but these, in turn, may be influenced by allies, legal restrictions, political commitment and consideration, bureaucratic politics, standard operating procedures, psychological factors, and group dynamics. Decision makers seldom begin decisions on issues with a blank slate. See Allison with Zelikow, *Essence of Decision*.

60. Indeed, Saddam's earliest contribution to the Ba'ath Party was to attempt an assassination of Iraqi president general Qassem in 1958. This bungled attempt brought him fame in the Ba'ath Party and exile in Syria and

Egypt for three years. His later climb to the presidency of Iraq is akin to Lee Harvey Oswald becoming president of the United States 19 years after assassinating John F. Kennedy.

61. Some estimate the total dead from the 1980–1988 Iran-Iraq War to have been in the neighborhood of 500,000 Iranians and Iraqis slain.

62. Karsh and Rautsi, *Saddam Hussein*, 2.

63. Author's interview with an Iraqi general who was under contract with the CIA after leaving Iraq.

64. Clancy and Horner, *Every Man a Tiger*, 374–75.

65. See "Gulf War," 6. Unfortunately, 183,000 US veterans of the Gulf War, more than a quarter of all who participated in the war, have been declared permanently disabled by the US Department of Veteran's Affairs as a result of Gulf War syndrome. "About 30 percent of the 700,000 men and women who served in US forces during the Gulf War still suffered an array of serious symptoms whose causes are not fully understood." See "Gulf War," 40.

66. Jervis, Lebow, and Stein, *Psychology & Deterrence*, 216.

67. Ibid.

68. "Gulf War."

69. This chart is an adaptation of one found in Clancy and Horner, *Every Man a Tiger*, xii.

70. See Bush, *Public Papers of George Bush*. See also Gordon and Trainor, *The General's War*, chapter 9, "The Mailed Fist," fn 17.

71. Freedman and Karsh, *The Gulf Conflict*, 332.

72. Ibid., 331–41.

73. Wikipedia, "Operation Desert Shield and Operation Desert Storm."

Bibliography

Allison, Graham, with Phillip Zelikow. *Essence of Decision: Explaining the Cuban Missile Crisis.* 2d ed. New York, Pearson Longman Publishers, 1999.

Baker, James A., III. *The Politics of Diplomacy: Revolution, War, and Peace, 1989–1992.* New York: G. P. Putnam's Sons, 1995.

Bush, George, and Brent Scowcroft. *A World Transformed.* New York: Alfred A. Knopf, 1998.

Bush, George H. W. "Statement by Press Secretary Fitzwater on President Bush's letter to President Saddam Hussein of Iraq." *Public Papers of George Bush: Book 1.* January to 1–30 June 1991. 12 January 1991.

Cheney, Richard, Secretary of Defense. *Conduct of the Persian Gulf War Final Report to Congress.* Washington, DC: US Government Printing Office, 1992.

Clancy, Tom, with Gen Chuck Horner, retired. *Every Man a Tiger.* New York: Putnam's Sons, 1999.

Davis, Paul K., and John Arquilla. *Deterring or Coercing Opponents in Crisis: Lessons from the War with Saddam Hussein.* Santa Monica, CA: RAND R-4111-JS, 1991.

Duelfer, Charles A., special adviser to the DCI on Iraq's WMD. *Comprehensive Revised Report with Addendums on Iraq's Weapons of Mass Destruction.* Washington, DC: CIA, 2004.

Dupuy, Ernest R., and Trevor N. Dupuy. *The Encyclopedia of Military History.* New York: Harper and Row, 1970.

Freedman, Lawrence, and Efraim Karsh. *The Gulf Conflict, 1990–1991: Diplomacy and War in the New World Order.* Princeton, NJ: Princeton University Press, 1995.

Gordon, Michael R., and Gen Bernard E. Trainor. *The General's War.* Boston: Little Brown and Company, 1995.

Haselkorn, Avigdor. *The Continuing Storm, Iraq's Poisonous Weapons and Deterrence.* New Haven, CT: Yale University Press, 1999.

Jervis, Robert, Richard Ned Lebow, and Janice Gross Stein. *Psychology & Deterrence.* Baltimore, MD: Johns Hopkins University Press, 1985.

Kahn, Herman. *On Escalation: Metaphors and Scenarios.* New York: Frederick A. Praeger, 1965.

———. *On Thermonuclear War.* Princeton, NJ: Princeton University Press, 1960.

Karsh, Efraim, and Inari Rautsi. *Saddam Hussein: A Political Biography.* New York: The Free Press, 1991.

Mearsheimer, John J., and Stephen M. Walt. "Can Saddam Be Contained? History Says Yes." *New York Times*, 2 February 2003.

Mullen, Adm Michael G., chairman of the Joint Chiefs of Staff. "It's Time for a New Deterrence Model." *Joint Force Quarterly* 48, 4th Quarter, 2008.

Powell, Colin, with Joseph Persico. *My American Journey.* New York: Ballantine Books, 1999.

Rubin, Barry. *Cauldron of Turmoil: America in the Middle East.* New York: Harcourt Brace Javanovich, 1992.

Schneider, Barry R. *Future War and Counterproliferation.* Westport, CT: Praeger, 1999.

Schwarzkopf, H. Norman, with Peter Petre. *Autobiography: It Doesn't Take a Hero.* New York: Bantam Books, 1992.

60 Minutes. "Interrogator Shares Saddam's Confessions." CBS Television, 27 January 2008.

Wolf, Barry. *When the Weak Attack the Strong: Failures of Deterrence.* Santa Monica, CA: Rand Report N 3262-A, 1991.

Chapter 12

Stymieing Leviathan
A Very Short Practical Handbook:
How Nonstate Actors Deter States

Paul Schulte

Deterrence will only be relevant to nonstate actors' (NSA) decisions when they find or believe themselves to be at risk from the discretionary actions of essentially hostile state governments. The organisations concerned will consequently tend to be on the competitor end of the spectrum of NSAs. That means they will seek to build alternative power structures bypassing or eventually replacing that government, as opposed to complementary NSAs, motivated by social, political, religious, or ethnic projects aimed at influencing or modifying the national political system, rather than replacing or destroying it.[1] In such adversarial conjunctions, where the competitor NSA is suspected of posing a significant threat to regime values or interests, state power will *already* be operating to deter a range of potential NSA choices by the threat of punishment ranging from legitimate legal action to physical denial or indiscriminate coercion.

Attempts by NSAs to deter states will therefore generally mean creating some form of mutual deterrent relationship by creating an expectation within the opposing state decision makers that they face overall costs from intensifying legislation, legal prosecution, repression, or military combat against the NSA that would exceed any resultant gains. They should consequently be induced to hold back from possible actions against NSA activities, organisations, or assets.

Disparities in physical power between states and nonstate organisations generally remain immense. Where government decisions are affected by the deterrence exercised by NSAs, this is therefore likely to come about through "self deterrence,"[2] based upon concerns over reputational damage or normative infractions. Few NSAs will be able to exert deterrence by physical denial or threats of kinetic punishment, except in the rare circumstances that are considered below. Self-deterrence will operate most strongly within those regimes that most value soft power and a positive international image.

What Kinds of State Actions against Which NSAs Might NSAs Want to Deter?

This question is best addressed in terms of a spectrum of NSA activities, assets, or personnel set out in figure 1. Where they are interested in deterrence rather than making a strategic or emotional choice of defiance or provocative escalation, NSAs will generally wish to induce hostile state decision makers to move up the list (or leftwards on the diagram) of possible actions towards the top (or left most) milder end, ideally taking always possible, frequently tempting, and sometimes prudent, default take-no-action positions.

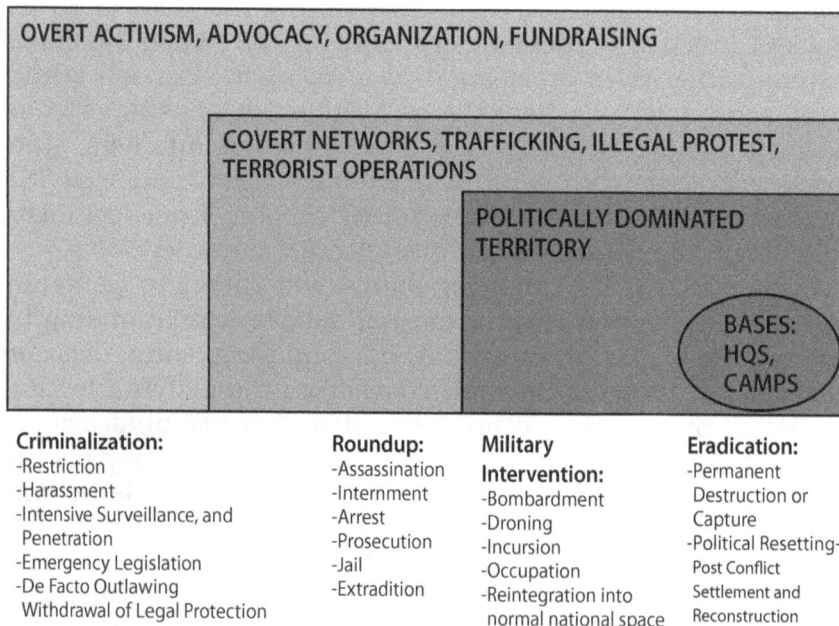

OVERT ACTIVISM, ADVOCACY, ORGANIZATION, FUNDRAISING

COVERT NETWORKS, TRAFFICKING, ILLEGAL PROTEST, TERRORIST OPERATIONS

POLITICALLY DOMINATED TERRITORY

BASES: HQS, CAMPS

Criminalization:
-Restriction
-Harassment
-Intensive Surveillance, and Penetration
-Emergency Legislation
-De Facto Outlawing Withdrawal of Legal Protection

Roundup:
-Assassination
-Internment
-Arrest
-Prosecution
-Jail
-Extradition

Military Intervention:
-Bombardment
-Droning
-Incursion
-Occupation
-Reintegration into normal national space

Eradication:
-Permanent Destruction or Capture
-Political Resetting- Post Conflict Settlement and Reconstruction

Figure 1. What state actions, against which NSA activities or targets, might be deterred?

Structural Factors

It follows from the graphic above that the ability of some NSAs to deter authoritarian and discriminatory states from

lawless and antidemocratic repression may be vital for the pro-
gressive achievement of democracy, stability, and prosperity.
Other NSAs may also seek deterrence—but only to prepare for
their own later escalation of violent politics as a method of compellence or as a step towards replacement of the state itself.
Alternatively, criminal gangs, as in the current Mexican narco
insurgency, who are apparently indifferent to formal or overt
politics, can attempt to create a hollowed-out system of nominal state authority, where real power and wealth operate be-
neath the surface "criminal free states," or " political spaces" in
which gangs can "move and act without governmental or any
other kind of hindrance."[3] By the highly credible threat of assassination, mixed with levels of corruption ("a form of non-
physical erosion of the state"[4]) that make personal risk-taking
appear futile, they seek to deter individual policemen or officials from enforcing laws that would constrain the criminal
transactions from which the gangs derive their hyper profits.[5]

Different NSAs' abilities to exploit ways to deter the state
from intervening against them will therefore have radically different implications for the welfare and political future of the
population concerned. Whatever their records or underlying
intentions, NSAs will often expend great efforts to ensure they
are treated, in at least some of their organisational manifesta-
tions, as nonviolent, inoffensively reformist, and unjustly per-
secuted. NSAs can seek to apply deterrence in enormously different contexts, potentially overlapping with political influence,
civil society campaigning, religious agitation, premeditated
subversion, criminal intimidation, or even asymmetrical war.

**NSA interest in deterrence will probably be temporary
and highly conditional.** Although there will be recurrent
structural incentives for NSAs to try to induce their adversaries
not to use all the capabilities at their disposal, they nevertheless often deliberately choose escalation—a strategy of deliberate provocation. They may, unpredictably, decide to switch to
enraged retaliation (perhaps by unauthorised factions), or towards deliberate, centrally planned escalation when the restraint required for deterrence appears to represent an unbearable acquiescence to intolerable enemy force, or, more
coolly, to a losing strategy. Serious interest in deterrence would
require a consistent strategic orientation, continuously apply-

ing a rational and instrumental calculus. NSAs driven by expressive, sacred, or emotional concerns are unlikely to think clearly or consistently in these terms. Expressive motivations may drive out strategic rationality while cloaking themselves with it. Any interest in achieving or maintaining deterrence risks being overwhelmed by what was called, in the northern Ireland troubles, the politics of the last atrocity, on the basis that "we will always defend our suffering people by showing we can hit back to hurt the enemy's most vulnerable interests and assets, too."

NSA leaders, like state authorities, have to preserve their internal credibility, which will frequently mean their reputations for toughness. Neumann and Smith suggest that the sum total of pressures acting on NSA leaderships once they adopt terrorism as a strategy tends to create an escalation trap, which would of course be incompatible with deterrence.[6]

Timing and Perceived State Vulnerabilities Will Affect NSA Deterrence Choices. Apart from the NSAs' underlying ideology, NSA interest in deterrence may depend on the stage of their operations and their vision of the end state. They will frequently have good reason early on in their campaigns to prioritise cautious, unhindered, organisational preparations, before risking strong state responses. Thereafter, they will continually update judgements on the deterrability of their opponents. These will rest upon their readings of the present situation and of the vulnerabilities of the opposing state.

Perceived State Vulnerabilities as Resources for NSA Deterrence Strategies. NSAs will be aware that, in responding to the challenges that they themselves could pose, states might well have to consider inhibiting combinations of the following:

- Legal challenges in national and international law
- Effects on budgets and economic development, international reprisals such as sanctions and boycotts, or foreign military assistance
- Domestic consequences for national politics and community cohesion—particularly the problem of inflicting mass humiliation by proxy[7]
- Religious and ethnic frictions

- Diplomatic and worldwide reputational damage
- Outcomes in the media and public diplomacy
- Geographical distances and topographical intractability
- Police and other government organisational competencies
- Military force-to-space ratios, risks, and predicted casualty rates

Strategic Culture

The relative importance and public salience of these vulnerabilities will help to frame national strategic culture—"a distinctive body of beliefs, attitudes and practices regarding the use of force, which are held by collective (usually a nation) and arise gradually over time, through a unique protracted historical process."[8] Strategic culture is a difficult and evolving concept,[9] but it is likely to be affected by the size, prestige, unity, and interconnectedness of different constituencies and interest groups and their relative influence over national decision makers. Significant groupings likely to influence the stream of decisions relating to competitive NSAs would typically include intelligence, police and military institutions, nationalist or liberal politicians and opinion formers, free and government-controlled media, ethnic or religious groups, antiwar or antimilitary organisations, the judiciary, foreign ministries, and business interests concerned about external condemnations, disinvestment, and boycotts or sanctions. Further relevant variables affecting NSA-related strategic culture might be the degree of economic dependence on aid, trade, or military assistance and the extent of public awareness or cultural acceptance of external comment or criticism. Two illustrative types of strategic culture appear in figures 2 and 3.

In softer strategic cultures, adherence to the legal process guarantees significant, though not infinite, forbearance. And, despite publicly voiced misgivings, nations with a highly legalistic character may be unable to prevent themselves from taking up hard positions by insisting on prosecuting offenders or refusing to enter into hostage deals. But democracies can also flip over into extreme and surprisingly disinhibited determination, as with the United States after 9/11.

219

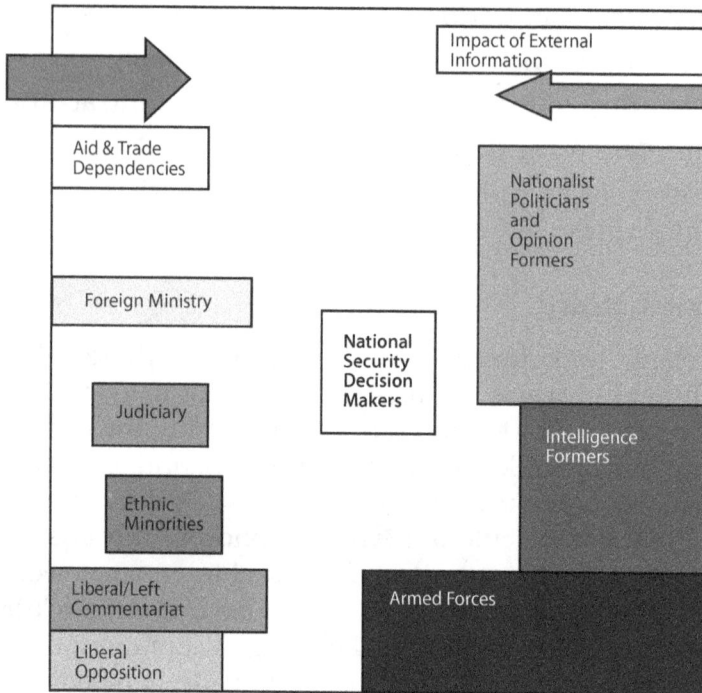

Figure 2. A hard-boiled, difficult-to-deter strategic culture.

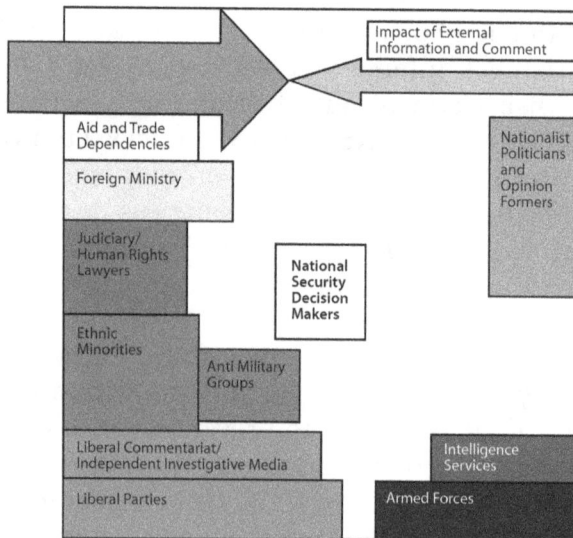

Figure 3. A softer, more deterrable strategic culture.

Remember that a government's deterrability by NSAs may differ profoundly from its deterrability by other states. (Russia is arguably a prime example of such differentiated deterrability.) Moreover, strategic culture may change importantly over time. The key constituencies will be variously strengthened, weakened, dissolved, separated, or unified by such different strategic and historical experiences as internal security successes, failures, or stalemates. (The most notable cases of profound changes in national strategic culture are probably Germany and Japan before and after World War II.)

The most ambitious NSAs may intend their campaigns to transform opponents' strategic cultures by strengthening constituencies for conciliation, negotiation, restraint, and discrediting hardliners. But they may very well get their judgements of current realities and potential vulnerabilities diametrically wrong. Muddled campaign strategies to enforce deterrence (or indeed coercion) by successful atrocity can lead to state reactions utterly opposite to those expected. Errors in estimation and planning are particularly likely to occur from conspiratorial thinking in which hostile governments are regarded as essentially fronts for shadowy hidden puppet masters or from the exaggeration of enemy cowardice and casualty aversion. Misjudgements may derive from historically or ideologically conditioned narcissistic or paranoid group thinking: self-infatuation, splitting, and stereotyping. For religiously inspired groups, the expectation of divine intercession may significantly complicate objective judgements.

Instability and Underlying Contradictions of NSA Deterrence

Deterrence by NSAs will often be fragile, provisional, and unstable—viewed on both sides as disreputable or unnatural. It will probably be implicit and therefore subject to mutual misunderstanding. Where it is formalised, agreements will probably have to be reached by back channels and remain unacknowledged, deniable, or indeed denied. Deterrence is likely to be a temporary stage before negotiated settlement, escalation, legally required or politically driven enforcement by the security forces, or state withdrawal.

Accepting mutual deterrence questions state legitimacy and competence. It will be widely taken to prove that the state is failing to maintain the Weberian requirement of exercising a monopoly of legitimate violence. Consequently, an NSA's success in demonstrating a capacity strong enough to deter may instead provoke state authorities into decisive action to stop it, thus increasing its challenge to regime credibility. Governments' need to show firm action to reassure their electorates and/or security bureaucracies and other states will conflict with any visible acceptance of mutual deterrence.

Measures, Methods, and Tactics to Enhance NSA Deterrence: A Short Practical Handbook with Examples, Escalatory, and Deterrence Choices for NSAs Confronting a Hostile State

To facilitate analysis of graduated deterrent methods and choices, the following rough typology of levels of NSA activity will be used. Several of these may be simultaneously combinable by different parts of the organisation, confederated groups, and front organisations. The following actions of operational and presentational possibilities are conceivable, and most have been tried by NSAs.

- Level I: Staying within domestic law
  - Cultivate widespread democratic legitimacy
  - Justify a popular self-description as part of global civil society—and the now-customary web presence to back up that claim
  - Provide welfare, educational, and medical services
  - Conduct cultural (especially ethnically or religiously based or youth) activities
  - Interconnect with, penetrate, and persuade other organisations (e.g., charities, churches, and legitimate political parties) of your movement's just and nonviolent intentions

- Enlist and then showcase sympathetic eminent or internationally prestigious figures
- Exploit every safeguard or delaying option available within the domestic law
- Build rainbow coalitions with all groups, minorities, and parties rejecting forceful state actions as inconsistent with responsible conciliatory politics
- Prove the willingness of your supporters to be imprisoned. Make the state authorities conclude that activists seek martyrdom to increase recruitment and polarisation
- Seek shifts in allegiance or commitment by security force personnel or national political actors through Gandhian-style nonviolence applied as consistently as seems productive
- Cultivate and display public support in highly visible displays, protests, or ceremonies, photogenically organised around symbolically important events, places, or commemorations. High-profile memorialisation of past state-inflicted wrongs can help deter their repetition. The repetitive public ceremonies of the mothers of the disappeared in Argentina and the Black Sash in apartheid South Africa, though they would not have described it in that way, generated future deterrence for a range of like-minded individuals and NSAs challenging state power and the secrecy that guaranteed it.
- Build international awareness and worldwide support
- Cultivate international media
- Build a sponsoring or at least supportive relationship with a sympathetic state. It should ideally be contiguous, generous, and powerful. If at all possible it should be a Security Council member who has a special ethnic or religious link to your country or to your specific ethnic group.
- Induce the UN or regional organisations, especially the European Union, to take up a transnational supervisory role

- Exploit diasporas for finance, lobbying, and active recruits
- Level II: Nonviolent lawbreaking (e.g., on funding, agitation, and recruitment)
- Level III: Limited public violence, such as rioting or intifada
  - Levels II and III: Low-level violations of security legislation coupled with limited public violence involve levels of confrontation with state authorities that indicate that the NSA is regarded as fundamentally competitive rather than complementary, although the NSA is holding back from deliberate violence
- Develop an account of the cause that intensifies the fervour and self-sacrifice of your supporters and is also explicable to world media and international nongovernmental organizations. It should ideally be linked to a wider, grander narrative. Effective and usually sincerely believed themes here include third world liberation, neo-colonialism, Islamophobia, and historic ethnic subordination
- Publicise (perhaps accurately) government blunders, partiality, incapacity, and corruption
- Stress (again perhaps accurately) the threat of violence from uncontrolled state security elements or hostile vigilante groups
- Seek sole representative legitimacy
- Organise, recruit, instruct
- Undermine, denigrate, and delegitimise rivals for the loyalty of potential supporters
- Threaten objectively inevitable rising tensions and violence if the authorities arrest or prosecute supporters or fail to concede demands. Attempt to ensure that as frequently as possible the authorities accordingly conclude, often in response to orchestrated public campaigns, that prosecutions or continued incarceration of organisation members would not be in the public interest.
- Ensure direct, and if possible real-time, media coverage of demonstrations. Classically, in the early days of live

224

TV news, when the Chicago police moved into Grant Park in August 1968, the antiwar demonstrators were able to chant "The whole world is watching" in front of the cameras.[10] There may in fact—as at Chicago and as at Tiananmen Square in 1989, where the Square was still violently cleared despite the media coverage—be no immediate deterrent payoff. But security forces and governments will be under greater pressure for restraint in subsequent years. And, encouragingly, the technical possibilities of ensuring footage reaches the outside world, via YouTube or similar websites, are improving year by year, despite corresponding governmental efforts to close off Internet access, as in China and Iran.

- Example: Lithuania in the 1980s to 1991, the Baltic Way, and Vilnius television station exemplify NSA deterrence campaign

  - Gorbachev's glasnost and perestroika softened the strategic culture of the Union of Soviet Socialist Republics.

  - During the 1980s, Lithuanian nationalist and democratic groups were able to develop a singing revolution below the threshold of Soviet repression based on folk song and national cultural traditions. The organisers were realistic and exceptionally self-controlled, but their transformative objectives made them regime competitors.

  - In August 1989, about 2 million people joined hands to form a human chain, "the Baltic Way," that extended more than 600 kilometres through Latvia, Lithuania, and Estonia to commemorate the 50th anniversary of the fateful Molotov-Ribbentrop Pact that began the forcible incorporation of the three Baltic States into the Soviet Union. The spectacular size, short duration, and nonviolent nature of this demonstration deterred action to break it up and rapidly accelerated the determinedly peaceful efforts to achieve the separation of all three countries from the Soviet Union. Lithuania declared independence on 11 March 1990. Open anti-Soviet resistance was nonviolent and loosely organised, frequently through mass rallies, rather than depending upon cell structures. A large number of individual citizens repeatedly accepted personal risk to oppose superior coercive force. Following provocations by pro-Russian demonstrators in January 1991, Lithuanian civilians started to encircle their major strategic buildings, including Vilnius TV tower, protectively, where, in the early hours of 13 January, a number of them were attacked by Soviet paratroopers. Fourteen were shot or crushed.

- But news and images were transmitted out of the country from another station, and large crowds were called out later that day to gather around the Supreme Council building. They were not attacked. Norway appealed to the United Nations on Lithuania's behalf against Soviet aggression. Forceful Western reactions and sympathetic statements from other former Communist states, together with prodemocracy movements within Russia itself, eventually led to evacuation of Russian forces from Lithuania and acceptance of her independence. Gorbachev had miscalculated the balance of forces within the strategic culture of the Soviet Union. The Swedish foreign minister, Carl Bildt, later described the asymmetrical encounter underneath the Vilnius TV tower as "one of the most important battles in Europe's modern history."[11, 12]

- The effectiveness of this kind of nonviolent, internationally supported, democratic, and secessionist campaign and its later evolution into colour revolutions is unlikely to have been forgotten by the Russian government in particular. A strong concern to counter attempted repetitions has therefore inevitably been incorporated into Russian strategic culture.

- Level IV: Limited terrorism, largely against legitimate state targets

  - Because this stage amounts to low-intensity conflict with the government, deception and disinformation become increasingly important to ensure that, while some activists are deeply engaged in violence, sympathisers can still benefit from government restraint.

- Simulate, merge with, and take over accepted religious/diaspora charities and political activities
- Invent and evolve but carefully coordinate separate, more aggressive factions or entirely peaceful front organisations and political wings
- Emphasise that your activists form a network, not limited in space or borders, which cannot be eradicated by surges or military offensives
- Conduct a graduated, controlled, and ambiguous campaign
- Maintain an operational profile just below what would provoke escalated security responses. This means planning operations that are unacceptable rather than unbearable.
- Develop a reputation for the NSA as a potentially responsible political actor, capable of becoming an indispensable negotiating partner if the conditions on which it has to insist were at least partially met. (It is not impossible that this might become true.)
- Project an image of a responsible leadership looking for a compromise while tenuously holding wilder elements in check.
- Denounce other organisations' atrocities (as Hamas did the 7/7 attacks in London)
- Conduct vigorous law fare[13] ("the growing use of international law claims, usually factually or legally meritless, as a tool of war") and integrated it into an intense information campaign. The aim should be to create an automatic international expectation that military force launched by states will be morally illegitimate and illegal in its inception and unlawfully applied in its practice.
- Launch legal actions for abuse of human rights, defamation, or ethnic discrimination wherever possible and ensure they are widely reported

227

- Recruit international volunteers to assist your terrorist campaign and encourage activists in your own organisations to link up and fight alongside sympathetic organisations in other terrorist theatres. Well-publicised links of this sort, however nominal, will strengthen the image of your own organisation as part of an unconquerable international network. It will also help to suggest to electorates on the other side that their security forces would have to face a potentially unlimited supply of reinforcements if the conflict is escalated or extended.
- Take hostages to limit government action by threats of reprisal
- Publicly stress and also arrange covert evidence that you precisely want the enemy to continue or even to escalate high-intensity security operations because they will further radicalise opinion and so recruit for you
- Form closer, symbiotic relationships with those sponsoring states willing to provide money, weapons, sanctuaries, and diplomatic support
- Agree, if necessary, to help cultivate international public opinion in their interest, and, if necessary, to conduct terrorist operations on their behalf
- Example: Northern Ireland, 1972—Bloody Friday, Operation Motorman, and the end of the no-go areas of Belfast and Londonderry
  - A failure to remain within a satisfactorily normalised deterrent relationship
  - By mid-1972, the provisional Irish Republican Army (IRA) was involved in secret peace negotiations with the British government, which was tacitly tolerating no-go areas in Catholic enclaves, beyond the reach of the security forces. These safe havens became practical and symbolic centres of paramilitary recruitment and organisation.
  - But, frustrated at stalemate in the political talks, the IRA decided to escalate its activities. On Bloody Friday, 21 July 1972, 21 bombs exploded in Belfast, killing 11 and wounding 130.

- This large-scale and highly publicised operation ended Her Majesty's Government's implicit policy of self-deterrence. Within 10 days, the British Army forcefully reentered the fray, with a forceful reentry into the Republican areas of Belfast and Londonderry in Operation Motorman on 31 July 1972. Policing was reestablished, as leading terrorist cadres were disrupted or imprisoned, and overall levels of violence began to drop.[14]

- Level V: Extreme and indiscriminate terrorism
  - Most of the measures in earlier or less-intense stages continue to apply, although the strategy of publicising indications of potential moderation will be less convincing.
  - Act to raise assistance, in technical capability and personnel, to and from other organisations practising terrorism. Increasing casualties to hostile (at present probably Western) security forces, particularly those involved in interventionary operations, will further benefit the general NSA deterrent calculus.
  - Make clear that you will also target development specialists and aid workers to frustrate stabilisation and reconstruction efforts. This should help ensure that interventionary wars are seen not only as illegal but unwinnable.
  - Consider indiscriminate car or suicide bombing of innocent civilians, including those from the NSA's own community, to deter public involvement in new state structures and/or reduce Western willingness to contemplate new interventions because the civilian death toll will be higher, even if casualties are not caused directly by their forces.

- Level VI: Territorial defence of fixed-liberated zones
  - Creation and maintenance of these NSA-controlled spaces will depend upon deterrent cost-benefit analysis to keep out national state authorities or their allies, particularly today the United States. Because these highest-intensity scenarios will involve conventional military assault, considerations here will most resemble defensive military calculations for kinetic deterrence by denial.
  - To help maintain a satisfactory balance of incentives that will help hold off military assault, avoid high-profile

provocations directly traceable to a base area (although, as in the murder of the American Blackwater employees in April 2004 at Fallujah, it may be impossible to exercise control over spontaneous events that the enemy will regard as intolerable).

- Especially when the enemy state lies across an international border, use shared ethnicity or religion to recruit and involve local people, and if possible their national army, so that an enemy attack on your bases would be confronted with combined resistance, as is widely expected in northwest Pakistan. In these circumstances, enemy decision makers would have to calculate that their operations would then face the determination of an aroused terrorist group, the numbers implied by local guerrilla resistance and the training, weaponry, and staying power of regular forces.

- In all cases, meld to the maximum with civilians so that locals automatically become continuous human shields

- Move where there are large numbers of people, or, in extremis, like the Tamil Tigers, move civilians with you

- Once the enemy attacks, claim disproportionate force and brutality. Dominate the media with exaggerated casualty claims. Each successively alleged atrocity will condition sympathetic world opinion and raise the political costs of the next assault on your sanctuaries.

- Cooperate in terrorist internationals, whether Jihadi, nationalist, or leftist (as with the cooperation between the Red Army faction and the Palestine Liberation Organization during the 1970s) to increase the number of combatants and reprisal attacks on which the enemy would have to reckon. Even if far from your operational theatre, wherever state efforts to apply comprehensive approaches to the military stabilisation, economic development, and permanent political reintegration of sanctuary areas can be defeated, the less chance they will be tried again elsewhere.

- Improving operational security will offer fewer tempting targets of key personnel or materiel.

- Keeping those critical assets mobile will still further diminish the attractiveness of the sanctuary as a military objective.
- Digging and hardening fortifications will decrease the effectiveness of attack by aircraft or drones and raise the number of casualties that the enemy must expect from a ground assault.
- Alliances with friendly sponsoring states will be even more important for positional defence. Only they can provide the most effective weapons, especially advanced shoulder-fired weapons including the following:
  - Man-portable air defence systems, capable of bringing down helicopters with enormous strategic consequences, as against the Soviet campaign in Afghanistan.
  - Such sophisticated antitank-guided weapons as the Russian Kornet, which was able to knock out previously invulnerable Israeli tanks in South Lebanon.
  - Self-forging IEDs, capable of destroying the most heavily armoured vehicles, which hugely complicate Western operations in Iraq and Afghanistan, causing a persistent drain of casualties, inexorably undermining public support.
  - Volumetric munitions, as a new and disturbing class of potential nonstate weapon.
- In the aggregate, all these measures should, as in South Lebanon, significantly lengthen the expected duration of any conventional offensive, with morale and publicity benefits, and further raise the casualties that the enemy must anticipate. And in these situations, most media commentators will now automatically quote some version of Henry Kissinger's much-mutated Vietnam aphorism that conventional armies lose if they do not win, but guerrillas and NSAs win if they do not lose and need only to survive. This will be a potentially self-fulfilling expectation. It can in itself constitute a major disincentive for government forces to engage in high-intensity assaults.

- Example: Jeningrad, the Alleged Jenin Massacre of April 2002
  - A contested entry into a terrorist sanctuary conducted amidst intense propaganda efforts, with widespread effects on global public opinion.
  - The so-called Battle of Jenin took place 3–11 April 2002 in the Palestinian authority–administered refugee camp of Jenin, in the West Bank, as part of Operation Defensive Shield during the Second Intifada. Israeli troops entered Jenin on the grounds that it had served as a base for numerous terrorist attacks against Israeli civilians. World attention focused on the operation, and Yasser Arafat compared "Jeningrad's" scale and significance with Stalingrad. Palestinian estimates of civilian casualties ranged from 3,000 to 5,000 and were widely republished with accusations of Israeli war crimes and massacres. A report by the UN secretary general[15] published at the end of July made criticisms of both sides' behaviour, but indicated that, while precision was unattainable, it was possible only to confirm that around 56 Palestinians had died, of whom about half might have been noncombatant civilians, as against 23 Israeli soldiers. Dispute has continued divisively since then, with repeated, apparently unstoppable, accusations that Palestinian losses had been underreported. Memories of this incident form part of the emotional background against which Israeli or other interventions against alleged terrorist sanctuaries in the Middle East have had to be considered.
- Level VII: Weapons of mass destruction (WMD) and mass casualty terrorism
  - This is an area of great speculative uncertainty, frequently explored in popular fiction. The threats involved would have to be both credible and cataclysmic to have a deterrent effect when the stakes were raised as high as they inevitably would be, even by the threat of such actions. This means that chemical, biological, radiological, or nuclear weapons are, inherently, highly risky for NSAs to attempt to use for deterrence. Any such scenarios

232

might trigger exterminatory international preemption or retaliation by many states. NSAs therefore seem much more likely to acquire WMD for escalatory provocation or "accelerated *engrenage*," rather than deterrence.

- But if they were prepared to adopt extremely high-risk options, NSAs might attempt to use WMD for deterrence by punishment in two main ways, depending on their reading of the leverages and vulnerabilities of opposing governments and publics:
  - Discreet blackmail, secretly revealing locations of actual, clandestinely emplaced, WMD to governments, as proof that there were more—which would, if necessary, be used.
  - Overtly publicised threats, with open displays of capability aimed at terrorising electorates into demanding that governments hold back from stated red lines (e. g., BW campaigns with additional outbreaks promised unless deterrence conditions were met).

- Yet the paradox haunting NSA deterrence would then bite still more strongly.

- Proven acquisition and actual deployment of strategically significant WMD would represent a huge increase in NSAs' power, even if the weapons were never used. Their nonstate owners would consequently have to expect extreme preemptive or punitive reactions from the society of states rather than any easy acceptance of a high-level mutually deterrent relationship.

- At any level: Cease-fires, hints of cease-fires, and indications of willingness to negotiate
  - The suggestion of negotiation, peace processes with tantalising glimpses of an end to agitation or violence, is a well-tried method to induce an antagonist to impose restraint in his prosecution of conflict. But the risks are also obvious. Governments may have little reason to trust a hostile NSA's good faith or to hold back if they judge its campaign to be faltering. Yet its supporters may not easily understand, or even tolerate, cease-fire offers if NSA efforts are still portrayed (as they may have

233

to be for recruitment and morale reasons) as headed for eventual success.

A Final Observation on Actors' Self-Understandings

Not all of the tactics and behaviours discussed here have been deliberately adopted for self-conscious strategic advantage. Nor would they necessarily emerge in that way in the future. Neither states nor their NSA opponents would often understand or calibrate their own choices through the neutral analytical optic of deterrence. They are more likely to experience either a frustrating struggle against subversion, lies, and interference while trying to maintain decency, civilisation, and the national interest or, on the other side, desperate efforts to improvise temporary stratagems to mitigate or evade oppression and unjust force. These intensely held interpretations of the situation may lead to interactive outcomes profoundly different from those predicted by cool deterrent analysis. In passionate and protracted struggles, especially within the same national community, chess-playing deliberations of equally cool strategic decision makers are evidently not impossible but are unlikely to be the rule.

Notes

1. I take this simple but fundamental distinction from Paul J. Smith, *The Terrorism Ahead: Confronting Transnational Violence in the 21st Century* (M. E. Sharpe: New York and London, 2008), 46. But I emphasise that there will be a complex spectrum rather than a simple dichotomy.

2. This understanding of self-deterrence is based upon the usage in T. V. Paul, *The Tradition of Non-Use of Nuclear Weapon*" (Palo Alto, CA: Stanford University Press, 2009), 203–4. Paul's analysis also emphasises (p. 32) the contribution that norm entrepreneurs, described as "reputation intermediaries and facilitators" made to nuclear self-deterrence in framing and calling attention to issues "using language that names, interprets, and dramatises" them. Presumably, today's best-known human rights and counterterrorist experts now play the role of norm entrepreneurs in the development of standards and expectations governing state responses to competitive nonstate actors.

3. Max Manwaring, *Insurgency Terrorism and Crime: Shadows from the Past and Portents for the Future* (Norman: University of Oklahoma Press, 2008), 104–28.

4. Ibid., 124.

5. In these cases, it seems to be expected that deterrence of the individuals at risk will be maximised by threatening not only death but extreme physical pain. Thus, a typical bulletin from the Mexican drug war reports "Anti-Narcotics Agents Tortured to Death by Gang" to describe the discovery of the bodies of 11 men and one woman in Pres. Felipe Calderon's home state of Michoacan. They had all been abducted while off duty by members of the La Familia drug cartel. See *London Guardian*, 15 July 2009, 17. Their bodies were found stacked on the highway with death threats that read "La Familia, join its ranks or leave" and "Let's see if you try to arrest another one." See "Drug Cartel in Deadly Challenge to Law," *London Times*, 16 July 2009, 31. On the same day, the mayor of a northern Mexican town was killed "in a revenge attack for a mass arrest of hit men." See *London Guardian*, 15 July 2009.

6. Peter R. Neumann and M. L. R. Smith, *The Strategy of Terrorism: How It Works and Why It Fails* (Routledge: London, 2008), 77–93.

7. This factor has been asserted as a contributory cause for Jihadi recruitment amongst Muslims throughout the world. See Peter R. Neumann, *Joining al-Qaeda: Jihadist Recruitment in Europe* (Routledge: London, 2009).

8. K. Longhurst, *Germany and the Use of Force* (Manchester: Manchester University Press, 2004), 17–18.

9. See Lawrence Sondhaus, *Strategic Culture and Ways of War* (Routledge: London and New York, 2006).

10. This incident was filmed by the cinematographer Haskell Wexler and later spliced into his feature release "Medium Cool" (1969).

11. Reported in *Baltic Times*, 17 January 2007, http://www.bafl.com/newsDetail.asp?idNews=368.

12. For a comparative overview of the Baltic experience in leaving the Soviet empire, see Roger D. Petersen, *Resistance and Rebellion: Lessons from Eastern Europe* (Cambridge, UK: Cambridge University Press, 2001).

13. On which, see, for example, David Kennedy, *Of Law and War* (Princeton: Princeton University Press, 2006).

14. Neumann and Smith, 89–90.

15. http://www.un.org/peace/jenin/index.html.

235

Chapter 13

The Madrid Train Bombing

Peter Neumann

Terrorists—even those of the supposedly irrational kind—are by and large rational actors. But the case of Madrid threw up some complexities that you may consider thinking about. I spent nearly a year in Madrid as adviser to the Club of Madrid, the association of former presidents and prime ministers. In the aftermath, I came to Madrid in May 2004, and although I was not there in March 2004, I witnessed very closely some of the aggravation and some of the very intense debates that happened in Spain. I also had the opportunity to speak to many of the protagonists.

So let me begin by putting in front of you the conventional wisdom. On 11 March 2004, a group of terrorists placed 13 improvised explosive devices (IED) on four commuter trains that were all travelling from suburbs to Otocha station, which is one of the main train stations in Madrid. The bombs exploded almost simultaneously at twenty-to-eight local time. By the end of the day, it became clear that the number of fatalities would be very large. The official figure is 191 dead, about 2,000 wounded, many of whom were severely wounded. That makes the Madrid bombings the most significant terrorist attack in Europe with the exception of Lockerbie. The number of dead could actually have been much larger if the terrorist's plan had entirely worked out. The plan was to have all these trains travelling into Otocha station and the bombs going off inside Otocha station, which at that time of day would have been packed with people, so it could easily have ended up with thousands of people dead. It is quite clear, therefore, that the intention of the attack was to cause mass civilian casualties.

Those are the facts that are largely undisputed. Now for the interpretation of what happened in the aftermath. The date 11 March was not just any other date. It was exactly two and one-half years after 9/11—the attacks against the United States. More important, in the Spanish context, it was three days before the general elections in Spain. Up to that point, the popular party, the Conservative Party, of Prime Minister Jose Maria

Aznar was leading in the opinion polls. The lead had been shrinking in the days running up to the election, but the party was still four or five points ahead of its Socialist rivals. People in Spain were quite happy with how the Conservatives had run the economy; Spain at that point was prospering. People were also happy with the Conservatives' hard line on ETA, the Basque Nationalist group in the northeast of Spain. A previous Socialist government had tried to negotiate with ETA; that had completely failed. A new government, the Conservative Government, came into power promising a hard line towards ETA, arguing that ETA could not change, could not be negotiated with, and that the only way to deal with them was to defeat them. The one Conservative policy that people were almost unanimously opposed to was the Iraq war. Aznar was one of the key allies of the Bush White House. Spain had committed significant numbers of troops to Iraq initially. Thirteen hundred troops had been taking part in the initial invasion of Iraq, and even though that number had come down significantly by the time of the Madrid attacks, Spain was still considered to be a significant contributor.

As soon as it became clear that the Madrid bombings had been directed or inspired by al-Qaeda, they were immediately interpreted by the Spanish population, the Spanish media, and key opinion formers as a punishment for Spain's participation in the Iraq war. Three days later, the last-minute swing that happened was seen as a direct response to the Madrid bombings because the Conservative Party was in favour. The Socialist Party had always been against the Iraq policy. Indeed, on the night of the election, when it became clear that the Socialists would lead the new government, Jose Luis Zapatero, the new prime minister, made an immediate announcement to the effect that Spain would pull out of the coalition in Iraq. That was unprecedented. Spanish political leaders normally do not make policy announcements during election night. Zapatero did not make any announcement on any other policy. He made that one statement during election night to the effect that Spain would pull out. Some have interpreted that as an indication of how al-Qaeda had intimidated the Spanish government. That Zapatero was making that statement was indicative, they said, of how scared the Spanish government had become of further attacks. Other interpretations say that Zapatero, rather than being scared of al-Qaeda, was rather scared of the allies and how they would put pressure on him in the following days to reverse his decision. That was stated in the party political manifesto—to pull out of Iraq—but he wanted to commit early to make it impossible for him to retreat on that election promise.

In any case, whatever the truth, the conventional wisdom is the attacks were seen as related to the Iraq war and prompted the election defeat of the one party that was supporting the Iraq war. The new government immediately pulled out of Iraq. That is indeed how supporters of the Iraq war perceived it. Look at what one leading politician, John Howard, said nine days after the attacks: "Countries cannot insulate themselves from terrorist attacks by opting out of the war on terror. We cannot buy ourselves immunity by changing our foreign policies. Apart from the moral cowardice of that position it can never work in practice." Similar statements were made by other supporters of the coalition.

The question is, Is that what actually happened? Let me introduce one or two layers of complexity here. The first one is about what actually happened in the three days between the bombings and the election. No one denies that there was a swing from the Conservatives to the Socialists. The question is, Why did voters change their minds? Conventional wisdom says it was because of Iraq. Many people in Spain would deny that. The truth is that for the first two days after the bombings, the Aznar government insisted that this operation had been carried out by ETA. It did not look anything like ETA, but on the day of the bombings, the Spanish interior minister came out and said, "Be in no doubt, there is no doubt, ETA is responsible, ETA has been looking for a massacre. In Spain today it achieved its goal." All Spanish embassies across the world were instructed to follow this line. In fact, the UN Security Council passed a resolution condemning ETA for these attacks. Aznar was personally calling the editors of all the main newspapers in Spain insisting that it was ETA and not al-Qaeda or any Islamist group. The day before the election of course, it became more obvious that this claim could not be sustained. Pursuing the various leads, police discovered more and more evidence of Islamist involvement. It eventually became clear just the day before elections that there really could be no doubt that Islamists had been involved.

As I said at the beginning, I was in Spain during that period, and even though I only arrived two months after the attack, I can tell you that people in Spain felt incredibly strongly about what they perceived to be a conscious effort of the government to mislead them. The government, they said, had lied to them about something as important as this, and it did so for completely self-interested reasons. The fact was that people literally could not believe that the government in a moment of national tragedy would deliberately set out to deceive its people. Even two months later, people were still extremely upset, not about the bombings necessarily but about the fact that their own government had blatantly lied to them. At least, that is how they perceived it. I think this factor, at least the intensity of this factor, is often overlooked. In fact, in contrast to this country, terrorist attacks in Spain, whether by ETA, Islamists, or others, have a huge mobilising effect. Whenever something happens, people go out on the streets. Indeed, within hours of the attacks in Madrid, hundreds of thousands of people were on the streets of Madrid and various other cities. Two million people were on the streets of the country that night. They were not demonstrating about Iraq; they were demonstrating against terrorism.

So no Spanish pollster denies that the Madrid bombings had an effect on the election. The question is, Did they produce that swing? Not necessarily directly. The electoral turnout was up by 12 percent, especially amongst younger voters. And most pollsters will happily admit that was because of the attacks. People, especially younger people, felt they had to participate in the elections as a result; these were young people who were opposed to the Iraq war of course, but they were young people who had also been incredibly upset about the government's supposed deception. So it is not really easy to separate these two factors. A lot of the people who turned up at the polling booth were in fact motivated by both. But, as much as Iraq might have been a factor, there is no doubt that people were also—I emphasise—extremely upset by what they saw as the government's lies.

Just as a footnote, did the government deliberately deceive its population? Having spoken to many of the protagonists, my

view is that first of all it seems quite clear that the security services themselves were split as to where the attack came from
with some saying that the kind of explosives were of the kind
that were typically used by ETA. There had been threats from
ETA and rumours about a radical splinter group. On the other
hand, of course, this was not looking like ETA at all. ETA in the
course of its entire 30- or even 35-year campaign had killed 800
people. In the most violent year of its history, it killed 100 people over an entire year; so, this was not the kind of attack that
even radical splinter groups of ETA would have carried out.

The fact is that even though perhaps the government was not
deliberately deceiving its population, the government certainly
was seizing every bit of information that would implicate ETA
and was ignoring every bit of information that would have implicated Islamists or al-Qaeda. If it was not deceiving the Spanish public—perhaps that is too strong a word—it was clearly
misrepresenting the state of the evidence. Clearly, it was not
justified in retrospect to make a statement on the evening of the
attacks, saying that ETA was the culprit beyond any doubt. At
that point, clearly there had been doubts, and in that sense, the
government was misrepresenting the evidence. It was also guilty
of certainly greatly exaggerating whatever indicators there were
of ETA's responsibility. That was undoubtedly an important factor in people's decision to vote for the opposition.

The second area of complexity that I would like to introduce—and there are only two, so do not worry—who was responsible? Was it really al-Qaeda, or was it in the words of
Mark Sageman, a leaderless network of grassroots Jihadists? If
the argument is that al-Qaeda had deterred or coerced the
Spanish government, clearly the underlying assumption is that
the attack had been directed by al-Qaeda, but was that really
the case? Again, the picture is quite complicated. A few days
after the attack, eight days to be precise, a document emerged
that had been posted on the Internet in December 2003. It had
been posted in one of the Web forms in which al-Qaeda typically posts its statements of responsibility or announcements;
it had been posted there three months before the attacks, a
strategy document that was published in one of the leading al-
Qaeda Web forums. It makes a very clear and logical case. It
sets out a very rational case for attacking Spain. It says, the

241

aim is "to make one or two of the allies to leave the Coalition because this will cause others to follow suit and the dominos will start falling." That is an exact quote from the strategy document. Then, the document goes through various countries that are supporting the coalition in Iraq. It goes through them one by one. It concludes that Spain is probably the most promising country to attack. Spain, in the words of the authors of that document, represents the weakest link because opposition to the war is almost total; the government is virtually on its own on the issue. That is pretty strong evidence of there being some rationale—clear, logical rationale—for attacking Spain, and indeed two months prior to that document coming out, bin Laden had used one of his video messages to call on attacks against, among other countries, Spain.

All this seems to suggest that al-Qaeda, if not directly steering the attacks, was at least doing everything it could to direct the attackers in the direction of Spain. Indeed, one of the leaders of the Madrid network upon hearing bin Laden's message entered 11 March as an important date into his mobile phone.

The people who were involved in the Madrid attacks clearly believed themselves to be part of al-Qaeda. They regarded bin Laden as we now know as an emir. They had watched copious amounts of Jihadist propaganda. Indeed, the roots of the Jihadist network in Spain go back to people like Abu Dada, who had been fighting in Afghanistan in the 1980s and who was certainly part of the Jihadist milieu. Abu Dada in fact was a close associate of Abu Qatada and had met him 17 times, quite often in London. They had people like Abu Dada—even though not directly personally involved as Bruce Hoffman would probably argue—engaged in the careful building, subversive action that would lead to the emergence of Jihadist structures in Spain. Clearly, the people who had carried out the attacks were keen to act on the strategic guidance that was issued by al-Qaeda central.

At the same time, there is no evidence whatsoever that al-Qaeda central ever ordered this attack, that it directed the attack in a close operational sense, or that al-Qaeda central had been in touch with the perpetrators prior to the attack. There is no evidence also that any of the attackers had read the strategy document to which I have just referred. In fact, the strategy document on the Internet concluded by saying that the most promising way forward was to attack Spanish troops in Iraq rather than civilian targets in Spain. Of course, what is often forgotten is that this was not a stand-alone operation. In fact, the campaign—or that is what the perpetrators saw it as—continued after the Madrid attack, and it even continued after the withdrawal from Iraq had been announced. They were quite keen to carry out further attacks, and indeed on 2 April, three weeks after the attack and almost three weeks after the announcement of the withdrawal from Iraq, the Spanish police found an explosive device on the track of a high-speed train. That bomb, not the investigation of the initial attack, then led to the dramatic scenes in Yaganis, the suburb of Madrid, where the remaining members of the network blew themselves up in a flat realising that they were surrounded by police. So it was that attack that actually led to the uncovering of the entire network, and that attack was meant to be carried out long after the withdrawal from Iraq had been announced.

So the operational relationship between al-Qaeda and the Madrid bombers was actually quite complicated; it was even more complicated than what I have just tried to explain. There is no doubt that this attack was inspired by al-Qaeda, that Iraq was an important part of the rationale, but it is by no means clear whether it was intended by the people who carried out these attacks as an act of coercion specifically directed towards Spain's participation in the Iraq war.

Let us go back to the conventional wisdom and reiterate some of the findings we have just made. First of all, it is not at all clear that al-Qaeda was directly responsible for the attacks. It is not clear that this was specifically meant to force a withdrawal from Iraq, and it is also not clear whether the Spanish people saw themselves as giving into al-Qaeda blackmail. That is how it was portrayed, but many Spanish people would tell you an entirely different story.

Let me conclude therefore by telling you something that is perhaps surprising, namely that *it all does not matter. The narrative, however true it is, has stuck.* The Jihadist movement, al-Qaeda included, has wholeheartedly embraced that narrative. If you look at Jihadist web sites, if you look at pronouncements of al-Qaeda leaders, Madrid is the operation that is most frequently cited as an operational success after 9/11. Ayman al Zawahiri, in almost every video message, cites the example of Madrid as the one that needs to be emulated, an operation that in his view had a clear and tangible result. People in this country who were involved in the Crevice plot described it as the perfect operation, one that needed to be imitated; and so did Dhirien Barot, another British terrorist, who also spoke of the Madrid attacks as, in his words, another beautiful operation that needed to be copied in other parts of the world.

So whatever we believe really happened, the narrative or, to use Lawrence Freedman's expression, the script within the Jihadist movement is that Madrid proves that this kind of operation works, that you can coerce Western governments through terrorist actions. It may be a mess, and it may be similar to the idea that foreign fighters expelled the Soviets from Afghanistan and brought down the Soviet Union. It may be similarly mythical to the idea that the Jihadists expelled the Americans from Somalia. These arguments, though strongly believed, are far from true when you investigate the facts. But they are strongly believed, and that is perhaps why they matter. Indeed, I want to conclude therefore by arguing that no amount of explaining by myself and others at RUSI conferences will change that perception. The Jihadist narrative has stuck, and whatever we believe, whether it is true or not, clearly with Madrid—not only with Madrid but certainly with Madrid—the idea that you can coerce Western governments through this kind of action has become a reality.

Chapter 14

Framing Strategic Deterrence
Old Certainties, New Ambiguities

Lawrence Freedman*

During the Cold War, deterrence worked better in practice than in theory. It became an article of faith that great-power war was virtually unthinkable because of the consequences; yet this conclusion was reached without ever working through the scenarios. Today, in a world of shrinking great power arsenals and proliferating small arsenals, we may now be moving away from the models that served us well during the Cold War.

My starting quote is attributed to both Yogi Berra and Albert Einstein: "In theory," one or both of them said, "theory and practice should be the same; in practice they are different." Deterrence has always worked far better in practice than the theory might suggest. This is because theorising about deterrence faces some fundamental problems.

Causation and Communication

The critical thing about deterrence is that it succeeds when nothing happens. This creates a real problem in working out cause and effect. If somebody moves forward or attacks, you have an effect and can worry about the cause. These might be distant causes, the structural changes that created this possibility, the factors that made an event likely, and the immediate triggers that turn it into a reality. Whatever the focus, there is something tangible to work on.

When something does not happen, or somebody does not do something, the question of causation is much trickier. Maybe they never intended to do it; maybe they had intended to do it some time ago and had put the thought quite out of their mind; maybe they had intended to do it and were dissuaded from doing it by something completely unrelated to anything you said or did; maybe it was something you did but not the thing that

*Published earlier in *RUSI* 154, no. 4 (August 2009): 46–50.

you thought had caused the noneffect; or maybe there was no direct relationship between your threat and their inaction.

How do we know about what matters to the deterrer? We can assume that an individual or a nation does not like to be hit without provocation or see property damaged or stolen. A sense of social norms tells us that a person, a minority group, or a state may find certain statements offensive or actions provocative. Our best clues, however, come from the deterrer's own utterances. In this respect, successful deterrence is a product of clear foreign policy, confirming what you care about and declaring and demonstrating vital interests. If either side is surprised by a turn of events—the would-be deterrer should be deterred at the ferocity of the response—then deterrence has failed. The threat has not been made, noticed, or believed. For deterrence to work, there should be a clear relationship between the prospective offence and the threatened consequences. If that is not understood, then something has gone wrong with the communication of the threat, which, given what we know about human cognition, is always possible.

Evaluating Effectiveness

This uncertainty over causation and communications causes real difficulties when it comes to evaluating claims about the effectiveness of deterrence. Consider the Cold War, when, for a long time and to considerable relief, not a lot happened. By the end of this not-a-lot-happening period, impressive tracts were being written about the long peace and what caused it, and the dispute is not yet over. During the Cold War, there were many competing claims to be the cause of the great nonevent. Diplomats claimed it, the arms controllers claimed it, those in charge of missiles claimed it, and those in charge of conventional forces claimed it. Everybody could say they were doing their bit for deterrence. We have seen something similar with the War on Terror over the last eight years. When pitching for resources, security and military agencies sought to demonstrate that what they were offering was in some way essential to the core mission, even though the origins of the particular programmes lay elsewhere, and actual relevance might be hard to discern. This was much a feature of Cold War deterrence.

At the other extreme, deterrence may be happening without any special effort. In some respects, it is ubiquitous. If I fancy a fight, I am deterred by a large person simply because he is bigger than I. He does not know he is deterring me, as he has no idea that the thought of a fight has occurred to me. But he deters because one look is all I need to know he can really hurt me. So deterrence works perfectly well without the deterrer having to make much of a deliberate, conscious effort. Palpable strength makes the point. Let us call this deterrence lite. This is a normal part of social life—the things that you go through the day doing or more importantly not doing, such as not drinking and driving. This is a consequence of deterrence, because of fear of the consequences of causing an accident but also of being caught by the police and having a criminal record, and then being stigmatised by friends, family, and neighbours.

Deterrence regular occurs when there is an explicit warning that hostile action would be unwise, a convincing explanation of why this would be so, and then nothing happens. The real issues with deterrence theory come with what we might call deterrence plus. The deterrer issues a very specific and dire threat in respect of potential hostile actions and demonstrates a readiness to implement them if the act occurs, even though implementation may add to the risks faced. Strategic deterrence is an example of deterrence plus.

Strategic Deterrence

Strategic deterrence is not just about nuclear weapons and post-1945 concepts. The antecedents can be found in the theories of strategic bombing developed in the 1930s, as described in George Quester's book, *Deterrence before Hiroshima*. The essence of strategic deterrence, whether with conventional bombers or nuclear missiles, is that (a) one side can impose great hurt on another; (b) the other side cannot stop that; (c) but it is capable of imposing great hurt back. As the conundrums this caused began to be addressed, and taking the very simplistic formula that deterrence depends on convincing the beholder that prospective costs will outweigh prospective gains, a whole series of theories were elaborated about the manipulation of gains as well as costs. Preventing gain by means of a credible ability to stop aggression in its tracks became known as deterrence by denial, while imposing costs became deterrence by punishment. (Glenn Snyder was originally responsible for the distinction.) Nonetheless, issues surrounding punishment really forged the conceptual framework associated with nuclear deterrence.

Credibility

One factor favouring deterrence was that it answered the stark exam question posed by the arrival of nuclear weapons: What role can there be for a capability that has no tactical role in stopping armies or navies but can destroy whole cities? An answer in terms of war fighting appeared distasteful and possibly ineffectual. An answer in terms of deterrence promised the prevention of future war. Though at first this offered a way to extract value out of a terrifying capability, doubts soon developed as the other side acquired its own capabilities and could respond in kind. If both sides had the capacity to hurt each other, then the only way out would be for one side to develop an ability to disarm the other in a surprise first strike. In the prenuclear era, this used to be called the blunting mission. This can be seen very clearly at that moment in the Battle of Britain, when there was a degree of relief that the German campaign had moved to cities and away from airfields. So long as the airfields were intact, the Royal Air Force could continue to function and prosecute the war. If the airfields were progressively knocked out, eventual defeat seemed inevitable. During the Cold War, the basic problem of credibility became more acute. Why would you implement a nuclear threat when this would lead to equally devastating retaliation?

There was another problem of credibility—not quite so severe then but probably more so now. Would rational, conscience-stricken policy makers ever really initiate nuclear warfare? At the end of the Second World War, after the blitz and the V-bombers, finding out about Auschwitz and Belsen, sanctioning Hamburg, Dresden, and the fire bombing of Tokyo, the atom bombs seemed to be a logical culmination of what had gone before and also brutally successful in bringing a total war to an end. The simplest (if depressing) assumption was that war was going to become pro-

248

gressively more murderous, with ever-more sophisticated means being found to slaughter people on a large scale.

Since then, we like to think that we have developed more humanitarian strategies that reject the idea that it is reasonable, fair, just, and even honourable to attack populations in war. Even when there is some agreement with the cause, methods that hurt civilians lead to strong objections. There have been three events in recent months—Gaza, Swat Valley (Pakistan), and Sri Lanka—where our side is putting civilian populations at risk, leading to complaints that a better way ought to be found, less careless of human life. Our doctrines stress attacking combatants rather than noncombatants, but there is a lingering question of whether we could switch, as we have switched before, into a position where we are prepared to put civilian populations at risk. You can always say your main target was elsewhere: Truman described Hiroshima as an important military base. The issue is not so much whether nuclear attacks would be illegal under international law but whether it would even be possible to get ourselves into the mind-set where we could make threats with any conviction in circumstances other than the destruction of our countries.

Protecting Friends

Another question of credibility, which was very important during the Cold War and is still present, is that of extended deterrence, which is the readiness to deter attacks on friends and partners as well as oneself. We may need better language to describe the issue now, but the idea is simple. It raises the problem of credibility in its most pure form. Would you unleash nuclear weapons in any circumstances other than an existential threat against your own state? During the Cold War, in part because of the superiority that the United States initially enjoyed, it got itself into the position—through such doctrines as massive retaliation in the mid-1950s—of threatening colossal nuclear war in response to a conventional attack against allies. As the Soviet Union acquired effective means of retaliation, the United States did not abandon that initial commitment. Indeed, theorising about deterrence developed precisely because of the problem about maintaining security guarantees to allies in

249

these circumstances. Without extended deterrence, the credibility problems would not have seemed so great. The French, for example, did not worry so much about it. They had a pure and simple doctrine of deterrence: if my country is attacked I will respond, and we will do what we can to hurt those who have hurt us. Only in the face of German objections to short-range weapons that seemed to envisage nuclear exchanges over German soil without any offer of extended deterrence in return did the French start to qualify their doctrine, and they got themselves in a considerable muddle as a result. Deterrence is much easier if you are just looking after yourself.

There is no good theoretical answer to the problem of extended deterrence as it is a matter of political judgment and will. It is a function of the strength of alliance commitment, and whether membership of an alliance, such as North Atlantic Treaty Organization (NATO), turns a country into a vital interest of the United States. NATO has acquired a number of new members since the end of the Cold War. Questions of political identity may have been more important than security guarantees at first, but now security concerns are more to the fore. It is striking how, in the face of Russian assertiveness in Europe and rising Chinese power in Asia, questions about the quality and durability of the nuclear umbrella are back on the agenda.

An assumption during the Cold War was that credibility could be added to nuclear threats through a demonstrable willingness to deal with aggression first by conventional means. Through conventional battles, the passion and the engagement would be generated that could create the momentum to propel the alliance forward to the next dire step on the ladder of escalation. The starting point—again going back to the mid-1950s—was the notion of the trip wire. When asked what conventional forces were needed on the inner German border to deter Soviet aggression, the answer was that there needed only be one soldier, but he must be American, and he must be killed, as if that would then trigger full-scale nuclear retaliation. In the face of growing Soviet nuclear strength, the trip wire notion seemed increasingly implausible.

By the time of the doctrine of flexible response in the 1960s, a serious conventional response was considered essential (even if not quite affordable) as an assertion of vital interests and as a means of creating conditions in which the use of nuclear weapons was just about conceivable. Therefore, nuclear and conventional capabilities were not separate but of a piece. They were joined together by so-called tactical nuclear weapons. The notion that these were truly tactical was always nonsensical, as if somehow these could be detonated as part of a regular war. This was the presumption when they were first introduced, as almost all types of conventional munitions were matched by nuclear versions. My favourite remains the Davy Crockett, the weapon with a lethal radius greater than its range. That was just an extreme version of the core problem with these weapons. They could not be used as if they were conventional weapons. In the event the blurring of the conventional/nuclear boundary became their vir-tue, they provided the powder trail from the conventional to the nuclear battle as field commanders sought to use them to get out of an otherwise hopeless situation. This helped to move the idea of the deterrent threat from the "If you do X, I will do Y" to "If you do X, you will set in motion a chain of events that may or may not include Y, but there is a risk that it might." This is what Tom Schelling called "the threat that leaves something to chance." If the Y was very large, the risk was probably not worth it, assuming that the X, the first blow, could not eliminate the possibility of Y.

Mutual Assured Destruction

By the mid-1960s, all of this was confirmed by mutual as-sured destruction (MAD). The language was supposed to be brutal and unambiguous. US Secretary of Defense Robert Mc-Namara rejected euphemism. He wanted people to understand that there would be destruction, it would be assured, and it would be mutual. The advantage was that it was absolutely clear to both sides where aggression might lead. It was therefore best to do everything possible to eliminate that chance and not try anything clever to get around this. Over time, MAD turned into crisis stability. Thereafter, a panoply of measures was de-veloped about how to coexist ideologically, resolve areas of dis-pute, regulate the military relationship to ensure that it remained stable, and maintain intense channels of communication, including a hotline at all times so that it was always possible to confer during a crisis.

Over time, this developed further into what Patrick Morgan called general deterrence. This was distinct from immediate deterrence, which refers to those situations when hostile intent is evident, and threats are issued with some urgency to prevent this turning into a hostile act. General deterrence is when there is no need to bother. Deep down, the hostile intent may still be present, but a hostile act has become so self-evidently foolish that it is no longer being considered.

Since the end of the Cold War, these issues have not really been revisited in anything like the depth and enthusiasm with which they were addressed during the golden age of nuclear strategy in the late 1950s and early 1960s. That period still provides the conceptual framework for thinking about deterrence and nuclear weapons. The question now is whether nuclear deterrence has outlived whatever value it might have had. Questions are raised about its relevance for nonstate actors and then for dealing with other so-called weapons of mass destruction— that is chemical and biological weapons. The term *weapons of mass destruction* is seriously misleading. Nuclear weapons are weapons of mass destruction, for they really do not have much use for anything else. Chemical and biological weapons may get used in lesser contingencies, and in terms of their destructiveness, they are not in the same category as nuclear weapons.

There is a purported example of nuclear deterrence working against chemical threats seen during the 1991 Gulf War. This illustrates the problem of explaining a negative—of why something did not happen. In this case, it was the fact that Iraq did not use chemical weapons. Tariq Aziz, then Iraq's foreign minister, said that the leadership was deterred by the threat of nuclear use. The actual deterrent threat issued by the administration of George Bush senior, however, was to topple the regime, delivered to Aziz in Geneva by Secretary of State James Baker just before the start of the war. It may also be that the Iraqis could not use any artillery very well, for they were completely disorientated, and even if an order had gone out, it would have been difficult to implement. Perhaps individual commanders were deterred by the threat of being prosecuted for a war crime. In stressing nuclear deterrence, Aziz may have been boasting, showing that this was the sort of regime that could only be deterred by the most severe of threats. If chemical weapons had been used, there would have been plenty of nonnuclear responses available and no intent to resort to nuclear weapons. So this case does not really prove anything.

A more important concern is whether there has been a revival of the risks of great-power war. Arguably, the great achievement of nuclear deterrence was to serve as a constant reminder of why such a war would be a terrible idea. It reminds us of how bad things could get. If we ever did have a third world war, it is hard to imagine how the restraints would hold. From the West's point of view, the conventional superiority of NATO in Europe and of US maritime strength in Asia provides good reasons neither Russia nor China would be tempted to cross the obvious red lines that alliance creates. That Georgia was picked on by Russia *before* it was a member of NATO is an indication that alliance still counts for something in these circumstances. It also invokes other requirements of stable deterrence, including clarity of vital interests and of military capabilities. If Russia attempted something similar to Georgia in Latvia, for example, it would know, whatever the uncertainties resulting from questions of timing and political will, that NATO forces would likely be involved in some form at quite an early stage.

Smaller Powers

The next concerns whether these essentials for stable deterrence might work for small nuclear powers, including rogue states. The issue of clarity of interest remains critical. If you are unclear about what matters, you cannot expect to deter. Is it also necessary to ensure a second-strike capability, encourage mutual assured destruction, have a serious conventional capability for flexible response to produce the escalatory pressures, have constant communication between potential adversaries to resolve disputes, manage military relationships, and prevent accidents and inadvertent escalation?

This is not necessarily only a matter of whether deterrence relationships might develop between NATO countries and these smaller powers but also the smaller powers' relationships with each other. This would include India and Pakistan or Iran and

Israel. Might such relationships develop into mutual deterrence? If Iran's nuclear capability cannot be stopped either by diplomatic or by preemptive military means, perhaps the Israelis would become much more explicit about their nuclear capabilities and address deterrence issues more directly. There are efforts now to move Indo-Pakistani relations to the point where they can cope with crises and reduce the risks of accidents and inadvertent escalation. Could the same be achieved with Israel and Iran? The reason for pessimism on this score is that the cases of nuclear proliferation involve countries that are chronically insecure and also, in a number of cases, potentially unstable internally. This is incidentally not a new issue. Recall the generals' revolt in France in the late 1950s while the *force de frappe* was under development or the Cultural Revolution in China in the 1960s at the same time as their testing. Now, we have to consider with Pakistan, North Korea, and maybe even Iran the possibility of nuclear assets getting caught up in internal turmoil. For both of these reasons, there is also a clear and constant interaction with nonstate actors, which are often active in and around these countries, stoking up dissent and conflict. A final factor is that these arsenals are tiny. It is hard to think in terms of mutual assured destruction as traditionally conceived, but it may also be a reminder that a few nuclear detonations would still have catastrophic consequences.

A further factor to consider is the pressure for radical disarmament. It is hard to object because there is a lot of surplus capacity around. At a certain point, continued disarmament will raise questions about deterrence relationships, particularly extended deterrence. This can already be seen with Japan, for example, which hates nuclear weapons for good reasons and would like them to be abolished. However, it is also scared of China and values its alliance with the United States because it does not want to look weak in relation to China.

Future Cares

In terms of a policy for the future, I would continue to stress the importance of alliance, for this removes ambiguity from security relationships. Alliance brings with it a form of extended deterrence, even if it is not nuclear. Refusing alliance can have

254

consequences, but so can accepting it, for that may cause a moral hazard all its own. The comparisons between banking meltdowns and nuclear meltdowns are questionable, but the ability of some to feel that whatever they do, somebody will rescue them, can create a dangerous situation, as was almost seen in Georgia. The reason for the Sino-Soviet split that occurred 50 years ago was that the Soviet Union would not underwrite every Chinese adventure. The biggest danger is too much ambiguity. That does not mean going round the world drawing red lines everywhere, but it is about being clear and honest if and when we are moving into dangerous situations. To go back to the 1991 war, when Iraq was threatening Kuwait, the United States had to say truthfully that "we have no defence responsibilities to Kuwait." It might have been better to raise the possibility that in the event of crude aggression, the issue is not a defence responsibility but the maintenance of international order. As crises develop in distant places, it is better to address the possibility of engagement before rather than after the act.

For the reasons already suggested, we may now be moving away from the models that served us well during the Cold War. To recap, deterrence worked better in practice than in theory to the point where we came to take it for granted that a great-power war would be an extraordinarily foolish thing upon which to embark. This conclusion was reached without really working out the scenarios. We are now thinking about a world of shrinking great-power arsenals but proliferating small arsenals and of ambiguous relationships in situations of insecurity and inner turmoil. For Western countries, deterrence remains, in the end, a problem of foreign policy. It is not necessarily a matter of capabilities or targeting—as our countries have no problems with either—or even what we do with nuclear weapons, for our conventional forces should be sufficient to have a deterrent effect in most contingencies. The fundamental issue remains one of whom and what we care about and how far we are prepared to go to follow our cares.

Chapter 15

India versus Pakistan
From Partition to the Present

*Rahul Roy-Chaudhury**

Mutual trust is in short supply between South Asia's two major rivals, India and Pakistan. The nuclear powers are bitterly divided on a host of issues, none more (seemingly) intractable than the future of Kashmir. Yet their nuclear arsenals have probably helped steer both countries away from all-out conventional war and even led to a thaw in bilateral relations. The key to better relations in the future will be how effectively India and Pakistan can cooperate to deter nonstate actors from carrying out major terrorist attacks.

The Indo-Pakistani rivalry dominates the strategic landscape of South Asia, where India serves as the major hegemon and Pakistan its principal challenger. In over 60 years of independence, the two countries have fought three (and one-half) wars with each other, mostly over the disputed territory of Kashmir, whose future status remains unresolved. Both countries possess nuclear weapons to deter each other, while expanding their conventional armed forces. Advanced military technology, including modern combat aircraft and ballistic and cruise missiles, are deployed alongside rising defence budgets.

Yet the prospect of another major state-versus-state war, akin to what took place between India and Pakistan nearly 40 years ago in December 1971, is unlikely. This is due to the probability of an all-arms conventional war escalating to nuclear use, which would result in mutual destruction. Far more likely is an increase in terror attacks by nonstate actors, which could generate greater Indo-Pakistani tensions with the risk of inadvertent military escalation by both countries. Such a state-versus-nonstate encounter would take place amidst their ongoing bilateral disputes and the potential for the threat of use of force by the two nuclear weapon states.

---

*Published earlier in *RUSI* 154, no. 4 (August 2009): 60–65.

Kashmir and Conflict

The dispute over the future of the former princely state of Kashmir, currently divided among India, Pakistan, and China, is largely, though not wholly, responsible for Indo-Pakistani tensions. In the past, this has led to wars and conflicts between the two countries.

The partition of British India in August 1947 was conducted on the basis of demography and geography, whereby predominantly Muslim contiguous areas went to Pakistan and the rest to India.[1] The princely state of Jammu and Kashmir, however, stood out with a Hindu ruling family governing a predominantly Muslim population in an area bordering both India and Pakistan. The only politically viable option for Kashmir was to opt for either India or Pakistan but not seek independence. India's claim over Kashmir rests on the Hindu ruler's accession to India on 26 October 1947 for fear of being overthrown by a pro-Pakistan Muslim tribal rebellion. Pakistan hotly contests this accession and claims that Kashmir is theirs on the basis of its Muslim-majority population.[2]

This led to the first India-Pakistan war from 26 October 1947 until the United Nations–mandated cease-fire on 1 January 1949, which left India with two-thirds and Pakistan the remainder of Kashmir. The cease-fire line (CFL) divided the Indian- and Pakistan-controlled parts of Kashmir. But following China's occupation of Aksai Chin—comprising a fifth of the princely state of Kashmir—during the 1962 Sino-Indian war, Pakistan ceded a portion of its own Kashmir-administered area to China the following year, thereby involving China in any final resolution of the Kashmir dispute.

The second Indo-Pakistani war from 1 to 23 September 1965 also took place over the Kashmir dispute. Pakistan's conventional attack across the CFL led to two weeks of bitter land and air warfare and culminated in a military stalemate. Following the UN-mandated cease-fire on 22 September 1965, the peace agreement at Tashkent in the erstwhile Soviet Union the following year led to both sides agreeing to exchange the territories captured by either side across the CFL, thereby restoring the status quo ante.[31]

The third Indo-Pakistani war on 3–17 December 1971 was the first that did not take place over Kashmir; instead, it had its origin in the Indian-aided secession of East Pakistan (now Bangladesh). Pakistan suffered a devastating blow with the loss of its eastern part; nearly 90,000 of its troops and citizens were held as prisoners of war by India. The Pakistani delegation to the peace talks in July 1972 in the northern Indian town of Simla was disappointed by the ensuing Simla Agreement of 3 July 1972, which *inter alia* converted the CFL into the line of control (LoC), reflecting minor variations in the CFL. The 460-mile (740 km) LoC was subsequently demarcated and reproduced in detail in two sets of maps by both sides in the Suchetgarh Agreement of 11 December 1972.

The most recent conflict over Kashmir took place 10 years ago in May–July 1999 in its Kargil sector. This was also the first time that both countries fought against each other after their nuclear tests, conducted a year earlier, which caused acute concern amongst the international community.[4] Nevertheless, it was precisely this nuclear dimension that largely confined the Kargil conflict to infantry and artillery operations by both sides, along with limited combat ground support air missions.

When Pakistan's clandestine military operation to occupy a series of high features along a 200 km trans-Himalayan front across the LoC was discovered in May 1999, India reacted strongly by putting its forces on alert and deploying troops and artillery guns to dislodge Pakistani troops and militants.[5] Pakistan's intrusion across the LoC came as a surprise to India, and India's determination and resolve to force the withdrawal of Pakistani forces back across the LoC was a surprise to Pakistan. Following several weeks of intense fighting and subsequent mediation by the United States, Pakistan announced the withdrawal of its forces from across the LoC in mid-July. India exercised restraint by ensuring that its own forces did not cross the LoC at any time of the conflict. Indian casualties included 474 men killed and over a thousand wounded; on the Pakistani side, an estimated 700 troops were killed, including 71 officers, and 243 militants.[6]

Clearly, the Kashmir dispute is not just about conflicting territorial claims but ideological compulsions as well. For Pakistan, created on the basis of the two-nation theory that Muslims

of the Indian sub-continent could not live alongside the majority Hindu population, the incorporation of Kashmir legitimises
its claim as a Muslim state. This became even more important
after having suffered the secession of East Pakistan in 1971.
For India, the incorporation of Kashmir legitimises its own claim
as a secular state for both Hindus and Muslims alike (since
1972 it has possessed the second-largest Muslim population
after Indonesia). Then, there is the future of the Kashmiri people themselves.

With both countries now possessing nuclear weapons and
delivery systems to deter each other, conventional major war
seems unlikely; the risks associated with escalation are too
grave. Indeed, the Kargil conflict was deliberately limited in
scale and operation by both sides to prevent such an escalation. To mitigate the possibility of another Kargil-type conflict
taking place in the future and to ensure peace and stability in
Kashmir, however, both countries have for the first time been
engaged in a comprehensive dialogue (begun in 2004) on the
Kashmir dispute. The joint statement of 6 January 2004 ensured the resumption of official-level bilateral talks after a
three-year hiatus. For the first time, New Delhi formally recog-
nised that the Kashmir dispute was to be settled to the satisfaction of both sides, and Islamabad pledged it would "not permit any territory under Pakistan's control to be used to support
terrorism in any manner."[7] The bilateral composite dialogue
that followed tackled eight key disputes and issues: peace and
security, Jammu and Kashmir, Siachen,[8] the Wular barrage/
Tulbul navigation project,[9] Sir Creek,[10] terrorism and drug trafficking, economic and commercial cooperation, and the promo-
tion of friendly exchanges.[11]

These talks have resulted in important confidence-building
measures in Kashmir, including for the first time the opening
of routes across the LoC for both passenger and trade traffic.
The 2003 cease-fire on the LoC and Siachen has also held despite allegations of violations by both sides. But even as India
feels emboldened by the 60 percent turnout in provincial elections in Kashmir in December 2008, it clearly needs to do more
to ensure peace and security in Kashmir.

To be sure, a final resolution of the Kashmir dispute involves
a host of complexities. Pakistan's preferred solution is the inde-

pendence or control of the Kashmir valley, something that is not acceptable to India, which currently exercises control. At the same time, India's preferred solution is to legitimise the LoC as the de jure international border, which is not acceptable to Pakistan as it sees the LoC as part of the problem and not a part of the solution. However, in a significant development in 2005–6, the president of Pakistan, Pervez Musharraf, and Indian prime minister Manmohan Singh put forward important proposals and counterproposals short of these maximalist national positions. In essence, they focused on making the LoC a soft border or making it irrelevant, while ensuring cross-border economic and people-to-people links among the Kashmiri inhabitants.[12] Special representatives of both countries have been working hard to further develop these ideas.

But the Mumbai terror attack in November 2008 stalled these talks. Despite the renewed tension, India seeks to reengage with Pakistan. Singh, at a meeting with current Pakistani president Asif Ali Zardari, poised on the sidelines of the Shanghai Co-operation Organisation's summit in Russia in June 2009, made it clear that he was willing to talk to Pakistan on terrorism if it cracked down on groups targeting India. In the joint statement at Sharm-el-Sheikh in Egypt on 16 July 2009, Singh and Pakistani prime minister Syed Yusuf Raza Gilani agreed that "action on terrorism should not be linked to the Composite Dialogue process and these should not be bracketed."[13] Although this appeared to imply that India was no longer prepared to halt official-level talks in the wake of another terror attack emanating from Pakistani territory, it was given another interpretation, namely, that Pakistan's actions to counter-terrorism should take place regardless of whether the bilateral peace process was suspended or not. The "composite dialogue" remains stalled.

Terrorism and Tensions

Even as the prospect of a major Indo-Pakistani state-versus-state war has receded, the prospect of a repeat of the December 2001 and November 2008 terrorist attacks is high. Following the terror attack on the Indian parliament on 13 December 2001, blamed on two Pakistan-based Islamist militant groups—

the Lashkar-e-Taiba (LeT) and the Jaish-e-Mohammed (JeM)—
India attempted to coerce Pakistan into complying with its demands to extradite the terrorist leaders and end cross-border
infiltration into Indian-controlled Kashmir and other parts of
India. As part of its coercive diplomacy against Pakistan, India
launched Operation Parakram [Valour] on 19 December 2001
and mobilised its armed forces in preparation for warfare. This
was a deliberate move, taking place amidst the global campaign
against terror, to threaten the use of force against Pakistan. It
included the deployment of India's three strike corps at forward
positions on the international border with Pakistan.

This 10-month military confrontation was the longest military mobilisation by both countries since independence in
1947.[14] At the height of the crisis (between December 2001 and
January 2002), over a million Indian and Pakistani armed
troops stood virtually eyeball to eyeball across the border for
several months. Facilitation by the British and American governments eased the situation.[15]

Tensions rose again after the devastating terror attack in
Mumbai on 26–28 November 2008, blamed on the Pakistan-
based LeT and its front organisation, Jamaat-ud-Dawah (JuD).
Although the LeT was formed as a group opposing Indian sovereignty in the disputed territory of Kashmir, it later acquired a
broader Islamist agenda. Ten men armed with guns and bombs
attacked multiple sites in a globally televised 60-hour siege
that killed 163 people and wounded over 300. Nine terrorists
were killed and one captured. While much of the killing was
indiscriminate, foreign nationals were specifically targeted, and
22 were killed. While India initially blamed elements in Pakistan for the attack, Singh raised the ante in January 2009 by
stating that the attack had the "support of some official agencies in Pakistan."[16] Though officially banned in Pakistan, the
LeT has been widely alleged to have links with Pakistan's Inter-
Services Intelligence (ISI) agency.

There was no military mobilization by either side in the aftermath of the Mumbai terror attack, even as both countries put
their armed forces on alert. There was intense media speculation that India would mount a surgical strike or carry out a
limited military operation against LeT/JuD camps and infrastructure in Pakistan, neither of which took place. While India

and the international community continue to press Pakistan to take action against the LeT/JuD, Pakistan has taken some steps in this direction. However, India believes that large parts of the LeT/JuD terror network remains untouched and views as a major setback the release of JuD chief Hafiz Muhammad Saeed from house arrest in early June on the orders of the Lahore High Court.[17]

Even though the Mumbai attack was the most spectacular in India last year, there has been a spurt in religious violence by both Indian Muslim and Hindu extremist groups. For the first time, India formally acknowledged the existence of homegrown jihadi groups following the simultaneous bomb blasts in the major cities of Jaipur, Bangalore, Ahmedabad, and New Delhi in the past year, killing over 150 people. In addition, six people were killed in bomb blasts in two western Indian cities last September. Eleven Hindu extremists of the radical group Abhinav Bharat were subsequently arrested and charged for these attacks, including a serving middle-ranking army officer.

At the same time, terror attacks in Pakistan occur on a weekly basis, if not more frequently; and, they continue to spread from the tribal areas bordering Afghanistan to the North West Frontier Province (NWFP) and other parts of the country. Most of these attacks have been attributed to Baitullah Mehsud (who was reportedly killed in an American drone attack), the leader of the Tehreek-e-Taliban Pakistan. The most prominent terror attack destroyed the landmark Marriott Hotel in Islamabad in September 2008, killing 54 people. The Sharm-el-Sheikh joint declaration referred to Pakistan's information on "threats in Balochistan and other areas,"[18] but India has denied it is linked to terror attacks in Pakistan. Terror attacks in both India and Pakistan are expected to continue, despite the strengthening of their national security structures. The likelihood of a Pakistan-based militant group carrying out another Mumbai-type terror attack in India to disrupt peace talks and provoke another India-Pakistan confrontation is high. This may not only fatally disrupt the peace process, but it would also generate considerable domestic pressure—in an already delicate nuclear weapons environment—for India to toughen its stance. The lack of mutual trust, along with possible misperceptions and misunderstandings, could result in inadvertent military escalation by both countries.

Nuclear Weapons and Threats

Since their May 1998 nuclear tests—when India's five tests built on its first in 1974 and Pakistan equalised with six of its own—both countries have announced voluntary unilateral moratoriums on further testing, even as they continue to expand their nuclear forces. Nuclear weapons and forces now serve as an integral part of both India and Pakistan's national security strategies and are expected to remain so for the foreseeable future.

India's rationale for testing was a mix of factors, including Pakistan's nuclear-capable missile and weapons programme as well as China's nuclear capabilities (the latter made clear in an official letter to then US president Bill Clinton in 1998), along with issues of national prestige. Pakistan's rationale was simply India's nuclear tests. India is currently estimated to possess 70–120 nuclear weapons to Pakistan's 60–120 weapons.[19]

India's 2003 nuclear doctrine formally enunciated a no first use (NFU) posture with second-strike massive retaliation. It contains two important caveats: first, in terms of a nuclear response against a nuclear attack on Indian forces anywhere, although this remains undefined; and second, in terms of a nuclear response to an attack by biological or chemical weapons. There is also speculation that by referring to a first strike designed to inflict unacceptable damage, India was actually conveying a flexible response rather than a massive retaliation posture.[20]

India also aims to build a credible minimum nuclear deterrent triad with aircraft, missiles, and sea-based capabilities. Testing of nuclear-capable ballistic missiles with longer ranges as well as cruise missiles takes place regularly. While parts of its land- and air-based assets are deployed, the first step towards its sea-based deterrent took place with the launch of its first ballistic-missile-capable nuclear-powered submarine on 26 July 2009. A Nuclear Command Authority has been established with the prime minister for the use of nuclear weapons.

Pakistan has not formally published its nuclear doctrine, but in view of its relative conventional arms inferiority with India, it can best be described as a non-NFU policy. It reportedly focuses on building a minimum nuclear deterrent and has had a National Command Authority since 2000. The head of its secretariat, the Strategic Plans Division (SPD), is an able three-star general, who recently retired from the army.

To stabilise their nuclear relationship, both countries agreed in June 2004 that their nuclear capabilities constitute a factor for stability. Since then, several nuclear confidence-building measures have been agreed upon and implemented. These include the June 2004 agreement to establish a dedicated hotline between the two foreign secretaries to reduce nuclear risks, the October 2005 agreement on the advanced notification of ballistic missile flight tests, and the February 2007 agreement focused on reducing risks from accidents relating to nuclear weapons. On 1 January 2009, both countries exchanged their lists of nuclear installations for the eighteenth successive year in relation to their 1998 agreement on prohibition of attack against nuclear installations and facilities. Yet, these nuclear confidence-building measures needed to be bolstered and institutionalised to ensure that misperceptions and misunderstandings are reduced during periods of tension. Hostile nuclear signalling has been carried out by both countries during past conflicts and crises. In the Kargil conflict, Pakistan conveyed only veiled nuclear signals to India, even as a former senior Clinton administration official claimed in May 2002 that Pakistan was preparing its nuclear-tipped ballistic missiles for possible deployment at the height of the conflict in July 1999.[21] In contrast, the 2001–2 military confrontation demonstrated unprecedented nuclear signalling—in the form of forceful public pronouncements and flight-tests of ballistic missiles—between the two countries, amidst the disruption of normal diplomatic channels of communication for much of the time. Both countries sent signals on nuclear as well as conventional matters with their public statements or deafening silences, with the issuance of provocative and inflammatory statements, and with subsequent denials or clarifications. These signals were multiple in nature, carried out at multiple levels, and addressed to multiple constituencies, to their domestic audiences, to each other, and to the United States and the United Kingdom. Whereas New Delhi wanted the United States and the United Kingdom to help pressure Pakistan to cease cross-border infiltration of militants into Indian-controlled Kashmir, Islamabad wanted the United States and the United Kingdom to restrain

New Delhi from taking military action. But it was not always clear that these signals, which were often confusing and ambiguous, were ever fully or even partially ascertained by either India or Pakistan.[22]

Some key concerns over the future of regional nuclear stability remain. These include, for Pakistan, the acquisition of Airborne Warning and Control System by India, the first of three having arrived in India in May 2009. They have the potential to identify nuclear-capable Pakistani F-16 combat aircraft and therefore erode Pakistan's nuclear deterrent. Another concern of Islamabad is the development of a ballistic missile defence system by India. In addition, Pakistan is concerned that the landmark India-US civil nuclear deal of October 2008 could provide India with additional stocks of weapon-grade fissile material from indigenous sources.

For India, its key concerns remain the clandestine spread of nuclear weapon technologies from Pakistan in the wake of the AQ Khan proliferation scandal, along with the related possibility of nuclear terrorism. There is also alarm about the possible infiltration of Pakistan's nuclear weapons establishment by Islamic extremists, despite the high priority Pakistan's SPD has given to countering this threat and the more general fear that the Pakistani Taliban will be able to extend its power base across the country. There are also questions over effective civilian oversight and command and control of Pakistan's nuclear weapons that have traditionally been controlled by the military, the key question being whether President Zardari has control of Pakistan's nuclear weapons. This uncertainty makes the nuclear environment considerably more fragile.

Conclusion

Mutual trust is in short supply between South Asia's two major rivals, India and Pakistan. Traditional rivalries and antagonisms have been exacerbated by the issues highlighted above. Peace efforts by civil society/nongovernmental organisations in both countries have not had much impact in times of tension, even though people-to-people contacts have dramatically increased. India continues to hold Pakistan responsible for the use of its territory by the LeT/JuD to carry out terror acts against India; it has also alleged official Pakistani links to the Mumbai attack of November 2008, which Islamabad denies. India urges Pakistan to act against the LeT/JuD in the same tough manner that it is currently doing against the Pakistan Taliban in the Swat valley and the Malakand division of the NWFP, which Islamabad appears unable or unwilling to do perhaps due to concern over provoking an LeT terror backlash in Pakistan itself.

For its part, Pakistan continues to seek additional evidence from India on the Mumbai attack that it describes as insufficient for its own investigations into the attack, even as it has made several arrests. Pakistan alleges that India is involved in the insurgency in Balochistan, which New Delhi denies, and claims that India's diplomatic and economic activities in Afghanistan are aimed at decreasing its own influence in the region. The key issue remains the ability of both countries to cooperate to deter nonstate actors from carrying out terrorist spectaculars like Mumbai. Both India and Pakistan have signed the South Asian Association for Regional Cooperation framework on the suppression of terrorism, as well as its additional protocol. It is therefore in the interests of both countries to ensure that terror organisations aiming to disrupt their peaceful bilateral relations are effectively prevented from doing so.

Notes

1. Rahul Roy-Chaudhury, "The Security Council and the India-Pakistan Wars," in Vaughan Lowe, Adam Roberts *et al.* (eds.), *The United Nations Security Council and War: The Evolution of Thought and Practice since 1945* (Oxford: Oxford University Press, 2008), 326.

2. Ibid., 327–28.

3. Ibid., 337.

4. Rahul Roy-Chaudhury, "India's Nuclear Doctrine: A Critical Analysis," *Strategic Analysis*, May 2009, 405.

5. Government of India, *The Kargil Review Committee Report: From Surprise to Reckoning* (New Delhi: Sage Publications, 1999), 16.

6. Ibid., 23, 97–98.

7. The International Institute for Strategic Studies, "India and Pakistan: Towards Greater Bilateral Stability," *Strategic Survey 2003/4* (London: Oxford University Press, 2004), 232.

8. The Siachen glacier, located in the Karakoram range of the Himalayan mountains, has never been bilaterally demarcated on a map; the 1949 Karachi

Agreement defined the cease-fire line in the area as running to map co-ordinate NJ 9842 and "thence north to the glaciers." From 1984 to 2003, this was the highest battlefield in the world—at heights of over 20,000 feet.

9. India's construction of the Tulbul navigation project on the river Jhelum is challenged by Pakistan on the basis that it violates the bilateral 1960 Indus Water Treaty as it aims to store water. This is denied by India on the basis that it simply maintains a better water level during the dry season.

10. Sir Creek is a 96-kilometre estuary that runs between the marshes of the Rann of Kutch in the Indian state of Gujarat and the Pakistani province of Sindh and opens into the Arabian Sea. The Indo-Pakistani boundary along this creek has not been demarcated.

11. The International Institute for Strategic Studies, "India and Pakistan: Cautious Engagement," *Strategic Survey 2004/5* (London: Routledge, 2005), 316.

12. The International Institute for Strategic Studies, "South Asia: New Possibilities, Old Problems," *Strategic Survey 2006* (London: Routledge, 2006), 312–13.

13. See "Text of Joint Statement of Prime Minister Manmohan Singh and Prime Minister Syed Yusuf Raza Gilani," 16 July 2009, http://www.hindu.com/nic/indopak.htm>.

14. Roy-Chaudhury, "India's Nuclear Doctrine," in note 4, 406–7.

15. Rahul Roy-Chaudhury, "The United States' Role and Influence on the India-Pakistan Conflict," United Nations Institute for Disarmament Research Disarmament Forum, 2004, 34–36.

16. Krittivas Mukherjee, "India PM Says Pakistan 'Agencies' Linked to Attack," 6 January 2009, <http://www.reuters.com/article/topNews/idUSTRE5030YB20090106>.

17. "Shock Win in India," *IISS Strategic Comments* 15, no. 5 (June 2009), http://www.iiss.org/publications/strategic-comments/past-issues/volume-15-2009/volume-15-issue-5/.

18. Text of Joint Statement of Prime Minister Manmohan Singh and Prime Minister Syed Yusuf Raza Gilani.

19. See the Nuclear Threat Initiative (NTI) website, http://www.nti.org/e_research/profiles/India/index.html and http://www.nti.org/e_research/profiles/Pakistan/index.html.

20. Roy-Chaudhury, "India's Nuclear Doctrine," in note 4, 409.

21. Ibid., pp. 405–406.

22. Rahul Roy-Chaudhury, "Nuclear Doctrine, Declaratory Policy, and Escalation Control," in Michael Krepon et al. (eds.), *Escalation Control and the Nuclear Option in South Asia* (Washington, DC: Henry L Stimson Center, 2004), 101, 116.

Chapter 16

Deterring Nonstate Actors
The Challenge of al-Qaeda

John Stone

It has frequently been suggested over the last few years that the concept of deterrence has had its day, that its previously important position within Western strategy arose from the particular conditions of the Cold War, and that these conditions are no longer extant. According to this line of argument, the efficacy of deterrence rested on our capacity to punish Soviet aggression by destroying targets that Moscow dearly wished to preserve. This made Soviet cities a vital target set, for not only was Moscow loath to place them at risk, but they were also remarkably vulnerable to attack. Today, however, the gravest strategic threat we face is from nonstate actors—shadowy and elusive groups that simply do not generate targets that can readily be held at risk and whose members are frequently more than willing to sacrifice themselves in pursuit of their objectives. This makes such groups essentially invulnerable to retaliatory measures, and thus strategies based on deterrence are powerless to affect them.

The challenge to deterrence is exemplified by al-Qaeda, which in 2001 proved both willing and able to attack the homeland of the world's foremost military power, killing upwards of 3,000 people in the process. In the wake of 9/11, the United States moved swiftly to smash al-Qaeda's infrastructure in Afghanistan and to topple the Taliban regime. But whilst this counteroffensive might conceivably have discouraged other states from extending help to bin Laden and his associates, it did not deter al-Qaeda itself from mounting further operations against the West, as the subsequent bombings in Madrid and London demonstrated. Indeed, military action could not hope to do so, because it could not threaten the *idea* of al-Qaeda. The events of 9/11 had already ensured that this idea was beamed around the world to lodge invisibly in receptive hearts and minds. And it is this idea that now represents the most important aspect of al-Qaeda; for even if bin Laden and his lieutenants were killed or captured tomorrow, the idea will survive, inspiring individuals or small groups to commit suicidal acts of violence against the very societies in which they live.

In what follows, I want to suggest that this line of argument is only partially correct. The Cold War model of punitive deterrence may not be relevant to the challenges posed by al-Qaeda, but this does not mean that deterrence *per se* is defunct. On the contrary, deterrence, in various guises, remains a potent tool for shaping al-Qaeda activity; indeed, it is helping to keep us safe as I speak today. By way of support for this position, I propose to explore two examples of deterrence at work. I make no special claims for these cases, which are two amongst many. They are, however, examples with which I happen to be familiar. Moreover, that there exists some modest evidence for their effectiveness also recommends their selection. As in most instances, it is notoriously difficult to demonstrate that an adversary's inaction is due to a specific deterrent threat. Before we move on to discuss these examples, however, it might be useful to say a little bit more about the activities they are intended to deter.

At root, al-Qaeda is a symptom of the Islamic world's unhappy engagement with modernity. It is the extreme reaction of a traditional society that feels its fundamental beliefs and values are under siege by colonial forces. It harks back to a past in which Islam was more readily capable of asserting itself in the face of such alien influences and indeed of prevailing over them. The key to regaining this past, it is argued, lies in a revolutionary political programme designed to create a geographical power base—a caliphate—within whose borders a radical interpretation of Islamic life can be practised. To the extent that obstacles to this project are encountered, force must be used to sweep them aside. These obstacles include the regimes that currently hold sway over the Middle East. They also include Western powers, such as the United States and Great Britain, who are charged with supporting the existing state structure as a means of maintaining their own anti-Islamic influence in the region.

A key problem facing al-Qaeda is that its capacity to generate force in relation to the states that oppose it is small, which means that direct confrontation would inevitably lead to crushing defeat. Direct confrontation is therefore avoided in favour of action intended—at least in the first instance—to augment al-Qaeda's strength. This involves the use of terrorism. The immediate target of operations is, in other words, not adversary states but the people who live within them. The effects of such operations are not an end in themselves. Rather, they are intended to convey a message to the global Muslim population—the umma. And, the message is that Muslims the world over need not languish under Western hegemony, that the United States and its allies are vulnerable to daring and determined attack, and that it remains only for the struggle to be taken up on a mass basis for victory to follow. All the better, therefore, if such operations encourage heavy-handed retaliation that falls on the heads of hitherto uncommitted Muslims. Such a response helps to unmask the true nature of the enemy, thereby encouraging further popular support for the cause. In short, al-Qaeda uses terrorism for *demonstrative* and *provocative* purposes.[1] Its function is to convert the umma from a traditional faith community into a modern political movement determined to pursue a shared goal in the face of adversity.

What role, then, does deterrence have to play in this strategic context? A risk with acts of terrorism is that they can alienate as well as galvanize popular support, that for each individual who is empowered by the spectacle of violence, another is revolted by it. Historically speaking, most terrorist organizations have been aware of this double-edged aspect to their strategy, and this awareness has exercised a constraining influence on the scale and scope of their violent activities. This, in turn, suggests that one potentially effective way of deterring al-Qaeda is to reinforce whatever normative barriers to terrorism exist in the Muslim world. The logic here is that the more terrorism is deemed to be unacceptable, the less readily will al-Qaeda resort to it for fear of alienating the popular support it requires to survive. Various interesting efforts to reinforce such barriers are, in fact, already under way both internationally and domestically. The one I want to focus on here involves highlighting religious injunctions against the indiscriminate use of violence. This is because influential charges of un-Islamic behaviour are something that al-Qaeda cannot afford to ignore.

Whilst it is a matter of record that the events of 9/11 led to scenes of jubilation in the Middle East, it is also the case that they elicited the strongest possible condemnation from prominent Muslim groups and individuals around the world. What so many found objectionable was the deliberate targeting of "innocents," which is to say individuals not directly implicated in US policy towards the Middle East. Acts of this kind, it was observed, are contrary to the dictates of Islam and therefore something that all right-thinking Muslims should eschew.[2] According to the Koran (17:15), "No soul laden bears the load of another." In the present context, this is interpreted as meaning that the people of a state are not accountable for the sins of their government.[3] This, by extension, rules out terrorism as a means of achieving one's political objectives.

That al-Qaeda is sensitive to this form of criticism is demonstrated by the fact that Osama bin Laden subsequently made a public effort to justify the 9/11 attacks on juridical grounds. On the specific issue of targeting civilians, he took refuge behind Koranic references to the principle of reciprocity in human affairs, such as sura 16, verse 125: "And if you chastise, chastise even as you have been chastised."[4] Al-Qaeda, he maintained, was only paying back the United States in kind for its past transgressions, and this it was fully entitled to do: "God, the Almighty, legislated the permission and the option to avenge this oppression [against Muslims]. Thus, if we are attacked, then we have the right to strike back. If people destroy our villages and towns, then we have the right to do the same in return. If people steal our wealth, then we have the right to destroy their economy. And whoever kills our civilians, then we have the right to kill theirs."[5]

A problem for al-Qaeda in this regard is that its justifications for terrorism are derived from a selective and highly contestable engagement with the dictates of Islam, which in theory is easy to refute. Bin Laden's position on the principle of reciprocity serves to illustrate this point rather well. Strictly speaking, the injunction to "chastise even as you have been chastised" applies not to acts of war but to acts of retribution for personal injury or murder. Thus, a murderer who kills his victim with a sword should himself be executed with a sword and so on. Moreover, even this basic principle of reciprocity is subject to qualification. Certain modes of killing—such as with fire, for example—are altogether forbidden. Thus, a murderer who immolates his victim may not himself be immolated.[6] Bin Laden's stance is therefore erroneous on two grounds. Not only is his use of the principle of reciprocity irrelevant to the question at hand, but even if it were relevant, it cannot be used to justify acts that in and of themselves are forbidden.

In practice, however, refutations of al-Qaeda's dubious brand of jurisprudence do require something more than orthodox rigour to gain credence. They must come from individuals who enjoy political legitimacy amongst Muslims and who cannot therefore be considered Western puppets. Such individuals must also enjoy a good command of the English language and of Western culture if their message is to be relevant to younger Muslims who are the ones most likely to support, and engage in, acts of terrorism.

A good example in this regard is Imam Zaid Shakir, whose blog supplied the qualifications to the principle of reciprocity we encountered a few moments ago. Originally named Ricky Mitchell, Shakir became a Muslim whilst serving in the US Air Force in 1977 and has subsequently emerged as a charismatic and erudite voice for orthodox Islam in the United States. He navigates between the twin worlds of traditional Islam and modern America with consummate ease, mixing lines from the Koran with rap lyrics as he goes.[7] Consequently, his rejection of terrorism enjoys both juridical rigour and immediate relevance to his burgeoning audience of young Muslims who currently flock to see him in the thousands.

Unfortunately, Shakir remains something of a rarity in the Anglo-Saxon world, where mosques tend to hire their imams from overseas. A recent poll of five hundred British mosques, conducted by the Quilliam Foundation, revealed that the overwhelming majority of their imams had been born and trained abroad. Whilst their knowledge of jurisprudence may be excellent, these imams tend to lack familiarity with the English language and with the cultural references necessary to engage a younger audience. Indeed, fewer than 10 percent of the mosques polled gave their Friday lectures wholly in English.[8] This, in turn, means that mosques are not typically the most influential source of inspiration for young Muslims seeking to navigate their own way through the twin worlds of Islamic tradition and Western modernity. Instead, they frequently turn to such sources as the Internet, where it is very easy to encounter the proterrorism message.

The lesson here would seem to be clear: whilst Western agencies cannot themselves hope to generate effective juridical prohibitions of terrorism, they can try to facilitate the activities of others, not the least by helping to resource them adequately. In this regard, the emphasis placed by the British government's new counterterrorism strategy on antiradicalization measures is to be welcomed.[9]

However it is attempted, the reinforcement of normative barriers against terrorism cannot be achieved overnight: it is something that will take time to come to fruition. My second example of deterrence in action is, however, one that can be achieved rather more quickly, as it is bound up with efforts to defend ourselves against attack. The fact of the matter is that the value of defensive measures derives not simply from their capacity for physically preventing attacks that would otherwise take place. Defensive measures also shape terrorists' perceptions of the likelihood of their operations being successful, along with the costs they will need to incur to maximize their chances of success. They impose, in other words, cost-benefit calculations whose results might well be a deterrent to action.

At this point, it might be objected that cost considerations are irrelevant to individuals who are willing to sacrifice their own lives to operational success and that the matter is all one of benefits so far as they are concerned; thus, deterrence cannot operate here. But the matter is more complicated than this. For the fact that such individuals are willing to sacrifice their very lives indicates that they do attach a great deal of importance to something, which is the contribution that a successful mission will make to the ultimate cause they espouse. And it is precisely this success that defences hold at risk. Defences threaten terrorists with the prospect not simply of failure but of costly failure. They threaten dead or captured personnel, the spending of money, and the commitment of precious resources— all to no good purpose. *The prospect of a well-publicized failure may also deter terrorists who are concerned to preserve their standing in the eyes of their supporters.* Failure risks detracting from the message that Western states are vulnerable to daring and determined attack; it risks entrenching a view that violent resistance is futile and that al-Qaeda is to be shunned rather than supported.

That such cost-benefit calculations do indeed shape terrorist behaviour is suggested by the case of Iyman Faris, a naturalized US citizen of Kashmiri extraction, who in 2002 was ordered to reconnoitre the Brooklyn Bridge with a view to establishing the feasibility of destroying it. As it happens, security in the area was particularly conspicuous in response to intelligence that bin Laden wanted to attack what was described as the "bridge in the Godzilla movie." Faris was evidently dismayed by conditions on the ground, for the National Security Agency subsequently intercepted a coded e-mail to Pakistan in which he declared that "the weather is too hot." In other words, that security was too tight for an attempt on the bridge to succeed. Here, in short, is an example of deterrence by defence in action.

Faris did, however, have ideas of his own that might have proved more practicable than those of his political masters. Drawing on his experience as a truck driver, he advocated a plan that involved attacking a stationary airliner with a lorry loaded with explosives.[10] And this highlights a serious problem associated with efforts to deter terrorism by defensive measures. The problem is that Western societies contain a vast array of potential targets that are vulnerable to attack and we cannot secure them all. To the extent that the prospects of successfully attacking a target such as the Brooklyn Bridge are deemed too slim to be worth the effort, al-Qaeda will be deterred from doing so. But terrorists will look for something more vulnerable to attack instead. By hardening point targets, we are therefore shifting the threat about, rather than removing it, although it might well be argued that shaping al-Qaeda activity in this regard is a valuable enterprise if it helps to secure targets that we feel must be absolutely protected.

On the other hand, defensive measures are by no means limited to the protection of point targets. There are other approaches that are much wider in scope. Tight border security offers prospects of deterring attacks by dint of its capacity for exposing the movement of key personnel or resources. Likewise, domestic intelligence services threaten the viability of all terrorist operations within the borders of a state. Needless to say, there is no panacea here. Just recently, British security forces experienced a series of misadventures in relation to the so-called "Easter Bomb Plot" that resulted in the arrest of 12 suspected terrorists. Whilst it was certainly Easter, there does not seem to have been either a bomb or a plot—or at least there existed no evidence of them that would have stood up in a court of law. Nevertheless, such high-profile events should not distract us from important facts that do not make it into news headlines. And one such fact is that the security service has been instrumental in achieving 86 successful convictions under antiterror legislation since January 2007. According to the head of MI5, Jonathan Evans, this "has had a chilling effect on the enthusiasm of the [terrorist] networks. They're keeping their heads down."[11] If Evans' analysis is correct, his organization is doing a good overall job of deterring al-Qaeda in Britain.

By way of conclusion, I should like to reiterate my central contention that al-Qaeda *is* amendable to deterrence, and raise an additional point for consideration. As we have seen, al-Qaeda's core leadership and its local operatives, alike, are cost-sensitive actors. And it is this cost sensitivity that provides us with opportunities to achieve deterrent effects.

My additional point relates to the role of the US Air Force in the foregoing. It might appear that the Air Force is irrelevant to the approach to deterrence I have sketched here, but this is not the case. On the contrary, airpower does have an important role to play, although this role derives from the fact that deterrence is only one component within a wider strategy for dealing with the threat posed by al-Qaeda.

Another important component consists of efforts to neutralize or destroy al-Qaeda's core leadership. It would be unwise to abandon such efforts because, left to their own devices, bin Laden and his lieutenants will only become more capable of supporting and directing local groups in their violent endeavours. And this would be the case well before the long-term deterrence measures I have described have had a chance to gain momentum.

A problem here, however, is that the twin goals of deterrence and destruction are potentially in tension with one another. Most obviously, overly enthusiastic efforts to hunt down bin Laden and his associates risk undermining deterrence by creating a climate in which an antiterror message cannot gain traction. Religious proscription is likely to fall on deaf ears if it must compete with noisy denunciations of collateral damage and flagrant breeches of sovereignty. Doubtless, technical advances will help to ease such tensions by providing the capability to apply force from the air with ever-greater accuracy and discrimination. Still, such advances will never in themselves remove the requirement to apply such force with great judiciousness. Clausewitz's message that war is a political act, and that acts of force must be shaped by the political context in which they are made, remains excellent advice. In this regard, the Air Force's contribution to deterrence is a vital—if negative—one: it must be able to apply lethal force effectively yet without undermining the deterrent elements of the campaign against al-Qaeda.

Notes

1. I borrowed these terms from Michael Howard, "Are We at War?" *Survival* 50, no.4 (August–September 2008): 253.

2. For a selection of Muslim responses to 9/11, along with links to other sites, see "Islamic Statements against Terrorism," http://www.unc.edu/~kurman/terror.htm.

3. Arthur J. Arberry, *The Koran Interpreted,* vol. 1, Suras 1:20 (London: George Allen & Unwin, 1955), 303.

4. Ibid., 301.

5. Bruce Lawrence, ed., *Messages to the World: The Statements of Osama bin Laden* (London: Verso, 2005), 165.

6. Imam Zaid Shakir, "Islam and the Ethics of War," http://www.newislamicdirections.com/nid/articles/islam_and_the~ethics_of_ war/.

7. "About Imam Zaid Shakir," http://www.newislamicdirections.com/nid/about/; and Laurie Goodstein, "U.S. Muslim Clerics Seek a Modern Middle Ground," *New York Times*, 18 June 2006. One assumes he is no relation of Billy Mitchell!

8. Anya Hart Dyke, *Mosques Made in Britain* (London: Quilliam, 2009), 11–14.

9. Cm 7547, *The United Kingdom's Strategy for Countering International Terrorism* (Norwich: TSO, 2009).

10. David Rennie, "Plot to Destroy Brooklyn Bridge," Telegraph, 20 June 2003.

11. Michael Evans, "MI5's Spymaster Jonathan Evans Comes Out of the Shadows," *Times*, 7 January 2009.

Chapter 17

Deterrence and the Israel-Hezbollah War Summer 2006

Shai Feldman

Israel is an interesting laboratory of deterrence theory. Since the state's establishment in 1948, its short history has provided enough tests for almost every type of deterrence. Moreover, from its very inception, the primary challenge of Israel's national security strategy was to find ways of addressing the basic quantitative asymmetry characterizing the country's relations with its Arab environment. One such imperative was that the few make every effort to avoid war with the many. And, central to the attempts to avoid war was the pursuit of effective deterrence.

One way of celebrating Israel's 61st anniversary is to note that it has achieved robust general deterrence—Israel is widely viewed as possessing the means to deter general threats to its existence and survival. These means are seen as including the development and deployment of every type of unconventional weapon and the means to deliver them to any target in the Middle East; the possession of the most advanced armed forces in the region—the only ones considered to have fully implemented the revolution in military affairs; the building of a national economy with a gross domestic product far larger than any of Israel's neighbors; the possession of a scientific and technological base that generates the most advanced military-industrial sector in the region; and, last but not least, an alliance with the only remaining superpower—the United States.

The result of Israel's robust general deterrence is that none of its adversaries can seriously contemplate the option of ending the conflict by military means—that is, by either totally defeating Israel Defense Forces (IDF) or by destroying Israel with nuclear weapons or other means. The extent to which Iran's possible acquisition of nuclear weapons will invalidate this proposition is a subject of considerable debate.

The most important consequence of such robust general deterrence is the conclusion reached by Israel's Arab neighbors that it cannot be defeated militarily and that, therefore, in one form or another, it must be accommodated politically. Thus,

279

Egypt signed a peace treaty with Israel over 30 years ago—an agreement that withstood the test of such rocky times as Israel's 1982 invasion of Lebanon and both Palestinian intifadas. While "only" 15 years old, Israel's peace with the Hashemite Kingdom of Jordan proved equally resilient.

Specific Deterrence

Conceptually, general deterrence is a fairly simple proposition: it rests on the capacity to promise a country's adversaries that attempts to destroy it would result in these adversaries paying unacceptable costs. Not so with specific deterrence: a country's capacity to deter specific threats is derived from a much more complex set of variables. Indeed, in the latter case, the importance of the relative capacity to inflict pain is matched—and often superseded—by the relative willingness to sustain punishment. As a result, a country possessing superior capacity to inflict pain may still find itself defeated in a deterrence-focused confrontation if its adversary happens to care more about the specific issue at stake, and, as a result, is more willing to sustain the costs entailed.

From Israel's standpoint, Egypt's launching of the 1969–70 War of Attrition, despite the IDF's superior capacity to inflict punishment, was precisely such a failure of specific deterrence. Israel failed because Egypt cared more about the issue at stake—liberating the Sinai Peninsula—and was willing to sustain high costs in pursuit of this objective. For the same reason, Israel also failed to deter Egypt and Syria from attacking on 5 October 1973.

Specific deterrence is much more prone to failure not only because it involves twice the number of variables associated with general deterrence but also because the additional variable—relative determination, which translates to the relative willingness to sustain punishment—is difficult to assess before a confrontation has taken place.

For example, Israel's defense minister, Moshe Dayan, was surprised both in 1969–70 and in 1973 because he believed that Egypt would not care enough to sustain the heavy costs entailed in challenging Israel's conquest of the Sinai Peninsula. Instead, Dayan seems to have believed that Egypt would "get used" to Israeli occupation of the Sinai. Dayan's miscalculations illustrate just how difficult it is to assess relative will in real time, because in retrospect, it seems baffling that in 1973 Egypt's determination could have been underestimated despite the clear signals it had sent through its conduct during the 1969–70 War of Attrition, including the evacuation and relocation of a million people from the Canal cities.

Paradoxically, however, in Israel's case, failures at specific deterrence did not detract from the country's general deterrence or even from its cumulative deterrence. This implies that the reputation Israel acquired for ultimately prevailing in every military confrontation contributed over time to the Arab states' conclusion that it cannot be defeated militarily. This explains the paradox: that Israel's failures at specific deterrence in 1969–70 and in 1973 did not deny it its ultimate prize: the decision of the most important of the Arab states—Egypt—to sign a peace treaty with the Jewish state.

The paradox can be made understandable if due appreciation is given to an important building block of cumulative deterrence: the pursuit and exercise of escalation dominance. Thus, Israel's reputation was based on its determination to prevail ultimately in every military confrontation, even those that began with a specific deterrence failure. Yet, the repeated exercise of escalation dominance is not cost-free. Conceptually, it is associated with the dilemma highlighted by Robert Jervis: "escalation exercised for deterrence purposes is prone to have the opposite effect: a spiral to greater violence." Thus, Israel's retaliatory raids in the mid-1950s ultimately led to the 1956 Sinai-Suez War.

Internationally, the pursuit of escalation dominance exposed Israel to the accusation that it was making "excessive use of force" by reacting disproportionately to Arab provocations. Israel found it difficult to respond persuasively to such accusations—a problem it faces to this very day—because in fact the pursuit of cumulative deterrence through escalation dominance requires that provocations be met with a disproportionate response.

Compellence

Israel's exercise of compellence strategy dates almost as far back as its deterrence efforts. While deterrence comprises dissuading an adversary from attacking, compellence is an effort to persuade a third party to take action to arrest a threat. Thus, Israel's retaliation raids against Jordan in the early 1950s were aimed at persuading the Hashemite Kingdom to prevent Palestinians from conducting cross-border raids against Israel.

Compellence necessarily implies an increase in the number of significant players—always a complicating factor. Whereas deterrence comprises one party's attempts to dissuade the other from attacking, compellence is associated with at least three parties. Country (A) attempts to persuade country (B) to take steps to arrest threatening party (C). Consequently, the aforementioned complications normally associated with specific deterrence are compounded by the distribution of power and will between the target country (B) and the threatening group or movement (C). For example, if state (B) is very weak, it would not be able to move effectively to arrest threat (C), even if state (A) threatens it with enormous punishment. Luckily for Israel, in Jordan of the early 1950s, the Arab Legion was relatively strong, and the Palestinian infiltrators were weak; so, Jordan moved effectively to arrest the Palestinian Fedayyin threat, crowning Israeli compellence strategy with success.

The opposite is the case if country (B) develops its own interests in allowing threat (C) to continue to operate. Thus, for Egypt during the early 1950s, Fedayyin raids against Israel served to boost Nasser's image as combating "the Zionist threat," thus enhancing his claim to lead a Pan-Arab Middle East. As a result, using the same means that produced effective compellence vis-à-vis Jordan, Israel failed to similarly compel Egypt to bring terror attacks to an end.

Deterrence and Compellence Against Terrorists

Compellence often becomes the preferred strategy in combating terrorism by default: that is, because terrorists rarely provide a clear address required for the exercise of deterrence. By contrast, host countries allowing terrorists a base from which to operate usually comprise a clear target. Unless the government of the base country has lost its "monopoly of force," thus becoming a "failed state," it can be persuaded to use its power to deny the terrorists the sanctuaries they need to launch their attacks.

During the Palestinian Second Intifada (2000–2005), Israel attempted a mixed-deterrence compellence counterterrorism strategy, ultimately and reluctantly finding itself adding an important component of defense. While initially its targeted killing of Palestinian terrorists comprised an attempt at preemption—killing terrorists and their "senders" before they succeeded to launch an attack—Israel increasingly moved to the killing of commanders and even their political leaders. This was partly an exercise of pure offense—an attempt to weaken terrorist organizations by depriving them of experienced commanders and by forcing their remaining commanders to spend more of their energy on self-preservation rather than on planning, preparing, and perpetrating attacks. But equally, it was an attempt at deterrence by directly punishing the leadership of terrorist organizations in an attempt to dissuade them from continuing to fight.

The compellence component of the strategy was directed at the terrorists' immediate environment. Thus, demolishing the homes of terrorists' families was at least partially aimed at persuading family members of terrorists to prevent them from launching attacks. Yet, these demolitions were also exercised as a form of deterrence: It was hoped that terrorists willing to sacrifice their own lives may yet refrain from actions that were bound to cause their family members to lose their homes. The strategy was later pronounced a failure: A study conducted by the IDF found that home demolitions had no discernable effect on the magnitude of the terrorist threat. With deterrence failing and compellence registering very partial success, Israel ultimately found itself compelled to supplement these measures by old-fashioned defense: the construction of a security fence—and in urban areas, a wall—aimed at preventing Palestinian terrorists from reaching Israel's metropolitan areas.

Confronting an Insurgency: The Case of 2006

Conceptually, insurgencies represent a middle-range case—somewhere between the threat presented by a well-structured state apparatus and the challenge presented by the elusive terrorist threat. While lacking the classical structure of a conventional force that normally includes armored, mechanized, air, and naval units, an insurgency usually fights in organized formations, often with each formation having distinct responsibility for a defined area. Indeed, the military arm of Hezbollah fought the IDF in such formation. Similarly, the same arm of Hamas divided the Gaza Strip among its units, with each responsible for some part of the strip.

When Israel withdrew from south Lebanon in May 2000, its strategy for dissuading Hezbollah from continuing the fighting by carrying the struggle into Israel was based on two forms of compellence. First, Israeli prime minister, Ehud Barak, announced that in light of Syria's large-scale military presence in Lebanon, Israel would hold it responsible for any Hezbollah attack. Thus, an attempt was made to compel Syria to prevent Hezbollah attacks. Accordingly, in the aftermath of its withdrawal, Israel responded to a number of Hezbollah attacks by retaliating against such Syrian targets as radar installations inside Lebanon.

The second target of Israeli compellence was the population of south Lebanon. Israelis reasoned that since the IDF had withdrawn from that area—and thus Lebanon had been "liberated" from "foreign occupation"——the population of the south would no longer support a continuation of the fighting. Under these new circumstances, it was argued, the population of south Lebanon would refuse to remain the victim of a cycle of Hezbollah attacks and Israeli retaliation. Thus, the withdrawal would deprive Hezbollah the legitimacy required to continue attacks against Israel; hence, the Lebanese population would no longer be willing to provide Hezbollah with the safe heavens required for an insurgency.

The months and years following Israel's withdrawal demonstrated that the aforementioned expectations were only partially warranted. Indeed, a balance of deterrence-compellence evolved between Israel and Hezbollah in the framework of which the populations of the Israeli north and Lebanon's south were both held hostage. Hezbollah attacks against Israel were few and far between, reflecting that the population of the south was no longer willing to sustain the costs of further Hezbollah provocations that would invite Israeli responses. The importance of legitimacy in this context was demonstrated when Hezbollah was

284

forced to limit its attacks—in justification, scope, and location—to the only part of the border that remained in dispute: the Shab'a Farms area at the northeastern edge of the frontier.

Yet, this legitimacy deficit was not sufficient to prevent Hezbollah from forcing the population in the south to allow it the safe haven it required. As a result, during 2000–2005 Hezbollah succeeded in transforming the towns and villages of south Lebanon into a robust line of defense.

Moreover, the magnitude of Israeli responses to Hezbollah provocations was now also limited, due to a number of factors. Primarily, Israel's 18-year-long presence in Lebanon—from which it has finally extracted itself in May 2000—made it extremely reluctant to respond to Hezbollah attacks in any way that risked the IDF becoming entangled again in what Israelis have come to regard as "the Lebanese quagmire." Second, Hezbollah's acquisition of thousands of missiles and rockets increased dramatically the possible price of Israeli responses. As such, it made Israeli exercise of "escalation dominance" highly problematic.

What for some years appeared to be a fairly stable balance of terror suffered two structural weaknesses. The first was the asymmetry in the two sides' sensitivity to costs. Israel's extreme sensitivity to the lives of its citizens and soldiers created a Hezbollah premium on taking Israeli soldiers hostage. This was buttressed by a gradual loss of Israeli reputation: Over time, the Israeli government demonstrated that it was willing to pay a very high price—measured in hundreds of prisoners released—to gain the release of a few Israeli soldiers, often some who were already dead.

The second structural weakness was the deterrence system's exposure to two sources of failures: miscommunication and miscalculation. Israel failed to communicate to Hezbollah the extremity of its likely response to a hostage-taking Hezbollah attack. And Hezbollah miscalculated: it convinced itself that Israel was a "paper tiger"—too constrained by its fears to administer very costly retaliation.

The result of this miscommunication and miscalculation was a total failure on Hezbollah's part to anticipate the magnitude of Israel's response to its 12 July 2006 attack. The attack, killing eight Israeli soldiers and taking another three hostage, led to a 34-day war between Israel and Hezbollah (only months later did it become clear that the three abducted soldiers also died in the attack or soon thereafter).

First, this twin failure was structural because Israel's failure to communicate likely response was rooted in, that its government did not know how it would respond to such an attack. This was the case even after the attack had already occurred; few if any of the members of the Israeli cabinet knew that the decisions they took on the evening of 12 July in response to Hezbollah's attack earlier that day would lead to war.

Second, the Israeli government would have been reluctant to advertise its likely response even if it did know how it would respond to such a challenge. This is because such a statement would have helped Hezbollah to design its counterresponse.

The summer 2006 war underscored a number of features of deterrence in counterinsurgency contexts. The first is that legitimacy matters. If it did not, Hezbollah leader Hassan Nasrallah would not have found it necessary to admit soon after the war that had he anticipated the ferocity of the Israeli response, he would not have been launched the 12 July attack. Clearly, his admission resulted from an assessment that in the aftermath of Israel's 2000 withdrawal, Lebanon's population was not willing to sustain the costs entailed in the continuation of violence against the Jewish state.

Second, Israel seems to have failed to realize that its post–May 2000 compellence strategy—that was based on holding Syria accountable for any attacks against Israel from Lebanese soil—needed to be revised in the aftermath of Syria's April 2005 withdrawal from Lebanon, a withdrawal conduced in the framework of Syria's forced compliance with United Nations Security Council Resolution 1559. Without its previous overt large-scale presence in Lebanon, Syria could no longer be held responsible for such attacks.

Third, in a struggle between a regional power (Israel) and an insurgency, the regional power is naturally expected to crush the insurgents. Hence, in such situations, to be considered victorious, it is enough for an insurgency to survive the confrontation. The insurgency's survival damages the regional power's reputation, and the latter becomes vulnerable to others' attempts to emulate the insurgency's success. Thus, Hezbollah's survival in 2006 allowed Nasrallah to market a narrative of victory, and two and one-half years later, Hamas was tempted to try the same recipe. Thus, a shattered reputation led to later deterrence breakdowns.

Yet, the Israeli experience also demonstrates that future deterrence breakdowns may be limited by adversaries' ability to discriminate between different types of reputations and to assess which ones were damaged and which ones were not. In the aftermath of the 2006 war, Israel's director of military intelligence (DMI), Maj Gen Amos Yadlin, was quick to express his assessment that Israeli deterrence eroded from the IDF's poor performance in the war. Yet, clear signs show that Syria's leaders did not share General Yadlin's assessment. That soon after the second Lebanon war Syria consented to the opening of peace talks with Israel indicates that Syrian leaders may have feared that the same Israeli military which found it difficult to deal with the Hezbollah insurgency might have easily destroyed the antiquated Syrian armed forces if they had opted for war instead of diplomacy. In this, they probably drew an analogy (in reverse sequence) from the US experience in Iraq: the armed forces that found it difficult to battle the Iraqi insurgencies were the same forces that in 2003 destroyed the huge Iraqi military within weeks.

By the end of 2007, General Yadlin is said to have assessed that Israeli deterrence had been restored. This followed the raid conducted by the Israeli Air Force in September 2007 that reportedly destroyed a nuclear facility in northeastern Syria. But the question remains: How did Israel's DMI know that Israeli deterrence had eroded in the aftermath of the summer of 2006 war, and on the basis of what evidence did he conclude that this lost deterrence was later restored?

Finally, once deterrence breaks down, a regional power may attempt to restore it based on a new equation. Indeed, soon after the summer 2006 violent confrontation began, the IDF's chief of staff asked the Israeli cabinet's approval to bomb Lebanon's infrastructure. This was a suggested attempt at compellence: the Lebanese population should be made to suffer extreme hardships so that it would force Hezbollah to cease the fighting. While the Israeli Air Force was denied the requested permission, its missions later ventured increasingly into the realm of infrastructure bombings.

To restore deterrence and compellence by bombing infra-structure targets was most pronounced in the case of the IDF's shelling and bombing of the Dahiya neighborhood in Beirut. Reportedly, these bombings resulted in many of the neighbor-hood's buildings destroyed. The concept of close-range compel-lence was based on the theory that clarifying the willingness and ability to extract heavy costs would lead the population to press the insurgents to cease their attacks. In the war's after-math, this was offered by the chief of the IDF's Northern Com-mand, Maj Gen Gadi Eizencot, as a preferred counterinsurgency compellence strategy. In Israel's national security discourse, General Eizencot's idea was now coined the "Dahiya doctrine."

Yet, the political costs of the Dahiya doctrine are consider-able. Whether by design or default, it was at least partially ex-ecuted during the Gaza confrontation in early January 2009. As was the case in the summer of 2006, the implementation of this doctrine in Gaza was filmed by every television crew and by hundreds of amateur photographers there. This led to huge international outcry that continues at this writing.

Finale

By the time of its 61st anniversary in May 2009, Israel had acquired a robust general deterrence capability and a reputation in cumulative deterrence earned through repeated demonstra-tions of escalation dominance. At the same time, the Hezbollah-Israel War in the summer of 2006 illustrated the complexities and limitations of Israel's ability to exercise effective specific deterrence and compellence as components of its counter-insurgency strategy. Unable to deter Hezbollah directly, Israel first attempted compellence through Syria. It later shifted the focus of its compellence strategy to a Lebanese population un-happy about the price of continued struggle against Israel now that the IDF had withdrawn from south Lebanon.

A number of lessons can be derived from this Israeli experi-ence: First, Hezbollah's 12 July 2006 attack shows how diffi-cult it is for a regional power to translate its robust general deterrence to effective specific deterrence against an insur-gency. Second, an insurgency's successful challenge to a re-gional power—measured by the insurgency's survival and its subsequent effective marketing of a narrative of victory—may lead to a loss of reputation by the regional power, tempting other insurgencies to try to emulate the challenger's success. This seems to be the effect of the 2006 war on Hamas' decision in December 2008 to refrain from extending the six months period of calm (the Tahdia) with Israel.

Conversely, while general deterrence is not easily translatable to effective specific deterrence, Israel's post-2006 experience also shows that failure at specific deterrence will not necessarily damage the regional power's robust general deterrence. Otherwise, why would Syria have agreed to conduct peace talks with Israel in the aftermath of the 2006 war? And, why did it call for the resumption of such talks in mid-2009?

Chapter 18

FRAMING DETERRENCE IN THE 21ST CENTURY

RUSI
www.rusi.org

Post-Conference Briefing Note

21 May 2009

KING'S
College
LONDON

Conference co-sponsored by
Royal United Services Institute for Defence and Security Studies

Centre for Defence Studies, King's College, London

United States Air Force Research Institute,
Air University, Maxwell Air Force Base, USA

This post-conference joint briefing note follows a two-day forum that took place 18 and 19 May 2009. Co-sponsored by the Royal United Services Institute for Defence and Security Studies (RUSI); the Centre for Defence Studies, King's College, London; and the United States Air Force Research Institute, the meeting was convened to discuss the issues surrounding the framing of deterrence in the twenty-first century.

The influence of nuclear weapons—and their arrival in the bipolar geostrategic context of the Cold War—served largely to confine the focus of deterrence debates to nuclear issues and to the Cold War itself, with discussion focused for internal politics and audiences. Following the conclusion of the Cold War, in broad deterrence terms, the preference of some policy makers has been to focus on using preemptive military force rather than deterrence in dealing with security challenges. Today, the nature and theory of effective deterrence in practical terms needs to be reframed. Therefore, a reexamination of the fundamentals of deterrence theory, its related strategies, and of what constitutes effective deterrence is particularly timely.

This conference provided the opportunity for such a reassessment and addressed four primary questions:

- What is deterrence?
- What are the instruments of deterrence?
- Why does deterrence fail?
- What are the consequences of deterrence policies?

Blending these major themes with specific case studies in two days of discussions, the conference brought together a community of officials, scholars, strategists, and national security experts from the United Kingdom, the United States and Europe to discuss how to frame deterrence in the twenty-first century. In particular, they explored if, why, and how deterrence is relevant in the more diverse and complex modern strategic environment, and scrutinised the political and military implications of deterrent postures as a means of illuminating and informing government policy choices.

The resulting conference report, to be released in the summer 2009, is intended to inform national policies and thinking, impending international strategic weapons and nonproliferation treaty negotiations, and the United States' impending Nuclear Posture, Quadrennial Defense, and Base Closure and Realignment Commission reviews. Another primary objective of the conference was to identify issues requiring further discussion or research.

Proceedings

"Framing Deterrence in the 21st Century", was structured around five general sub-topics:

- deterrence in general terms
- deterrence and counterproliferation
- deterrence relative to nonstate actors engaging state actors
- deterrence relative to state actors engaging other state actors
- deterrence relative to state actors engaging nonstate actors.

The 40 conference participants examined each sub-topic area employing a three-part process:

- keynote presentations
- case studies
- workshops to further address the four primary questions, listed above.

The conference's case studies examined:

- the 2008 Russian War in Georgia and the implications for deterrence
- policy instruments for deterring proliferation
- the 2004 Madrid train bombings
- the implications of the India/Pakistan situation
- the 2006 Israeli-Hizbullah War.

Themes and Findings

- In general, participants agreed that a generationally rigid Cold War perception frames "deterrence" as a nuclear face-off between the United States and the Soviet Union. The participants agreed also that deterrence is about much more than nuclear weapons: it is essentially a core activity which guides relations between actors in dealing with crisis and conflict

- Deterrence is a status quo equation, vital to promoting international stability
- Deterrence is the product of one entity's ability to influence the behaviour of another entity; but the targeted entity decides whether or not they can and will be deterred
- In the new multipolar world, multiple behavioural/cultural elements of every potential adversary must be thoroughly understood to devise strategies to effectively influence behaviours favourable to the influencer, and in a worst case scenario, generate unanticipated and unfavourable results for the adversary
- Evolving notions of "deterrence" that necessarily reflect the dynamics of the current national security environment have been slow to surface, and adjusting deterrence strategies to fit this new process will take time

  o One participant opined, "We will look back on the Cold War as the heyday of the unitary actor"

- Since the fall of the Soviet Union, the primary challenges confronting many states have expanded beyond traditional state-on-state, force-on-force strategic *calculi*

  o The implications of this expanded range of threats should be considered in the context of an increasing level of globalisation, an international "interconnectedness" which presents a new strategic paradigm

  o The desired effects, probable costs, and unanticipated consequences of any future military or political deterrence strategy should be examined in the context of an apparent decline in the effectiveness of normative deterrence—a process in which states or actors are deterred by the simple existence of established international norms of behaviour

  o Participants agreed there remains no consensus on how to utilise deterrent theories, policies, and force structures developed in the Cold War nuclear context in today's complex security environment

294

- The concept of deterrence (and subsequent strategies) must be framed within the new paradigm of warfare
- The participants acknowledged the continuing risk of major state-on-state crisis and conflict, for which deterrence —and understanding how to apply it in political, military, and other contexts—is still relevant
- After much discussion, the participants agreed nonstate actors generally cannot be deterred by state actors employing traditional deterrence strategies, and that new processes and understandings must be found

    o States have a shared interest in stability; certain non-state actors have an interest in instability; this situation has the potential of aligning traditionally adversarial state actors with a shared interest in stability and drive them into a collaboration in response to the instability generated by nonstate actors

    o State actors must devise strategies to communicate with nonstate actors

    o State "narratives" (actions and words) are often in conflict and incongruent; nonstate actors and those they wish to influence employ these incongruent state "narratives" to validate their actions to destabilise international security

- There is a danger that deterrence concepts and strategies may be levied with unachievable expectations

    o Nonstate actor–generated insurgencies are an example— once an insurgency is under way, the generally accepted understanding is that deterrence strategies and methods of persuasion, inducement, and threat have failed

    o But within this context, there are opportunities to deter nonstate actors engaged in an insurgency from taking subsequent extreme actions

    o Participants debated whether or not state actors can harness and deter nonstate actors by overtly and covertly threatening extremist idealism—there was no consensus on this issue, but it posed an important question requiring significant further research

- Within the context of a globalised, interconnected world, deterrence will increasingly rely on established alliances, trusted communication, improving understanding of different strategic cultures and engagement that establishes credibility with various actors
- Established alliances, both formal and informal, permit the use of extended deterrence by the possessors of nuclear weapons to cover and protect the non-nuclear weapon states within that alliance. However, in a multipolar world, does extended deterrence still apply, and in the same way, moreover are the traditional "rules" of such relationships understood as before?
- Moves towards restarting arms control and disarmament processes are welcomed but, as these processes move forward, their principles must be developed while taking into full account their potential impact upon proliferation and deterrence.

Conference proceedings will be released in a variety of formats over the summer. Individuals interested in further information regarding this conference can contact either Daniel Sherman, Royal United Services Institute in London, at + 44 (0) 20 7747 2617 or Robert Potter, US Air Force Research Institute, in the United States, at + 1 334 953 3969.

Joint Briefing Note Issued By

Prof Michael Clarke, Director, Royal United Services Institute for Defence & Security Studies, London, UK

Dr John Gearson, Director, Centre for Defence Studies, King's College, London, UK

Gen John A. Shaud PhD, USAF (Ret'd), Director, US Air Force Research Institute, Air University, Maxwell Air Force Base, USA.

Chapter 19

Quick Look
Deterrence in the Twenty-first Century

Anthony C. Cain, PhD

Issue/Question

The challenges of the international security environment coupled with a continuing global financial crisis set the context for renewed interest in deterrence. After nearly a generation of operations since the end of the Cold War, however, scholars and strategists continue to struggle to adapt the theories and vocabulary of deterrence to the existing and emerging contexts.

Background/Discussion

The overarching structure of the bipolar conflict between the United States and the Soviet Union constrained notions of deterrence to nuclear power balancing. Other strategic interactions were discussed using terminology that did not derive from the nuclear war context. Although such theorists as Hermann Kahn, Bernard Brodie, and Thomas Schelling have indicated that conventional conflicts could escalate into nuclear war, thus requiring careful attention on the part of statesmen, the special circumstances of the Cold War have kept attention focused on preventing nuclear war rather than analyzing the continuities between that type of war and the "lesser included" types of conflicts.

The watershed events represented by the end of the Cold War and the terrorist attacks of 11 September 2001 called into question the relevance of the deterrence paradigm. Nuclear operations seemed less relevant in a world characterized by such diverse challenges as failed states, humanitarian and environmental disasters, genocidal conflicts, counterproliferation, terrorism, and conventional wars. The questions related to deterrence now should center on linking deterrence to desired effects. In other words, states that adopt deterrence as part of a comprehensive strategy should be able to link particular deterrent policies and initiatives to specific adversary behavior modifications. This is where the notion of deterrence in the twenty-first century begins to break down.

Theorists and practitioners agree that at its core, deterrence is about achieving a change in an adversary's behavior while preserving the status quo. This requires an understanding of the adversary's motives, decision-making processes, and intentions. While the Cold War structure may have evolved to give strategists some degree of confidence that the principal adversaries were deterred by capabilities, force structures, and the network of alliances, the diversity of challenges today increases the complexity of formulating deterrence strategies. In fact, there seems to be a consensus that not all situations lend themselves to deterrent postures. This is especially true when examining nonstate actors.

Some analysts postulate that globalization has transformed the security environment to an extent that makes unilateral policies and actions by states impractical and possibly ineffective. Analysts who adopt this perspective argue that the punitive nature of deterrence creates a foundation of conflict that precludes constructive conflict resolution mechanisms. Others claim that the costs of deterrent systems and structures are unsustainable, removing resources from the global economy that could be better invested in more constructive ways. Still others see the primary utility of deterrence remaining in the nuclear arena, relegating the conversation to one of nuclear arms control and warhead reduction.

The lack of focus and clarity that prevails among theorists and practitioners, combined with the nuclear-focused Cold War legacy, has produced a situation in which there is no common foundation for understanding what deterrence means and how it applies to national security. The result is a lack of clarity and rigor in policy making that could result in ineffective and inefficient investments—and, ultimately in failed policies. Force structures that rely on the Cold War legacy without the existential threat represented by the Soviet Union have the potential to be too expensive to maintain in the long term while also removing capabilities that would be better employed against other threats in the short term. Attempting to apply deterrence as a template without understanding the specific social, cultural, governmental, and military characteristics of the adversary could be futile at best and disastrous at worst, depending on the intentions and capabilities of the adversary of the moment. In other words, deterrence, as any strategy, must be specific to the context and characteristic of the threat.

Findings/Recommendations/Way Ahead

To make progress in this field, we must first constrain the debate to profitable discussions. Those who expect quick, concise, and immediate practical answers from this area are destined to be frustrated by the highly conceptual tone of the products of deterrence conversations. Others may experience similar frustration as the conversation quickly becomes constrained to notions of nuclear deterrence, arms control and limitation, and counterproliferation. There are, however, several insights that can inform policy discussions.

First, deterrence is probably not applicable to all situations. Some adversaries are probably not likely to be deterred by any practical means at the disposal of state actors—such challenges must be either contained or eradicated.

For those situations in which statecraft does apply, some situations can and should be shaped without resorting to the conflict inherent in deterrence interactions. This implies that states adopt coherent, comprehensive approaches that are relevant to the global security environment and that they purposely employ all instruments of power to achieve desired goals. In such a context, states would focus and tailor their strategies according to the demands of the threat.

Second, for those situations where deterrence may apply, policy makers must determine the appropriate instruments that work in concert with military preparation to ensure that the object of deterrence can receive, understand, and value the deterrent aims of the policy. Additionally, the success of deterrence depends on being able to assess the adversary's behavior and likely counter moves. Without such assessment measures, deterrence will remain a theoretical construct with little relation to actual conditions as they exist in the adversary's camp.

Third, there may be ways to deter nonstate actors. This area requires further research to develop an understanding of these actors' motives and values. To the extent that criminals, insurgents, terrorists, and other groups that represent challenges to state and international security value political goals and outcomes, they may possess levers of vulnerability that states can hold at risk and thus can use for deterrence purposes.

Fourth, as long as states possess nuclear weapons and as long as there are states that seek to proliferate weapons of mass destruction (WMD) and delivery technologies, deterrence remains a valid strategic approach. Where states have acquired such systems, deterrence is the dominant paradigm that provides a foundation for governing interaction with competitors. Where states seek to acquire nuclear or WMD capabilities, deterrence strategies provide robust theories and approaches for other states to delay or prevent proliferators from developing and deploying such systems.

In conclusion, policy makers and strategists should consider deterrence seriously as an essential tool for confronting the complex security environment of the twenty-first century. But, rather than applying the theory and template developed in the Cold War, they should encourage and sponsor more study, exploration, and discussion of how deterrence can be enriched for the conditions that prevail today.

Chapter 20

Quick Look
Deterrence and WMD Counterproliferation

Adam Lowther, PhD

Issue/Question

Counterproliferation is perhaps the most opaque aspect of deterrence. States historically have had difficulty preventing the spread of chemical, biological, nuclear, and radiological materials, technologies, and weapons. States and nonstate actors frequently see value in developing weapons of mass destruction (WMD). The rationale for their acquisition and/or development can vary widely.

In the case of Iran, nuclear weapons are seen as a solution to a perceived threat from the United States. Iranian leaders view acquisition of nuclear weapons capabilities as an insurance policy for its own survival. For Pakistan and India, the calculation is different. Intense hatred and a recent history of persistent conflict drove both powers to invest in expensive and resource-intensive nuclear weapons programs, which proved successful. The list of additional proliferators includes states and nonstate actors worldwide and is only eclipsed by the list of reasons behind proliferation. The Royal United Services Institute (RUSI), King's College London; and the Air Force Research Institute co-sponsored a conference on 18–19 May 2009 to explore this question and others related to deterrence.

Background/Discussion

Conference participants found it difficult to place counterproliferation within the construct of deterrence. Unlike traditional nuclear deterrence, where, for example, the United States issues a retaliatory threat should another country attack the United States or its allies, counterproliferation is rarely threat-based. Thus, participants sought to determine whether counterproliferation is part of deterrence at all. Is it dissuasion? And, if it is, what is the relationship between dissuasion and deterrence?

301

There was a great deal of concern surrounding the language often used in declaratory statements in which American political and diplomatic leaders express that an action or policy related to proliferation is "unacceptable" or "grave," for examples, and then take no punitive action when the proliferator does that which is unacceptable. The "diplomatic speak" that such language symbolizes was widely seen as undermining the credibility of dissuasion/deterrence.

A second point discussed by the participants dealt with the role treaties play in dissuading/deterring WMD proliferation. While there appeared to be an innate efficacy toward a system of nonproliferation treaties, there was also doubt as to their effectiveness. The inability of participants to provide a viable alternative may explain the continued support for treaties, such as the Nonproliferation Treaty. A majority agreed that counterproliferation treaties, of any type, are unlikely to prevent a determined proliferator from pursuing weapons that are often perceived as necessary for state or regime survival.

As previously noted, proliferators often attempt to acquire WMD when there is a perceived threat. A robust discussion explored the potential for a more inclusive extended conventional and nuclear deterrence umbrella as a means to address real or perceived security threats. Could this serve as one way to reduce the demand for chemical, biological, nuclear, and radiological weapons?

Findings/Recommendations/Way Ahead

A number of findings/recommendations emerged from the various group discussions:

- Export controls are useful tools in counterproliferation efforts and are often underutilized.
- Be careful when choosing language or communicating "redlines." Do not characterize a potential act as unacceptable if you have no intention of preventing or reacting to it.
- A better understanding of the rationale for proliferation is needed if the United States and its allies are to dissuade/deter individual proliferators.

- Nonproliferation treaties need teeth. Absent punitive measures, they are unlikely to be effective.
- Formal statements of US desires may be as effective as a formal treaty.
- A long and unpopular Iraq war is less effective in deterring future proliferation than a short war may have been.
- Cyber should be included in WMD discussions because of its potential to cause mass casualties and economic loss.
- Current adversaries should be attributed with the same seriousness and rationality that was once attributed to the Soviet Union.
- In the end, proliferation will not be stopped. Deterring the use of WMD may be the most effective approach to this problem.

Chapter 21

Quick Look

Deterrence in the Twenty-first Century
Nonstate Actors versus State

Dale L. Hayden, PhD

Issue/Question

The terrorist attacks on the United States on 11 September 2001 changed the perspective in the United States and in much of the world on what constituted a threat to security and the applicability of deterrence to the changing strategic environment. In the post–9/11 era, the question becomes, "How do nonstate actors (NSA) change our understanding of deterrence and can their actions deter states?" The Royal United Services Institute (RUSI), King's College—London; and the Air Force Research Institute co-sponsored a conference on 18–19 May 2009 to explore this question and other issues related to deterrence.

Background/Discussion

Paul Schulte, senior visiting fellow, Centre for the Study of Global Governance, London School of Economics, addressed how we should define deterrence of states by NSAs, the kinds of state action that might deter NSAs, and how the strategic cultures of states might affect the interaction between states and NSAs. We must first define what deterrence against NSAs might look like. NSAs may be criminals, simply wanting to provide an illegal product, or insurgents, wanting to overthrow the government. In either case, NSAs have certain common factors: they must portray states as illegitimate; they can talk about cease-fires as deterrent strategy; they fear threats to their legitimacy such as being branded as criminals or vigilantes by states, roundups, preventive arrests, imprisonment, removal from the "battlefield"; and they fear military intervention in areas they control. More importantly, they value survival and fear eradication. Often, NSAs want to escalate levels of violence, or they want the benefits of deterrence and may switch back to provocation. They constantly evaluate their adversaries, and often they get it wrong. NSAs may not be deterred solely by military power.

Those who may seem to take irrational action may, in fact, have a logic—a rationality defined by their beliefs or ideologies— that, if understood, may provide insight into how to construct strategies to deter or defeat them. They may attack civilian populations to protect their leaders or those under their control. NSAs can attempt to infiltrate governments or society. They may attempt limited terrorism while presenting the appearance of being reasonable parties to negotiations or masquerading as partners in legitimate reform efforts. These strategies could afford them access to decision-making processes while they wait for the right moment to point out the illegitimate nature of their adversaries. NSA agents in such roles may attempt to deter states by highlighting the unpredictability of radicals within their own organization. As they gain access to adversary strategies and decision-making processes, they can play a double game of inciting fear among state leaders and the populace while gathering valuable intelligence about their enemies.

Weapons of mass destruction (WMD) are problematic for NSAs. The threshold of WMD use raises the cost to NSAs. Unless the WMD attack is wildly successful in decapitating the retaliatory apparatus available to states, the likely outcome is a response that will spell the end for the NSA leaders and fighting forces. The acquisition and threatened use of WMD may, however, represent risks worth taking for NSAs if the outcome is increased deterrent or coercive power over the state adversary. But, even when applied as a bargaining chip, the threat posed by WMD may provoke state intervention.

While scholars may present plausible arguments to suggest that NSAs seek to deter their adversaries, evidence suggests that this may have already occurred. The conference organizers asked Dr. Peter R. Neumann, director of the International Centre for the Study of Radicalisation and Political Violence, to present an analysis of the 2004 Madrid train bombing. The bombings occurred during rush hour on 11 March 2004, killing 191 and wounding 2,000. The strategy was to kill thousands three days before the national elections, but bombs exploded prematurely, failing to catch the four trains in station. At the time of the bombings, the governing party was ahead in the polls. People were pleased with the conservative government in the area of economics and its hard-core policy against the Basque separatists (ETA). However, one policy that was not popular was Spanish participation in the United States–led coalition in Iraq. Conventional wisdom holds that the attacks caused the downfall of the conservative government and intimidated the new liberal party into removing the Spanish contingent from Iraq; the real story may be more complicated.

No one denies the swing from conservatives to socialists. Immediately following the bombings, the Spanish government announced that ETA terrorists, not al-Qaeda operatives, had launched the attacks. However, the day before the elections, it became clear this was not the case. The public perceived that the government had deliberately manipulated the facts surrounding a national tragedy for political gains. The result was a dramatic increase in polling numbers—12 percent more than in recent elections. This increase, a symptom of dissatisfaction with the government's handling of the investigation, determined the outcome of the election.

In the end, determining a direct link to al-Qaeda central proved difficult for Spanish authorities. Al-Qaeda leaders called for attacks against one or more coalition members to increase domestic pressure to withdraw from Iraq. Web pronouncements indicated that Spain was the weak link with the greatest public support against the war. Clearly, the bombers believed they were part of al-Qaeda and saw Osama bin Laden as their leader. At the same time, there is no evidence that al-Qaeda was in touch with the bombers or directed the attack (or that the bombers read the Web-site strategy document that called for attacks against Spanish troops in Iraq rather than in Spain). Even after the newly elected government announced its intent to withdraw troops from Iraq, the terrorists continued their actions against Spanish civilians.

In summary, it is not clear if the bombers intended to force a withdrawal from Iraq or whether Spanish public opinion reflected fear and outrage over the attacks or their anger at the overt deception by their government. Ironically, it no longer matters because jihadists claim that the Madrid bombings were a great strategic and operational victory. That the terrorist attacks represent a model for success, they could serve as a template for a deterrent strategy by NSAs aimed at adversary states.

Findings/Recommendations/Way Ahead

This topic was met with a great deal of skepticism by conference participants. Deterrence by NSAs is a complex issue and may require new models to enhance understanding of how NSAs and states interact. NSAs may use deterrence tactically en route to a larger strategic goal; states often see deterrence in strategic terms. NSAs will often frame their narrative in its cultural context or framework. They attempt to present themselves as legitimate actors in opposition to an illegitimate state. Ultimately, states may be more vulnerable or susceptible to deterrence initiatives taken by NSAs than the reverse.

The Madrid train bombing illustrates that states must have a better understanding of NSA motivation and goals. When states do not carefully evaluate their actions, the mere proximity in time to an NSA action can result in a public relations success for NSAs, thus creating a narrative where none might exist. States may need to look at immunization in relation to the action of NSAs rather than hoping to eliminate or preclude all actions. For example, Israel continues to operate as an open society, despite the threat of attacks against civilians—malls remain open, restaurants serve meals. The Israeli people continue to gather in public places and see placing themselves potentially in harm's way simply as the cost of living.

Including NSAs in the larger context of deterrence raises certain questions to which there are no clear answers. Can NSAs deter states? Do NSAs use deterrence against states, or is what states see as deterrence simply an action in support of NSAs end goals? Are NSAs actions best evaluated in a confrontational context rather than using a model that relies on deterrence calculations?

Chapter 22

Quick Look
State versus State Deterrence in the Twenty-first Century

Larry G. Carter

Issue/Question

We live in interesting times, complicated by post–Cold War politics, post–9/11 attention on terrorists and nonstate actors, global economic recession and financial crisis, numerous global environmental challenges, and domestic health, education, and social issues. In the midst of all these important concerns, we must also refocus on deterrence, a critical long-term, stability enhancing element of our national security strategy. Deterrence is examined in the categories of counterproliferation, state on nonstate, nonstate on state, and, in this quick look, state on state.

Background/Discussion

One state deterring another is a familiar strategy to those who lived during or studied the Cold War. They will recognize such strategies as mutually assured destruction, commonly known as MAD. Prof. Sir Lawrence Freedman framed the conference discussion of state versus state deterrence by reviewing some of its history, characteristics, and observations. He noted one problem in understanding deterrence, "In theory, theory and practice should be the same; however, in practice, they are different." Sir Lawrence continued, "It worked much better in practice than in theory." Deterrence succeeds when nothing happens. It is difficult to show exactly what kept the nonevent from happening. While champions of the many possibilities that could have prevented an adversary's action will certainly take credit for having done so, no cause can be absolutely proven. He noted that states, as well as individuals, affect the choices of others by their conscious and unconscious actions. For example, a stated threat of retaliation would deter the actions of others if the threat were credible, which is the product of capability and will. During and after World War II, the thought of using the atomic bomb was an evolution of the bombing operations and effects of that war, particularly fire bombing. The demonstrated ability to build weapons and the willingness to use them generated an opportunity capability for the United States to deter other nations from taking actions that were not in its interests.

However, attitudes change as weapons become significantly more powerful and the consequences of their use becomes more extreme, both to the nation being attacked and to the world's environment. Western civilization has become increasingly uncomfortable with killing civilians, even if it is unintended and incidental to the targeting of military targets. These combined factors may cause a potential adversary to question whether the United States or any other nuclear-armed Western nation will use such a destructive and indiscriminate weapon. If that adversary feels the risk of retaliation is low, it may no longer be deterred. Additionally, a nation that depends for its security on the extended deterrence provided by a nuclear-armed state must also question that state's willingness to fulfill its treaty commitments if it is not also directly threatened. Sir Lawrence noted that deterrence is easiest to understand if one state is only looking after its own interests and becomes increasingly more difficult with the addition of a first-use policy, trip wire deployment of forces, extended deterrence, deterring the use of chemical and biological weapons, and additional nations being added to alliances. These complicating factors served to move the idea of a deterrent threat from one of "if you do X I will do Y," to, "if you do X you will set into motion a chain of events that may include Y." However, if Y is sufficiently horrible, the aggressor will still be deterred. These consequences must be clearly stated and unambiguous to be effective. During the 1960s and in support of the MAD deterrence strategy, Secretary of Defense Robert S. McNamara said that the effects would be massive brutal destruction, it would be assured, and it would be mutual. The great achievement of nuclear deterrence reminds the world how terrible a great-power war would be. It has discouraged adversaries from trying something clever to get around the strategy, and it has led to crisis stability. Measures were developed to communicate between potential adversaries and manage problems and issues at the lowest possible level. Clear communication between potential adversaries is critical between major and minor nuclear-armed states.

The world is moving away from the deterrence models used in the Cold War. Many subtle and overt threats can be used to deter an adversary and do not require nuclear weapons. For example, the conventional superiority of NATO and the US naval superiority in the Pacific are two of the means by which the probability of great-power war is minimized. Another indication of change is the discussion of radical disarmament, which could have significant implications for those countries that benefit from extended deterrence. For example, Japan hates nuclear weapons but is also concerned about China. Sir Lawrence advised that we maintain a broad range of military capability and be very clear that alliances matters. He said that deterrence is finally a matter of foreign policy, not a matter of capability or targeting. It is about what we care about and how far we are prepared to go to protect it

Findings/Recommendations/Way Ahead

State-on-state deterrence is the strategy implementation of one state to prevent an adversary state from taking a particular action because of its fear of undesirable consequences. It is a state of mind brought about by the perception of a credible threat of the application of unacceptable counteractions and/or an engineered range of undesirable consequences. That threat uses the instruments of deterrence, which include a full set of options derived from any of the elements of power extending from a threat to reduce foreign aid to using nuclear weapons. If successful, the risk of the adverse consequence convinces the potential adversary to forego that action. The instruments of deterrence are numerous, many predate nuclear weapons, and all can be manipulated to disadvantage an adversary.

Deterrence can fail to dissuade an adversary for several reasons. A lack of clarity in transmission or reception of the warning statement can lead to bad judgments and a failure to deter when the other necessary elements are present. If the practitioner misunderstands what motivates the adversary—what he will tolerate and what he can't—the deterrence effort can fail. It will also fail if the importance of a deterrent objective changes and was no longer considered important enough for the nation to carry out the threat. The practitioner may have misjudged the complex variables and chosen to use the wrong deterrent instrument. Likewise, the reactions of Western democracies are often hard to figure out due to the complexities of their governance and societies; therefore, other states may get things wrong when trying to deter or respond to a deterrence strategy. Practicing deterrence is an art that requires expertise and diligence.

The political environments and various scenarios in several geographical areas could be studied to determine if the development of additional alliances could further deterrence objectives and potentially aid in crisis stability. In addition, we should research likely ways the United States can offer extended deterrence and similar actions to reassure NATO's eastern members, which could free up some of their forces for other activities such as NATO operations in Afghanistan.

Finally, peace, stability, and the protection of life are always among America's objectives, but it also happens to be much less expensive to deter war than to fight it. We find ourselves generally in an asymmetric advantage with respect to nuclear weapons and most nations. Policy makers should therefore ensure that our current strategy is appropriate for the global political environment, our national objectives, and potential adversaries. We have a great opportunity to continue to use that deterrent advantage to help ensure peace and stability in the world.

Chapter 23

Quick Look

Deterrence in the Twenty-first Century
State versus Nonstate Actors

Jeffrey B. Hukill

Issue/Question

Since the end of the Cold War, the impact of nonstate actors (NSAs) at regional and global scales has grown. This has been especially evident since the start of the twenty-first century with the 9/11 attacks and the Madrid and London train bombing. These events along with others have caused many nation-states to examine their traditional security measures to discover methods applicable to NSAs for preserving security. With this growth in NSA influence on nation-states, one of the most relevant questions pertaining to deterrence theory is "can nation-states deter NSAs." The Royal United Service Institute (RUSI), King's College London; and the Air Force Research Institute cosponsored a conference on 18–19 May 2009 to explore this question and other issues related to deterrence.

Background/Discussion

Keynote speaker Dr. John Stone, senior lecturer at King's College's Department of War Studies, stated that NSAs can be deterred. By way of illustration, he focused on ways that nation-states can deter al-Qaeda (AQ). His major theme was that punitive deterrence is ineffective against AQ but that other forms of deterrence hold substantially greater potential. He suggested that nation-states should focus, for example, on the vulnerabilities inherent in the illegitimacy of AQ's religious message used during recruiting. AQ is dependent upon a steady flow of new recruits; so, deterring new recruits has substantial consequences for the organization. It is, by effect, an attack on AQ from within. In concert with information strategies aimed at deterring potential recruits from joining the network, Dr. Stone advocated effective defensive measures that would force potential terrorists into unfavorable cost-benefit decisions.

Case Study: Prof. Shai Feldman, director, Crown Center for Middle East Studies at the University of Brandeis, focused on deterrence issues surrounding the 2006 Israel-Hezbollah war. Israeli deterrence strategies failed for several reasons. First, Israeli deterrence doctrine for the Lebanon region was based on Syria when that nation-state occupied Lebanon. When Syria withdrew, the doctrine was not updated. This created a strategy and planning disconnect with the changed circumstances of 2006. In other words, actions aimed at deterring Syria, a state actor with traditional nation-state equities, were applied against Hezbollah, a nonstate actor with wholly dissimilar equities. Second, after withdrawing in 2000, Israeli weakness made Hezbollah feel stronger. Third, there were unbalanced prisoner exchanges between Hezbollah and Israel. Hezbollah received many more prisoners for the number of prisoners they took. Fourth, Hezbollah underestimated Israel's response to the capture of two of its soldiers. Israel had failed to communicate its intent, thus losing the deterrent value of its military capability. Deterrence was finally restored through successful compellence. The cost of punishing attacks on Lebanon's infrastructure forced Lebanon to move its military into the south to stop the rocket attacks and create a "safety zone."

Findings/Recommendations/Way Ahead

The keynote and case study speakers presented evidence to suggest that nation-states can deter NSAs. This notion was met with skepticism on the part of many of the conference participants. The conventional view seemed to be that most NSAs, particularly actors that used terrorism or violence to pursue their goals, do not respond to deterrence attempts.

The presentations and the workshop discussions that followed highlighted many key concepts when it comes to nation-states' attempts to deter NSAs. These concepts, while similar to traditional deterrence theory, have notable differences. When states attempt to apply deterrence strategies to deter NSAs, they must abide by the following:

- Be more flexible and adaptable than traditional deterrence constructs.

314

- Take into account NSA's varied motivation for existence, culture, and structure.
- To be relevant, deterrence strategies must be more time-sensitive in their reaction to NSAs that can maneuver inside nation-state decision-making cycles.
- Address the deterrence of NSAs as well as any nation-state sponsors—to address one without the other only addresses one-half of the problem
- Create credible "redline" issues tailored to specific NSAs
  - NSAs are more likely to probe redlines; so, nation-states should not threaten some kind of punishment if they are not willing to carry out the threat
  - Have a more sophisticated redline structure so a nation-state does not box itself into a corner with an unrealistic response to an NSA crossing a redline
  - Unlike the Cold War, when our deterrent efforts focused on one country, we now must understand the motivations of each NSA and find effective means to deter
  - Develop a detailed understanding of each NSA
- NSA deterrence is less about nuclear confrontation and more about using all instruments of power to deter and then respond if a redline is crossed
  - Have a different set of military capabilities for effective deterrence (i.e., irregular warfare capabilities may have the greatest military deterrent effect)
  - Develop ways to communicate with NSAs, which is difficult to do because of varying degrees of organizational structures between NSAs

Further research is needed in multiple areas to create effective state deterrence of NSAs. These areas include the following considerations:

- Broad standard deterrence theory definitions to fit a multidimensional world.
- Are there specific contextual situations that would make deterrence against NSAs more effective?

315

- Can the complex relationship between NSAs and their sponsors be affected through deterrence?
- Can purely defensive measures deter NSAs?
- How does a nation-state effectively communicate intent toward NSAs?
- Develop measurement constructs of deterrence effectiveness.

Deterrence theory has always been a complex issue. Today's environment does not simplify the problem.

Attendee Roster

Co-Sponsors

Prof. Michael Clarke
Dr. John Gearson
Gen John A. Shaud, USAF, retired

Work Group Facilitators

Sarah Sewall
Beatrice Heuser
Wyn Bowen
VAdm Charles Style, CBE
Maj Gen Donald C. Alston, USAF
Kirk Augustine
Keith Britto
Gp Capt Al Byford
Malcolm Chalmers
Rahul Roy-Chaudhury
Michael Codner
Denis Corboy
Col Kirk L. Davies
Maj Ryan Eastwood
Lt Gen Robert J. Elder, Jr., USAF
Shai Feldman
Prof. Sir Lawrence Freedman, KCMG CBE FKC
Julie George
Christina Goulter
Gen Eugene Habiger, USAF, retired
Christopher Hobbs
Prof. Sir Michael Howard
Mary Kaldor
Joanna Kidd
Lt Gen Frank G. Klotz
Ben Lambeth
Jack Macdonald
Peter Neumann
Sir David Omand, GCB
James Quinlivan
Michael L. Rance

Nick Ritchie
Capt Guy Robinson, Royal Navy (RN)
Ruth Saunders
Thomas Scheber
Barry Schneider
Paul Schulte
Eric Sikes
John Stone
Trevor Taylor
Cdr Hamish Tetlow, RN
James de Waal
Ian Wallace
Lee Willett
Ken Young

Deterrence in the Twenty-first Century
Proceedings

General Editors

Anthony C. Cain, PhD
Air Force Research Institute

John Gearson, PhD
Director, Centre for Defence Studies, King's College, London

Lee Willett, PhD
Royal United Services Institute for Defence and Security Studies

Air University Press Team

Project Editor
Richard Bailey, PhD

Copy Editors
Tammi Long and Darlene Barnes

Cover Art and Book Design and Illustrations
Daniel Armstrong

Composition and
Prepress Production
Vivian D. O'Neal

Print Preparation and Distribution
Diane Clark

www.ingramcontent.com/pod-product-compliance
Lightning Source LLC
Chambersburg PA
CBHW080412270326
41929CB00018B/3001